# Effective
# Egoism

# Effective Egoism

## An Individualist's Guide to Pride, Purpose, and the Pursuit of Happiness

## Don Watkins

ISBN: 979-8-3974503-6-2

Design by Simon Federman and Tom Bowden

*A quote misattributed to Oscar Wilde:*
*You don't love someone for their looks, or their clothes, or for their fancy car, but because they sing a song only you can hear.*

To Samantha, for all the music

"As man is a being of self-made wealth,
so he is a being of self-made soul."

—From *Atlas Shrugged* by Ayn Rand

# CONTENTS

# CONTENTS

# CONTENTS

## Lesson 1

# Your Life Matters

IT'S ALL ABOUT YOU.

Has anyone ever told you that? Probably not. Instead, you're born into the world without a say in the matter, and from day one people are telling you how *unimportant* you really are, as if you were an uninvited guest intruding on a party. "Think of others first." "Don't be selfish." "Do as you're told." "It's *not* all about you."

And yet the people you're supposed to serve and sacrifice for? They're all being told the same thing. Servants serving servants serving servants. None of us has a right to exist for our own sake. It's servants all the way down.

Few people really believe that, of course. Most parents want their kids to be happy, to find fulfilling jobs, passionate romances—not join a monastery or start a soup kitchen. I've yet to meet a parent who thinks *of other people's children* first. They say things like "think of others first" because they believe they're supposed to say it—and because they believe that thinking of yourself is a given. Telling people to value their own happiness is supposed to be as pointless as telling

1

them to breathe. They do *that* automatically. The real challenge in life is learning to rein in their innate selfishness for the sake of others.

Really?

As a parent, coach, mentor, and long-time human being, nothing is more obvious to me than that people do *not* automatically value their own lives and happiness—and that, even when they do, knowing how to make the most of their lives and *actually* achieve their happiness is the most daunting challenge a person will ever face.

As I write this, headlines are announcing that drug overdose deaths have reached a record high. Were the addicts hooked on fentanyl treating their lives as if they mattered? What about the people who stay in abusive relationships? The people who smoke too much, drink too much, and exercise too little? The people who join cults and crusades demanding selfless obedience to the leader or the cause? What about the millions of people sitting in their therapist's office wrestling with feelings of shame, self-doubt, and self-contempt? Is the problem they value themselves too highly?

Even when people *do* seek the best for their lives, it's not as though it's obvious what to do. Most of the people I know well are active, ambitious, and reasonably self-confident. Yet they, too, struggle. How *do* I find a career that I love? What do I do when my parents' values don't align with mine? How can I restore my self-respect after I've taken an action unworthy of me? How should I move forward when what I want and what I think I should want clash?

Sacrifice is easy. You just give up what you want. But knowing what you want? Coming up with a vision of who you want to be and the life you want to live, figuring out how to realize it, staying true to that vision over the course of years and decades while overcoming distractions, obstacles, and outside pressure? There is nothing more difficult, more rare, or more heroic than building a self and a life that you love.

But there's a science that exists to teach you to do it.

Philosophy.

# Check Your Assumptions

My dad was a Navy pilot, and when I was nine, his job took us from Virginia to Japan. It was like moving to a different planet. People didn't shake hands—they bowed. People didn't drive on the right side of the road—they drove on the left. Wearing shoes in the house was taboo, but openly looking at porn on the train? Just fine.

We take so much of human behavior for granted: this is just the way people do things. We never question many of the assumptions behind our beliefs and behaviors because it doesn't feel like we're selecting among alternatives. We're just believing and doing what comes naturally. But there are alternatives.

Some of the alternatives people face are completely optional conventions. It doesn't matter what side of the road you drive on, so long as everyone in the area drives on the same side. But other alternatives matter. They can be right or wrong—good or bad. We take it for granted that slavery is evil. Not everyone in history has.

*Philosophy* is the subject that examines our deepest assumptions about life: about what we are, where we are, how we know, how we should live. In fact, philosophy got its start precisely when different cultures started interacting on a mass scale. The ancient Greeks never questioned that they worshipped the right gods, or that their conceptions of the good, the just, and the noble were correct. But they kept running into cultures that didn't share their outlook. Cultures that worshipped different gods. That had different conceptions of virtue. That organized society in wildly different ways.

Suddenly, the Greeks faced a real question: how do we know we're right?

If you've studied any philosophy, you've probably read some of Plato's Socratic dialogues. In those dialogues, Socrates goes around Athens asking one very basic question: do you know what the hell you're talking about? He happens upon Athenians debating whether this or that thing is just, and he says: "Hold on. What *is* justice? If you don't know that, you'll never be able to say for sure whether a particular action is just or not."

That was the beginning of philosophy. Philosophy doesn't just identify your most basic assumptions. It allows you to question them. To think about them self-consciously and critically so that you know your most basic assumptions are true. And, once you know they are true, philosophy leaves you with an explicit framework you can use to solve all the particular real-life problems you face.

Why does all this matter? Because if you aren't aware of the assumptions you're making, *you're out of control.* You're acting blindly, in the grip of ideas that are invisible to you. Ideas that, all too often, are contributing to your fears, self-doubts, frustrations, conflicts, and regrets.

Here's one example. Are you in control of your life? Do you have the power to choose—or are you at the mercy of the invisible forces of nature and nurture, your genes and your environment? Even if you've never taken a formal position on the issue of free will versus determinism, you can't escape making certain assumptions about whether you're in control of your life and responsible for your actions. It's no accident that even the most uneducated criminal will appeal to determinism to rationalize his crimes and subdue his guilt. "I couldn't help it, that's the way I was raised." (Never mind that his siblings managed to stay out of prison.)

This book is about self-creation. It's about taking ownership of your life, refusing to bow to routine or conformity or conventional wisdom, and instead making the commitment to actively create your life—and your soul. Here's how my greatest philosophic influence, Ayn Rand, once put it:

> Just as man's physical survival depends on his own effort, so does his psychological survival. Man faces two corollary, interdependent fields of action in which a constant exercise of choice and a constant creative process are demanded of him: the world around

him and his own soul (by "soul," I mean his consciousness). Just as he has to produce the material values he needs to sustain his life, so he has to acquire the values of character that enable him to sustain it and make his life worth living. He is born without the knowledge of either. He has to discover both—and translate them into reality—and survive by shaping the world and himself in the image of his values.[1]

My deepest conviction is that each of us is a being of self-made soul. And the only way to make your soul consciously and deliberately is through philosophic inquiry. It's philosophy that puts you in the driver seat of your life. If you ignore philosophic issues, you will still be in the grip of philosophic ideas—but you'll take over those ideas blindly and accidentally from the people around you. You *will* be the product of your environment. To be self-made—to design your life on your own terms—you have to examine your deepest assumptions. And be willing to change them.

# The Anti-Self Assumption

In my judgment, the assumption that's done more damage to self-creation than any other is the one that equates being moral with being selfless. It's the assumption that says: to live a fulfilling, moral, meaningful life, you must serve a cause greater than yourself. I call this the dictum, and you hear it everywhere.

- "The richest men and women possess nothing of real value if their lives have no greater object than themselves," said the late senator John McCain.[2]
- "It's only when you hitch your wagon to something larger than yourself that you realize your true potential and discover the role that you'll play in writing the next great chapter in the American story," Barack Obama told students at Wesleyan University.[3]

- "Purpose is that sense that we are part of something bigger than ourselves," agreed Facebook's Mark Zuckerberg.[4]
- "Get out of the shallow waters of selfishness and give yourself to causes greater than yourself," Mitt Romney told Coe College graduates. "Launch yourself into the deep waters of great causes."[5]

To serve a cause greater than yourself is to act "in ways that are beyond personal concerns and direct personal gain."[6] In the terminology of psychological anthropologist Richard Shweder, it is to embrace an ethic of community or of divinity. Meaning is to be sought in the group or in God—in society or the sky. Not the "I."[7]

And who could disagree? The alternative, we're taught, is to be self-centered: to be, in *Urban Dictionary*'s trenchant description, "The asshole that won't offer a hand to anybody."[8] And assholes aren't happy. They project, not joy, serenity, or confidence, but fear, touchiness, and neediness. They can, if clever and ambitious, achieve the trappings of success: money, status, power. But there is *nothing to them*.

What the "self-centered" fail to recognize, and what lends the dictum plausibility, is that you do need to live *for* something. You do need to set your sights beyond your transient desires and fears. You do need to aim at the highest possible good. In short, you need to *live for a moral ideal*. In his book *The Happiness Hypothesis*, psychologist Jonathan Haidt hints at the issue:

> Aristotle asked about areté (excellence/virtue) and telos (purpose/goal), and he used the metaphor that people are like archers, who need a clear target at which to aim. Without a target or goal, one is left with the animal default: Just let the elephant graze or roam where he pleases. And because elephants live in herds, one ends up doing what everyone else is doing. Yet the human mind has a rider, and as the rider begins to think more abstractly in adolescence, there may come a time when he looks around, past the edges of the herd, and asks: Where are we all going? And why?[9]

It is a moral ideal that helps you answer these questions: Where am I going? And why? It is what sets your proper aim and establishes the virtues that will realize your aim. It helps you decide what kind of person you should strive to become by outlining an inspiring and ennobling vision of *what is possible to you*—a vision that you acquire first and foremost through art.

You hear Cyrano de Bergerac declare that he has "decided to be admirable, in everything, for everything" . . . You witness a fugitive declare in open court, "I am Jean Valjean" . . . You listen as Scout is exhorted, "stand up. Your father's passin'" . . . You gaze at Michelangelo's *David* or David's *Death of Socrates* . . . You are swept away by the first movement of Tchaikovsky's first piano concerto or the last movement of Rachmaninoff's second.

These experiences, and the deep, soul-changing emotions they evoke, elevate you. "Elevate" means: inspire you to live for a moral ideal.

Philosopher Allan Bloom argues the point eloquently in *The Closing of the American Mind*, writing that idealism

> should have primacy in education, for man is a being who must take his orientation by his possible perfection. . . . As it now stands, students have powerful images of what a perfect body is and pursue it incessantly. But deprived of literary guidance, they no longer have any image of a perfect soul, and hence do not long to have one. They do not even imagine that there is such a thing.[10]

This is tragic. And it explains, at a much deeper level, the "self-centeredness" that you see in those who do not live for a moral ideal. Their failure is not that they attend only to their own desires—it's that they do not attend to their own souls.

And so you do not see in such people the ambitious self-improvement of Ben Franklin, the proud dignity of Abraham Lincoln, the principled courage of Harriet Tubman, the indomitable will of Winston Churchill, the all-consuming curiosity of Bill Gates, the intense passion and demanding quest for beauty of Steve Jobs.

The "self-centered" *have no self on which to be centered*—only a hazy canvas of self-doubt and a palette of pretense. What we call their desires are only the unexamined impulses given to them by nature or copied from neighbors. What we call their "ego" is precisely the cloak that conceals an empty hole where genuine self-respect could have grown. They cannot show gratitude, appreciation, or admiration because those are marks, not of humility, but of spiritual abundance.

Art has the power to show us what it looks like to live up to a moral ideal and give us the spiritual fuel to seek the ideal in our own lives. What art cannot do is *validate* any particular ideal or elucidate its principles. That is the task of ethics.

What ideal should you pursue? Should you live for God, as religion says? Should you live for pleasure, as the hedonists say? Should you live for society, as everyone today says?

I believe that the moral ideal you should strive for is an ideal of self-interest or *egoism*. The full argument for that claim will have to wait. For now, it's sufficient to observe that the very reason you have for seeking an ideal gives a clue as to what kind of ideal to embrace. For if it is your happiness that is at stake in deciding whether to pursue a moral ideal at all, then that suggests that your happiness *is* the proper goal of morality.

Today "happiness" has been castrated and no longer carries deep meaning. We equate it with momentary satisfaction or an ephemeral sense of "feeling good." Jordan Peterson calls happiness "fleeting and unpredictable," like "cotton candy."[11]

This is deeply wrong. Happiness is not weather—it is climate. It is the emotional undertone of a life well-lived. Happiness is not something you lose when life gets difficult: happiness, and the promise of it, is what sustains you in choppy waters.

Even worse than confusing happiness with fleeting satisfaction are the false idols of happiness: an addict getting his fix, a preacher shouting hosannas, an Instagram "influencer" hash-tagging a sunset, a self-help guru sporting a phony perma-grin.

My God.

Years ago I took my six-year-old swimming. She was petrified—then she became brave. She stopped clinging to the side of the pool. Eventually, she would doggy paddle as I held her. When I let her go, she at first reached for me in fear. The next time, she *tried*.

"I'm swimming! I'm swimming!" She could not stop yelling it. "I'm swimming!" I cannot communicate that tone of voice, except to say that it was ineffable in the literal meaning of that term. I cannot communicate what I felt, except to say that only once had I felt it in so intense a form—when, at the climax of *The Miracle Worker*, Annie Sullivan ecstatically cries out, "She *knows!*"

That is a glimpse into happiness. Happiness is a life of unadulterated joy in existence, in your capacity to live, and in your worthiness of living. And it is the conviction, in those moments when you suffer terribly, that suffering is not your proper state but an aberration to be fought, endured, conquered, and forgotten.

This rich, enduring concept of happiness was endorsed by Aristotle as our proper moral end, to be served by the cultivation of virtue. Virtue, he and other ancients held, is not a detour sign leading you away from your interests, but a golden road showing you the way to happiness.

What virtues do lead to happiness? The ancients' list included reason, courage, honesty, justice, pride. They, however, had not lived through the Industrial Revolution but in aristocratic societies reliant on slavery. This masked for them the role of *production* in human life—production as the central rational activity allowing us to flourish.

This was one of the gaps filled in by Ayn Rand. Building on the Aristotelian tradition, Rand emphasized that the pursuit of creative, productive goals should not be relegated to some amoral "practical" sphere of life. It is at the heart of a moral, flourishing, happy existence.

The virtue of Productiveness is the recognition of the fact that productive work is the process by which man's mind sustains his life, the process that sets man free of the necessity to adjust himself to his background, as all animals do, and gives him the power to adjust his background to himself. Productive work is the road of man's unlimited achievement and calls upon the highest attributes of his character: his creative ability, his ambitiousness, his self-assertiveness, his refusal to bear uncontested disasters, his dedication to the goal of reshaping the earth in the image of his values.[12]

That is the path to happiness: to live for an ideal—but an *earthly* ideal that treats your life as sacred and teaches you to thrive through your own thought and effort.

The most important question you face in life is not *what is its meaning?* It is: What do I *want?* And that question is to be answered, not by staring blankly at your desires, but by *examining them.* Are they consistent with reality? Are they consistent with each other? Do they reflect the highest aspirations of which you can conceive? What are the virtues required to achieve them?

For most moralists, this is blasphemy. "It's not all about you," begins the best-selling *Purpose Driven Life.*[13]

Religion's contribution to ethics was to declare that when you ask, "What do I want?" about your life, you are asking the wrong question. As philosopher Onkar Ghate has pointed out, religion replaces an earthly father demanding blind obedience with a Heavenly Father demanding blind obedience. Morality isn't about doing what you want, it's about doing as you're told.

Jordan Peterson has made the point that even atheists believe in God, if judged by their actions. I half agree: most atheists believe in God if judged by their ethics. They accept a secularized form of the Christian morality, wherein it is not God who issues commandments that trump what you want, but other people. Auguste Comte called this "altruism," meaning "other-ism." It means self-sacrifice: placing other people and their demands above your own personal happiness.

Whatever the differences, religious ethics and social ethics agree on one thing: the good must be some form of subordinating the self to an outside authority's orders.

The ugly meaning of this doctrine—that what matters to you doesn't matter—is whitewashed by equating religious morality and altruism with love, benevolence, and generosity.

This is madness.

Other people are very obviously an enormous source of pleasure. Aristotle devotes two chapters in his ethics to friendship, and Rand viewed romantic love as life's greatest reward. That has nothing to do with the anti-self moralities of religion and altruism. Who would want to be considered a friend or a lover not for the personal pleasure that we give our companion, but out of charity or duty?

The central issue in ethics is not whether to love and help others. It is whether you are committed to achieving personal values— or whether you are committed to surrendering personal values and serving impersonal causes because some external authority says so.

Serve a cause greater than yourself? Creating a self that is worthy and capable of happiness is the greatest cause there is.

# Our Agenda

In this book, you'll discover a new view of morality, a view that says your life matters, and your job is not to serve and sacrifice, but to learn how to build a self and a life that you love.

I've titled this book *Effective Egoism* because its goal is to help you make the most of your own life—and because its principles *are* effective. I've seen these ideas give people born into poverty and abuse the power to become happy and confident. I've seen these ideas give people born into dictatorships the courage to flee to freedom. I've seen these ideas help people launch great careers, end bad marriages, stand up for justice, and build characters of iron. And I know that everything good in my own life, from my career to my relationships to moments of quiet joy spent with my favorite works of art, I owe to the philosophic principles you're about to discover.

But since this book's title is also taking an obvious jab at the "Effective Altruism" movement, let me clarify a potential misunderstanding.

Effective Altruism is a movement claiming to advise people on how to do the most good. In the words of the Centre for Effective Altruism:

> It is a research field which uses high-quality evidence and careful reasoning to work out how to help others as much as possible. It is also a community of people taking these answers seriously, by focusing their efforts on the most promising solutions to the world's most pressing problems.[14]

My critique of Effective Altruists will come in Lesson 3. For now, I want to note that Effective Altruists assess the value of different projects through a utilitarian-type calculus guided by empirical data. For example, they ask: What kinds of activities save the most lives for the lowest cost? What existential risks does mankind face, and what are the best ways to mitigate them?

So you might expect that a book titled *Effective Egoism* would propose something similar. That we'd be poring over data concerning which jobs have the highest earning potential or which dating strategies yield the most attractive romantic partners. Or that we'd be examining the kinds of "happiness studies" beloved by psychologists and social scientists. Nothing could be more alien to my approach.

What you'll find here is a *philosophical* argument. Because, as we'll see, philosophy *is* the science of happiness. Here, then, is the book's basic argument:

- Lesson 2: You have free will, and that free will gives you the power to build a self and a life that you love.
- Lesson 3: To fully realize that power you need moral guidance—not the guidance offered by today's anti-self

moral theories, but the guidance offered by a morality of self-interest.

- Lesson 4: Your self-interest demands living a life of reason.
- Lesson 5: Your self-interest demands living a life of purpose.
- Lesson 6: Your self-interest demands achieving self-esteem.
- Lesson 7: You experience happiness through rational pleasures—above all, the pleasure offered by work, art, and love.

Let the journey begin.

## Lesson 2

# Take Charge

## You Control Your Mind

It's 2006, and I'm relaxing on a cruise ship, celebrating my parents' 25th wedding anniversary. I'm 23, and I've just graduated from night school with a business degree. I have a decent job editing business proposals, but the work itself is mind-numbing. My main source of joy is writing about philosophy on the internet, with dreams of someday making it into a career—only I have no idea how to actually make a living writing about philosophy. That's when I pull up my email and find a message from someone at the Ayn Rand Institute. How would I like to apply for a job writing about philosophy?

"I think you're making a mistake," my dad tells me a week later, after I've been formally offered the job. He's not crazy to think so. I had just purchased a nice condo, I was making good money, and I was on track for a promotion. Taking the Ayn Rand Institute position would mean moving across the country, from Virginia to California, and taking a 25 percent cut in pay to work at a job that didn't offer any obvious long-term career prospects.

And truth be told, although I desperately wanted to say yes, I was scared. I had almost no savings, I knew exactly zero people in California, I had never truly been on my own. I cannot remember precisely what most worried me, but I distinctly remember wanting to back out at a certain point. To cling to the safe and the known. But I said to my dad, ignoring the fears and doubts swirling through my mind: "If I don't do this, I'm going to regret it for the rest of my life." (To Dad's credit, once he saw that my decision was final, he did everything in his power to support me.)

It was the most important decision I've ever made, and the reason you're reading this book.

We face choices in life. Some are big, life-changing decisions. Others are small, even trivial. But it's our choices that define who we are and how we live. It's our choices that shape our soul and our life.

Much about who we are is innate. Our genetic sex. Our hair and eye color. The shape of our nose and fullness of our lips. Other factors are influenced by innate characteristics: our height, weight, muscle mass, flexibility, hand/eye coordination, energy levels. Perhaps our raw intelligence (though not what we do with it) and our temperament (though not how we exercise it). But what about the soul?

Your soul is your deepest convictions and value judgments—your core estimate of yourself and the world. The basic claim of this book is that your soul is self-made: you create it—and can re-create it—through your choices. Free will is what is responsible for your convictions, your values, your emotions, your character, your happiness, the overall shape and texture of your life.

No, I do not agree with the self-help gurus who say that "you are responsible for everything that happens to you." Such statements aim to encourage people to stop making excuses and take an active role in improving their lives. But a child born in poverty isn't responsible for being born into poverty. A sexual assault victim isn't responsible for being raped. A person enslaved in the Antebellum South or communist North Korea isn't responsible for his chains. You are not responsible for every misfortune and injustice that befalls you. You are responsible only for what is open to your choice (including how you respond to misfortune and injustice).

But so much *is* open to your choice. And to unlock the magnificent power of free will, you have to understand what free will is, and how it shapes your soul and your life.

# The Challenge of Free Will

Nothing is more terrifying than being out of control. If you've ever hallucinated, or hydroplaned in your car, or been the victim of a violent crime—there's an overwhelming sense that your fate is no longer in your hands. Whether or not you live or die feels like a matter of chance. You're a passenger in your own life, rather than the driver.

But are you ever *really* in control? And if so, what's the nature of that control?

The belief that you don't genuinely have control over your own life is called "determinism." Determinists say that if we actually had sufficient knowledge, we would be able to predict a person's every thought and action. Human beings, on this view, are nothing more than complicated rocks rolling down a hill—only the force moving us along isn't gravity, but nature and nurture, our genes and our upbringing.

Yes, they'll say, it *feels* as though you make choices. If *feels* as though you could have done this when instead you did that. But that choice is an illusion. Here's how philosopher Sam Harris puts it:

> Free will *is* an illusion. Our wills are simply not of our own making. Thoughts and intentions emerge from background causes of which we are unaware and over which we exert no conscious control. We do not have the freedom we think we have.[15]

The determinists are wrong. You do make choices. You do this when you could have done that. Stalin was evil because he enslaved and murdered millions of people when he could have chosen not to be a ruthless killer. Frederick Douglass was admirable because he fought for the liberation of blacks when he could have chosen to remain silent. And you? You are who you are because of the choices you've made—and you'll become who you'll become through the choices you make in the future.

That, anyway, is my conclusion. But why think it's true?

Though common sense tells us we are making choices, when we probe into the nature of choice, we run into difficulties. Take a familiar choice. It's Thursday night and you sit down to watch Netflix. You spend a few hours scrolling through your options and then you settle on *Stranger Things*. At one level it feels like you made that choice. But if someone asked you why you chose that show, how would you answer?

One answer might be, "For no reason at all." But that doesn't sound like control. That sounds like being out of control. That sounds like your so-called choices are as random as a card shuffle. If free will means, "I do random stuff for random reasons," then what good is free will?

Another answer might be, "Because *Stranger Things* is my favorite show." But that doesn't sound like control. That sounds like your so-called choices are determined by your values and preferences. You don't control your life. You just do what you want—and you don't have control over what you want.

So on the one hand it feels like we make choices. But on the other hand, when we try to articulate the source and nature of our choosing, we come up empty. We seem trapped between determinism and indeterminism, with no space left for free will.

The problem is, we're looking in the wrong place. Choosing what show to watch, or what meal to eat, or what brand of shampoo to buy—these are choices between *content*. They do involve real acts of choice. But to see that, we have to go deeper: we have to identify the basic choice, our locus of control. And that turns out not to be a choice about content: it's a choice about process. Our primary choice has to do, not with *what* but *how*.

It's an issue of mental management.

## To Think or Not to Think . . . That Is the Question

Have you ever found your mind drifting off while reading a textbook for class? Your eyes kept following the words on the page, but none of it registered? What did you do? You probably stopped yourself and made a deliberate effort to focus on the words and their meaning. Maybe you decided to go more slowly over the material, looking up definitions of unfamiliar words, underlining key passages, jotting down questions to ask your professor.[16]

That's what I mean by mental management. It's your ability to raise your level of awareness and regulate how your mind functions. Your default mental state is one of *drift*. It's the state of your mind when you were looking at the words on the page of the textbook, but not registering their meaning. When you're drifting, you're still seeing things, hearing things, and even having sub-verbal conversations with yourself. But you're mentally passive. As when your eyes are out of focus, the world is there but it's blurry.

Your basic choice, the root of your free will, is your ability to take control of your mind and raise your level of awareness—to move from a passive state of drift to a state of purposeful alertness. Free will is your freedom to think—or not.

Self-control is really mind control. It's your ability to regulate the functioning of your mind. You can set your mind to the task of understanding reality—or you can be pulled along by your subconscious. When you do take control of your mind, you're aware that you chose to do it—it's something you made happen, not something that happened to you. Nothing *compelled* you to raise your level of awareness.

The clearest indication of this is *effort*.[17] It takes effort to raise your level of awareness. It takes effort to pay attention. It takes effort to manage your mental processes. And inherent in the exertion of effort is the awareness: "I didn't have to expend that effort." Some energy you expend effortlessly. Think of when a bug flies toward your eyes and you flinch. Your automatic actions—your *deterministic* actions—don't involve effort. Effort is what's required to perform volitional processes. It is the self-evident insignia of the fact that you do have free will.

But isn't this conception of free will vulnerable to the same objections I raised earlier to choosing to watch *Stranger Things*? It's not.

The choice to focus isn't random. You don't mysteriously find yourself in focus. You're aware that it came about through a deliberate act of will: you exerted the effort required to increase your level of awareness. Nor is focus a result of passively following your desires. It's true that in some sense you desired to know what was going on in reality, and that you adopted focus as a means to that end. But the value of knowing what's going on in reality is omnipresent: that's *why* being out of control is so frightening. Implicit in every waking moment is the knowledge that awareness is better than confusion. But this knowledge has no causal efficacy apart from your choice to act on it. Your sense that it would be good to know what's going on doesn't *compel* you to exert the effort to know what's going on. That remains a sovereign choice.

The choice to focus is your primary choice. But it's not your only choice.

If you continue to drift passively, then you don't face any further choices. Your actions *will be determined*—they'll be determined by your emotions and whatever mental content comes up from your subconscious. Maybe you've had the experience of drinking a few too many. You're still walking around and speaking, but when you look back the next day you think: "I wasn't in charge last night." The reason people make dumb decisions when they're drunk isn't only because their inhibitions are lowered. It's because, once they reach a certain point of intoxication, *they're not making decisions.* The less cognitive control you exercise, the more your emotions are in charge.

But if you are mentally alert, if you take control over your mental operations, then you face all sorts of further choices about how to think and how to act. Go back to our textbook example. If you're passively reading your textbook, then whatever content drifts through your mind is pure accident. But once you take charge, you face further decisions.

*Should I read this more slowly? Should I go back and re-read earlier material that might clarify this material? Should I set the textbook aside and look at my class notes, or watch a YouTube video on the topic, or email my professor? Should I take a nap so I can revisit this material fresh? Which strategy will be most effective for learning the material?*

Each of these decision points gives rise to further decisions. You decide to read the text more slowly and come upon a statement: "The Industrial Revolution was a time of poverty and worker exploitation." You don't accept the statement and move on. You start asking probing questions to connect the claim to other things you know in order to judge it.

*Did the Industrial Revolution create poverty? Or did it inherit poverty? What does it mean to say workers were exploited? If they were being exploited, why did people keep moving from farms to factories, from countries that weren't industrializing to countries that were?*

Suddenly, you feel a sense of discomfort. You've always considered yourself a progressive and all your friends are progressive. You sense that continuing this train of thought could lead you to challenge your evaluation of capitalism and put you in conflict with your professor and your peers. You decide: *I want to know what's true, come what may.* You press forward with more questions, following reason wherever it leads.

Your basic choice is to think or not. If you choose to think, you face further choices about how to implement that resolve: what to think about, how to think about it, what actions to take. All of these choices have reasons, but you select the reasons that will govern you. You are a self-programmer.

# Evasion

I've said that your basic choice is to raise your level of awareness or not. But there is a third basic alternative open to you: not effortful awareness but effortful blindness. You can purposefully turn away from reality and try to cloud your own vision. You can shut off your mind, induce an inner fog, and pretend that if you don't face the facts, that will erase the facts. You can, in short, *evade*.

Awareness as such is experienced as a positive. But sometimes when confronted with unpleasant or painful facts, people choose not to confront them. Your romantic partner tells you you're being cold and aloof, your boss criticizes your sloppy work, you feel a pain in your chest and worry that it might be a sign of a heart attack. In each case, you can seek to understand the truth—or you can struggle not to know the truth. You can give in to fear, guilt, discomfort, or sheer laziness and work to push the facts out of your mind.

Typically, evasion works by means of rationalizations—false reasons and spurious justifications people use to conceal from themselves and others that they're evading. "I've just been tired," you tell your partner, even though you dimly sense the truth: you're unhappy in the marriage. "I got sidetracked by other assignments," you tell the boss, trying not to think of the hours you've frittered away on social media. "That's probably just acid reflux," you tell yourself, trying to erase the terror that something more serious is going on.

But evasion, like focus, is a choice. In the very act of exercising effort not to know, you grasp that you could exercise the effort to know. It's no accident that 12-step recovery programs start by demanding that people acknowledge they have a problem. Addictions thrive off of rationalizations and evasions. You cannot act self-destructively with your eyes open. You have to actively work not to see into the future, not to see the obvious consequences of your actions, not to acknowledge the guilt, shame, and disappointment that's driving you to play Russian roulette with your life. Change is only possible once you make a choice. Not, in the first instance, a choice to alter your future behavior—but the choice to face the truth about where you are today.

One of the most prominent rationalizations people use to evade reality is *determinism*. Criminals love to say, "I couldn't help it." They talk about their tough upbringing. They talk about their temper. They talk about their dire financial situation. In one way or another, they argue: *don't blame me, I didn't choose to rob, rape, and kill.*

One thing that makes the determinist rationalization so compelling is that, insofar as you don't think, you *are* controlled by mysterious inner and outer forces. The determinist feels that determinism is true because, in a sense, he is not self-made. His motives and the source of his desires are a mystery. In a deeper sense, however, he *is* self-made. He *elected* to be controlled by something other than his own will. The truth he cannot escape is: he could have done otherwise.

## What Do We Introspect?

Sam Harris would deny all of this. He goes further than other determinists. They argue that when you experience yourself making choices, the sense that you are doing so freely is an illusion. Harris argues that you don't actually experience yourself making choices.

> [T]he deeper truth is that free will doesn't even correspond to any *subjective* facts about us—and introspection soon proves as hostile to the idea as the laws of physics are. Seeming acts of volition merely arise spontaneously (whether caused, uncaused, or probabilistically inclined, it makes no difference) and cannot be traced to a point of origin in our conscious minds. A moment or two of serious scrutiny, and you might observe that you no more decide

the next thought you think than the next thought I write.[18]

Harris acknowledges that some states of consciousness "seem self-generated, deliberative, and subject to our will."[19] If you hear a leaf blower outside your window, that's a state of awareness that arises automatically—yet when you try to ignore the noise and direct your attention somewhere else, that feels very different from passively hearing a sound. It feels like you're deciding to do something. In reality, it's just that: a *feeling*. "The phrase 'free will' describes what it *feels* like to identify with certain mental states as they arise in consciousness."[20]

Harris asks us to look closer.

When you seemingly choose to try to ignore the sound of leaf blower, what's actually happening? In Harris's view, your subconscious is sending up a thought: "Hey, ignore that leaf blower and focus on your writing!" Did you choose that thought? No, it just popped into your conscious mind. And why did you listen to the thought? Say, because your subconscious sent up another thought, "You'll get fired if you don't finish this article!" But you didn't choose that thought either. The ultimate reason for any of your decisions is "utterly mysterious" to you.[21]

> You have not built your mind. And in moments in which you *seem* to build it—when you make an effort to change yourself, to acquire knowledge, or to perfect a skill—the only tools at your disposal are those that you have inherited from moments past.
>
> Choices, efforts, intentions, and reasoning influence our behavior—but they are themselves part of a chain of causes that precede conscious awareness and over which we exert no ultimate control. My choices matter—and there are paths toward making wiser ones—but I cannot choose what I choose. And if it ever appears that I do—for instance, after going back and forth between two options—I do not *choose* to choose what I choose. There is a regress here that always ends in darkness. I must take a first step, or a last one, for reasons that are bound to remain inscrutable.[22]

But Harris's whole description of what it's like to think flies in the face of what we actually introspect. In Harris's view, if you look closely at your mental life, you'll see that your conscious mind is being controlled by thoughts coming from an invisible unconscious. "If you pay attention to your inner life, you will see that the emergence of choices, efforts, and intentions is a fundamentally mysterious process."[23]

But that's a bald assertion that in no one way describes what you're actually aware of when you think. What you're actually aware of is *directing* and *controlling* your thought process. Yes, thinking involves an interaction between your conscious mind and your subconscious. But it's your conscious mind that sets your intentions and passes verdicts on what your subconscious feeds you.

When you choose to focus on your writing and not the sound of the leaf blower, it's not some thought from your subconscious that makes you focus on your work—it's your *decision*. Can you give reasons for that decision? Yes. But you had to endorse those reasons and carry them out in action. And when it comes to the fundamental choice, the choice to engage in reasoning, there is no prior cause that *could* constitute a mysterious force directing your choice: there is only the sheer act of you willing your mind to pay attention and engage in mental management. Far from your thought processes being passive, you're aware of being in the driver's seat—and you're aware that you *put yourself* in the driver's seat.

## Free Will and Causality

The fact that you control your thought processes is self-evident. You can directly introspect it. It is no more open to doubt than that you're now looking at these words. And yet many people—and most professional intellectuals—deny it. Why?

Usually it's because they think there's a conflict between free will and cause and effect. Harris, for example, argues that "events have causes. Everything that arises seems to be born into existence by some previous state of the universe." And that includes consciousness. "[A]ll of our conscious experiences—our thoughts, intentions, desires, and the actions and choices that result from them—are caused by events that are not conscious and which we did not bring into being." He goes on:

> You didn't pick your parents, you didn't pick your genes therefore, and you didn't pick the environment into which you were born, and yet the totality of these facts determines who you are in each moment and what you do in the next. And even if you think you have an immaterial soul that somehow animates this machinery, you didn't pick your soul. The next thing you think and do can only emerge from this totality of prior causes, and it can only emerge in one of two ways: lawfully, that is deterministically, like one domino just getting knocked over by another—or randomly.[24]

Well, yes, if the law of causality means that events are necessitated by previous events, then there's no room for free will. But that's just one perspective on what causality is. Harris's argument amounts to: "If we assume that the only alternatives are deterministic causation or randomness, then human beings don't have free will." It assumes free will out of existence.

If we actually look at where our concept of causality comes from, however, it doesn't come from seeing events following inexorably from previous events. It comes from grasping a relationship between an entity and its actions. The world is causal, not because events necessitate other events, but because the things in the world act according to their identities. Our walking is caused by the movement of our legs. A bird's flying is caused by the flapping of its wings. A ball's rolling is caused by the nature of the ball as a solid, spherical object.

A thing's nature determines how it can act. And that's as true of human beings as it is of rocks. But our distinctive form of action is *choosing*—selecting among alternatives. You have no choice about the need to choose to raise your level of awareness or not—that is inherent in the identity of your mind—but *what* you choose is up to you. Your actions *are* caused—but they are *self*-caused.[25]

Is that a different form of causality than we see in inanimate objects? Absolutely. But so what? Quantum mechanics suggests that subatomic causality works differently than the familiar mechanistic causality we find among rocks and plants. Why would we think that the phenomenon of consciousness has to operate in the same manner as the non-conscious world?

One reason you might think that is because the mind is dependent on the brain: it has a material source and therefore must obey the deterministic causal laws matter is subject to. But that doesn't follow. As neuroscientist Kevin J. Mitchell notes, "Thoughts and feelings and choices are mediated by the physical influx of molecules in the brain, but this does not mean they can be reduced to it. They are emergent phenomena with causal powers in and of themselves."[26] The mind depends on the brain, but it isn't identical with the brain.

Harris and other determinists offer a false choice: determinism or randomness. But that leaves out a third alternative: self-causation. You are the cause of your choices. Free will, on this view, doesn't conflict with the law of causality—it is a type of causality.

## Free Will and Neuroscience

Determinists will sometimes trot out research from neuroscience to undermine the case for free will. Harris, for example, writes:

> The physiologist Benjamin Libet famously used EEG to show that activity in the brain's motor cortex can be detected some 300 milliseconds before a person feels he has decided to move. Another lab extended this work using functional magnetic resonance imaging (fMRI). Subjects were asked to press one of two buttons while watching a "clock" composed of a random sequence of letters

appearing on a screen. They reported which letter was visible at the moment they decided to press one button or the other. The experimenters found two brain regions that contained information about which button subjects would press a full *7 to 10 seconds* before the decision was consciously made. More recently, direct recordings from the cortex showed that the activity of a mere 256 neurons was sufficient to predict with 80 percent accuracy a person's decision to move 700 milliseconds before he became aware of it.[27]

Science, in short, has shown that we *think* we're making decisions, but in reality our brain has already made the decision for us. "These findings," Harris concludes, "are difficult to reconcile with the sense that we are the conscious authors of our actions."[28]

No, they're not. The fact that brain activity precedes a conscious choice doesn't show this activity causes the conscious choice. This brain activity could reflect the brain gearing up for a decision yet to be made by the mind. (In fact, Libet found that after the brain *seemed* to show test subjects had made the decision to move, they could inhibit that decision—which suggests that the brain activity didn't reflect a decision at all.)[29]

More important, all of these experiments assess random, arbitrary, meaningless decisions. But that is not what free will is. Free will isn't your power to press a random button at a random time. It is perfectly conceivable that when we set our mind to that sort of task, we wait for some random signal from our brain. Free will is our power to *think*— to engage in active mental management. None of these experiments are relevant to that activity.

## Free Will, Genes, and Environment

One indication of just how prevalent determinism is comes in the very concept of the "nature/nurture" debate. Scientists go back and forth over whether we're determined mostly by innate factors or environmental factors, with no one asking: are we determined by *anything?*

Psychologist Eric Turkheimer surveyed the scientific literature and found that about 40 to 50 percent of the variance in character traits scientists had studied could be attributed to heredity, while a tiny sliver more could be attributed to family upbringing. And between 40 and 60 percent couldn't be explained by either. Even if we take the scientific literature at face value, there's nothing remotely resembling evidence that human behavior is determined.[30]

And in fact it's not even obvious that what scientists are measuring when making claims about nature versus nurture are the kinds of things we have in mind when thinking about free will. For example, intelligence could theoretically be fully determined by nature, nurture, or some combination. That would say nothing about how a given individual exercises their cognitive ability.

Personality traits—openness to experience, conscientiousness, extroversion, agreeableness, and neuroticism—are more complicated. These traits are supposed to measure habitual patterns of behavior, thought, and emotion, and so cover (to some extent) the kinds of activities where free will is operative. The strong evidence these traits are partly heritable does pose a challenge. But the challenge is not to the existence of free will. Instead, the challenge is to explain how biology can influence volitional thoughts and behaviors, as well as emotions (which, as we'll see, aren't directly under our control but are ultimately explained by our volitional mental activities).[31]

Mitchell argues that biology creates "predispositions that make us more likely to act in certain ways in certain situations, but that doesn't mean that on any given instance we *have* to act like that. We still have free will, just not in the sense that we can choose to do any random thing at any given moment."[32] What Mitchell seems to have in mind is that our circuits for neuromodulators like dopamine and serotonin "work differently in each of us, thus influencing the habitual behavioral strategies we each tend to develop."[33] To oversimplify, certain kinds of actions are easier or more rewarding for some people than for others, and so we tend to develop different habits. To take an analogy, a person who takes opioids and doesn't experience the typical euphoric sensation is probably not going to become addicted, whereas the person for whom the euphoric rush is incredibly strong will have to exercise more self-control to keep from getting hooked.

I find Mitchell's account plausible, but for our purposes we can set the whole issue to the side. The point is that when it comes to your thoughts and actions, you are never determined by factors outside of your control, even if you are influenced by them. And there is nothing to suggest that your *basic* choice—to seize control of the reins of your mind and raise your level of awareness—is subject to such predispositions.

What, then, about environmental influences? Your environment can obviously have an impact on what you think about. But it can also make thinking easier or harder. Your environment can encourage independence, it can provide opportunities for a solid education—or it can preach (and demand) obedience to authority and replace education with indoctrination. But aside from extreme cases, such as severe instances of child abuse, what your environment cannot do is stop you from thinking. It cannot take away your ability to think, to judge, to question (nor can it compel you to think, judge, or question).

When I was in college, I remember talking to friends whose parents smoked cigarettes. And I can think of half-a-dozen times when my friends said, "I smoke because my parents smoke." But I can also think of half-a-dozen times when my friends said, "I don't smoke because my parents smoke." It wasn't the actions of their parents that determined their behavior—it was what they concluded about their parents' actions that determined their behavior. Their environments gave them the material for decision-making—their minds used that material to reach an independent judgment.

What is true is that to the extent you *don't* choose to think, you will be a product of your environment. That's why we do see a correlation between a person's environment and his ideas. It's why we find most Catholics had Catholic parents and most Muslims had Muslim parents. It's not that their environment determined their ideas—it's that, on some important issues, many people don't think. And if you don't think, you usually conform.

Environment matters. But the key to a person's soul is not the environment they are raised in, but how they characteristically choose to use their mind.

## You Control Your Emotions

If free will is your ability to think or not, to follow reason or not, that leads to a crucial question: What is the relationship between reason and emotion?

Since Plato, there has been a widespread view in philosophy that human nature is made up of warring elements: reason and emotion—logic and desire—mind and body. Free will, on this view, amounts to your ability to override your irrational desires. To shove aside what you want in the name of the true and the good.

It's not a crazy view. Reason and emotion can conflict. You know that you shouldn't eat a whole bag of Doritos—but you do. You know that you should hit the gym—but you don't. You know that you shouldn't spend four hours a day on social media—but you do. You know you should start working on that school assignment—but you don't. You know that you shouldn't sleep with that guy or girl—but you do. You know that you should ask that guy or girl on a date—but you don't.

Reason and emotion can conflict—but *they don't have to*. You aren't made up of two warring elements. Your desires need not be mysterious forces pulling you to act in ways that harm you, subvert your long-range goals, fill you with anxiety and guilt. Free will isn't about quieting or overriding your emotions—it's about bringing your emotions into harmony with reason.

No, you cannot control our emotions directly, the way you control your mind—but you can shape your emotions through how you use your mind so that they reflect your considered judgment. To see this, we need to take a closer look at what reason is and what emotions are.

## What Reason Is

Animals share our power to perceive the world; what they can't do is identify abstract relationships between the things they perceive. My cat Alfie can see a mouse. But he can't form the idea of "mouse." He can't study mice, learn about their biology, and start a mouse farm to mass produce thousands of tiny victims. Alfie just sees something that entices him and pounces.

Human beings do have the power of abstract thought. As Ayn Rand observes: this power

> does not consist merely of grasping a few simple abstractions, such as "chair," "table," "hot," "cold," and of learning to speak. It consists of a method of using one's consciousness, best designated by the term "conceptualizing." It is not a passive state of registering random impressions. It is an actively sustained process of identifying one's impressions in conceptual terms, of integrating every event and every observation into a conceptual context, of grasping relationships, differences, similarities in one's perceptual material and of abstracting them into new concepts, of drawing inferences, of making deductions, of reaching conclusions, of asking new questions and discovering new answers and expanding one's knowledge into an ever-growing sum. The faculty that directs this process, the faculty that works by means of concepts, is: *reason*. The process is *thinking*.[34]

By actively conceptualizing the world, you are better able to deal with the world. Reason is not some mysterious, mystical substance welded on to your body. It is a *biological* faculty. It's a vital organ—and just as your other organs have a survival function, so does your mind.[35] Reason doesn't exist for the sake of pure contemplation, but for the sake of helping you navigate through your environment to meet your needs.

Plants survive by taking in light and nutrients from their immediate surroundings. Consciousness expands the range of actions open to a living organism. Animals can perceive objects at a distance and use that awareness to move toward potential resources or away from potential threats. Reason allows human beings to act over far greater distances and timescales. You can have food delivered to you from miles away using phones that were built through a global supply chain. You can work on projects that won't pay off for a decade. As a human being, your potential environment consists of the entire universe, and your relevant timescale is not minutes or days but your entire lifespan.[36]

The incredible advances we've made since the Enlightenment in scientific knowledge and standard of living testify to the awesome power of the human mind. We can achieve unlimited knowledge—about the stars, atoms, chemicals, life, history—and translate that knowledge into technological marvels and life-sustaining processes. We turn ideas into buildings, theories into computers, thoughts into food, inductive inferences into vaccines, syllogisms into airplanes. Reason turns poverty into plenty. It's what expanded our lifespans from 30 to 80.

These grand scale achievements highlight the power of reason—but they don't exhaust it. Reason is what you use to set your goals and navigate your way toward them. It's what you use to learn and grow and make good decisions. It's what you use to understand and evaluate the people and things around you so that the world becomes intelligible. And it's what you use to make sense of your inner world, so that you can identify and fulfill your mental and emotional needs, as well as your physical ones.

Reason isn't just your tool of cognition—it is your basic means of survival, your capacity to invent and use technology, the source of human creativity, the source of human achievement, the tool that enables you to achieve joy, serenity, and exaltation.

## What Emotions Are

Reason is your volitional faculty: willpower is mind-power. To understand the world, solve problems, identify your needs and formulate strategies for meeting them, you have to exert effort and set your conscious mind to the task of understanding reality.

But your conscious mind is not the whole of your mind. You also have a subconscious. The subconscious isn't some mysterious realm with its own secret agenda. It's simply stored material that once was conscious and can be brought back into conscious awareness. For example, a friend asks (as friends often do): "Who did America fight in the War of 1812?" Your conscious mind queries your subconscious memory: "Who *did* America fight in the War of 1812?" Your subconscious feeds you a fact you learned way back in history class: "Britain." Then your conscious mind has the power to judge the answer. "Was it Britain? Were other parts of the empire involved, as well as Native American tribes?" All thinking involves a constant interaction between the conscious mind and the subconscious.

Abstract knowledge isn't the only thing that's stored in the subconscious. The subconscious also stores behaviors and skills. Think about what it was like to learn to drive. You didn't just study a manual and then start racing down the highway. Like all complex skills, learning to drive consists of consciously and deliberately performing certain actions until, over time, those actions become automatic. *Automatization* is what allows an activity like driving to become "second nature," so that you don't have to consciously think about each part of the process. You just drive, and your mind can focus on other things, like where you're going or who won the War of 1812. The same process accounts for your ability to walk, to tie your shoes, to play the piano, to throw a baseball.

This is the key to understanding emotions: just as you have automatized knowledge and automatized skills, so you have automatized *value judgments*. Your values are the things you choose to aim at, commit yourself to, take action to create, achieve, and maintain. Every emotion you feel—love, hate, anger, joy, sadness, etc., etc.—is a verdict on your values. The emotion tells you, in effect, "I want this" or "This will help me get what I want" or "I got what I want" or "This threatens what I want" or "I lost what I want" or "I don't want that." *"An emotion,"* in psychologist Nathaniel Branden's definition, *"is the psychosomatic form in which man experiences his estimate of the beneficial or harmful relationship of some aspect of reality to himself."*[37]

Joy, for instance, reflects the judgment that I've achieved a value. Love reflects the judgment that a value is a deep source of pleasure. Pride reflects the judgment I've lived up to my standards, especially my moral standards. Fear reflects the judgment that something threatens me. Sadness reflects the judgment that I've lost something I care about. Guilt reflects the judgment I have not lived up to my standards, especially my moral standards.

Your first awareness of values—of what's good for you and what's bad for you—comes from your physical pleasure/pain mechanism. A baby feels hunger pains and cries—the milk tastes delicious and feels good in its belly. Getting a hug from Mommy feels good. Getting a whack from the family cat feels bad. Your pleasure/pain mechanism is hardwired from birth and it's designed by natural selection to encourage you to act in ways that promote your life and protect you from danger.

But your physical pleasure/pain mechanism is extremely limited. It can tell you that a bullet entering your chest is bad—but not that the gun pointed at your chest is bad. It can tell you that a massage is good—but not that a promotion at work is good. Pleasure/pain depends on an immediate physical interaction between you and your environment. And it does not take into account long-range consequences. A brownie smothered in ice cream tastes incredible—even if it's moving you toward a heart attack at age 50. Going to the dentist feels like torture, even if it's protecting your dental health.

Your emotions have a function similar to your physical pleasure/pain mechanism. They too are feelings, but instead of working by a hard-wired physical mechanism, emotions are mediated by your ideas. This allows them to account for a much wider scope of benefits and harms.

For example, you decide that you want to work as a software engineer at Apple. That's your value—that's what you're going after in life. For years, you get out of bed at five in the morning and race to the computer to improve your coding skills. You turn down better paying jobs in favor of roles where you can build a track record of solving difficult, high-stakes programming challenges. You're driven by a conscious value judgment—"Working at Apple would be amazing"—and that judgment creates the emotional desire that propels you forward over the course of years. Then one day, you get a call: "You're hired." You feel elation. Think about that: nothing in your physical situation has changed. Just a few words uttered over a cell phone. And yet the emotional experience is more powerful and more pleasurable than the best massage.

Whereas all human beings share roughly the same pleasure/pain responses, our emotional reactions can vary enormously precisely *because* they depend on our ideas. Take Bitcoin. In March 2022, the price of a Bitcoin surpassed $47,000. But by June, it had crashed to $20,000. Speculators hoping to make a quick buck felt frustration, disappointment, even despair. True believers saw the crash as an opportunity to "buy the dip" and felt excitement. Bitcoin critics saw the crash as vindication and felt a sense of satisfaction and triumph. People who didn't understand cryptocurrency heard the news and felt nothing in particular, except perhaps confusion and relief that they hadn't missed out on an opportunity after all. Same event, different emotional reactions based on different ideas.

So while your pleasure/pain responses are programmed by evolution, your emotions are programmed by you. This imposes a tremendous responsibility: you cannot take your emotions as infallible guides to what's true or what's good. You have to check the programming.

The two basic questions you face about the external world are: "What do I know?" and "How do I know it?" When it comes to understanding your inner world, the two basic questions you face are: "What do I feel?" and "Why do I feel it?"

Here's the basic cause and effect chain that produces an emotion:

*Awareness* —> *Identification* —> *Evaluation* —> *Feeling*

The process of identification and evaluation that generates emotions is performed with lightning-like rapidity by your subconscious. To ask, "Why am I feeling what I feel?" is to slow things down and ask, "What is the subconscious identification and evaluation producing the emotion—and do I agree with it?" This last part is crucial. Emotions aren't infallible: you can mis-identify something, or you can mis-evaluate it, or both.

*Mis-identification.* You see the girl you just started dating at a restaurant with a guy you don't recognize. My God, she's cheating on you. You feel a surge of anger, jealousy, and, underneath it, hurt. But as you march over to their table she smiles and introduces you to her brother. You feel relief and mild embarrassment as you realize you completely misread the situation.

*Mis-evaluation.* Let's say you're a crackhead. You see some crack. You (subconsciously) identify it as crack. You (subconsciously) evaluate the crack as desirable because of the elation it has evoked in the past immediately after smoking it. You feel the desire to smoke it. So you smoke it and the police catch you and throw you in jail for five years. Your emotions told you the crack was good for you because the subconscious evaluation didn't take into account the long-term consequences of using crack.

If that was the whole story, introspection would be easy. But your subconscious identifications and evaluations are not independent from one another, like blades of grass arrayed on a field. You don't have a "girlfriend having dinner with a strange guy" blade and a "girlfriend texting" blade and a "girlfriend not returning my calls immediately" blade, all being interpreted in unrelated ways and sparking unrelated emotions. Rather, you have a more generalized set of beliefs that will encourage you to interpret and evaluate whole clusters of situations in similar ways. A jealous person *characteristically* will interpret situations in ways that will provoke jealousy. To make sense of your emotional life, and to improve it, requires understanding the source of these emotional patterns.

The automatized value judgments that produce emotions usually come in the form of automatic thoughts. You encounter a situation, your subconscious generates automatic thoughts about the situation and its positive or negative impact on you, and you react: emotionally, behaviorally, and physiologically. For example, you see a couple walking hand-in-hand down the street, have the automatic thought, "I'll never find someone," and experience sadness. You're singing in the car and realize people in the next car over can see you. You have the automatic thought, "I look like an idiot," and feel embarrassed.

Where do automatic thoughts come from? From a complex structure of ideas and values that starts with *core beliefs*. Core beliefs are beliefs about yourself, other people, and the world you form growing up that thereafter shape all of your emotions. Psychologists typically classify these in negative terms: helpless core beliefs ("I am incompetent," "I am weak," "I am out of control"), unlovable core beliefs ("I am unattractive," "I am bound to be rejected," "I am bound to be alone"), worthless core beliefs ("I am bad," "I am immoral," "I don't deserve to live") and external danger core beliefs ("The world is dangerous," "People can't be trusted," "Nothing ever goes right").

These core beliefs (and their positive counterparts) shape your attitudes, rules, and assumptions—your *intermediate beliefs*. Take someone with the core belief, "I'm incompetent." This could break down into the attitude, "It's terrible to fail." It could lead to the rule, "Give up if a challenge seems too great." It could produce the assumption, "If I try to do something difficult, I'll fail. If I avoid doing it, I'll be okay."[38]

This network of core and intermediate beliefs can become activated in specific situations, generating situation-specific automatic thoughts. Take the person who believes "I'm incompetent." She sits down to read a challenging new book. The material is difficult, and she finds herself having to re-read the same page multiple times. This generates the automatic thought, "This is just too hard. I'm so dumb. I'll never master this." She feels discouragement, and her default rule is, "Give up if a challenge seems too great" because "If I avoid doing something difficult I'll be okay." She sets down the book, and watches television.[39]

Notice how these negative thoughts and feelings lead to coping strategies—strategies that from the outside appear self-sabotaging to a person's welfare (if you watch TV instead of reading a difficult book, you could fail a class or lose your job), but which, from the inside, are experienced as routes of self-protection. Substance abuse, procrastination, binge eating, conflict avoidance, approval-seeking, and blaming (yourself and others) are just some of the traps you can fall into if you act blindly on your emotions. Emotionally, it feels like you're taking care of yourself. But existentially, you're harming yourself; psychologically, you're ignoring and reinforcing the *cause* of your negative emotions.

Emotions are crucial to life. They encourage you to act to achieve values and reward you for achieving them. They encourage you to change course if you're encountering frustrations and setbacks. In short, they provide crucial material for thinking and the motivation to act. But they are not infallible guides. Your subconscious doesn't automatically take into account a complete picture of the facts, and your value premises may or may not be true. Acting on them blindly *is* acting blindly.

How, then, should you deal with your emotions?

## Aligning Emotions and Reason

You are constantly experiencing low-level emotions—feelings of comfort or discomfort, engagement or boredom, irritation or tranquility, hope or worry, confidence or self-doubt, desire or aversion. These emotions are subtle and usually make up the background of your day—they don't consciously register unless you attend to them. When you "find yourself" rushing to the kitchen for a bag of Doritos when you're not actually hungry, or logging on to social media when you should be working, or snapping at your partner without knowing why, you're being moved by low-level negative emotions and the desire to numb them, escape them, release them, or replace them with a jolt of pleasure.

Other emotions are powerful. When they are triggered, *you know it*. This triggered state is so strong, in fact, that it can sometimes feel overwhelming. You can't focus on anything but the feeling. Calm deliberation can be impossible. These are the emotional states where acting on your feelings tends to leave you bewildered by your behavior and filled with regret. Your willpower, in such cases, doesn't vanish, but it can be reduced to sheer inhibition: you can choose to act on the emotion or not, to lash out or cool down, but you cannot do much else.

Whether it's low-level emotions or triggered states, when your thoughts and emotions conflict, what you're actually experiencing is a conflict of *ideas*: your conscious judgment versus an automatized, subconscious judgment. Instead of thinking of reason/emotion conflicts as warring elements within your soul, where victory requires squelching emotion or silencing reason, you should think about such conflicts as "misalignment." When your car is misaligned you don't go to war with your car's suspension. You just have it adjusted so that your steering wheel and tires are in harmony.

How does reason/emotion realignment work? By transforming

your reason/emotion conflict into a conflict of ideas and assessing those ideas rationally.

## Identification

The starting point for reason/emotion realignment is to become at home with your emotional world. That means first and foremost learning how to identify what you're feeling.

That's not as easy as it sounds. Most people repress their emotions to one degree or another. If you habitually push painful facts, conclusions, and feelings out of awareness, this can become automatized so that it happens without you even noticing it. To the degree you repress, you feel very little—and to the extent you do feel, you do not know what you're feeling or why.

One insignia of repression is an impoverished emotional vocabulary. Even if you decide you want to become more familiar with your inner life, you may find that when you try to identify what you're feeling you can't come up with much more than "happy," "sad," and "angry." I certainly had that problem. I literally had to print out a list of emotions and their definitions and study it like I was preparing for a test. But once I did, it was like discovering a whole new world.

Once you identify what you're feeling, you can start to articulate why you're feeling it. Whenever you have a notable emotional experience, put into words (a) the situation, (b) your automatic thoughts (i.e., the identifications and evaluations producing the emotion), (c) your emotion, and (d) your behavioral response.

The goal here isn't change, but the precondition of change: to understand the reality of your emotional life.

## Conscious questioning

Because emotions are "first take" reactions that don't automatically take into account all of the relevant facts, we can all have out-of-context emotions. No matter how confident you are, if you find yourself in a high-stakes, unfamiliar situation, you can experience self-doubt. No matter how healthy your relationship, you can experience sexual attraction to someone other than your partner. No matter how realistic you are, you can catastrophize a setback on a crucial project.

In these cases, aligning your thoughts and your feelings is relatively easy. Psychologist Judith Beck recommends some basic questions you can ask about any automatic thought:[40]

1.  What is the evidence that supports this idea? What is the evidence against this idea?
2.  Is there an alternative explanation or viewpoint?
3.  What is the *worst* that could happen (if I'm not already thinking the worst)? If it happened, how could I cope? What is the best that could happen? What is the most realistic outcome?
4.  What is the effect of my believing the automatic thought? What could be the effect of changing my thinking?
5.  What would I tell [a specific friend or family member] if he or she were in the same situation?
6.  What should I do?

Typically a few moments of thinking is enough to resolve these passing clashes. The greater challenge is enduring clashes between reason and emotion—cases where you have a pattern of feelings that are inappropriate or coping mechanisms that are self-destructive. This requires harder, more sustained work.

## Deep mining

Enduring conflicts are rooted in core (and intermediate) beliefs. These can be incredibly hard to identify and change. People's core beliefs, Beck points out, are "enduring understandings so fundamental and deep that they often do not articulate them, even to themselves. The person regards these ideas as absolute truths—just the way things 'are.'"[41]

Worse, core beliefs are self-reinforcing. It's easy to take in evidence that confirms your core beliefs, but disconfirming evidence gets reinterpreted so that it is confirming, or it just gets ignored. A person who believes "I'm incompetent" will not be attentive to their successes, or they'll see their successes as failures. They won't celebrate making the football team—they'll focus on the fact that they're not a starter. They won't recall all of the difficult books they did manage to read and understand—their mind will be flooded with the few books they tossed aside in frustration.

That said, you aren't a captive of your false beliefs—not even your core beliefs. But it takes work to identify and challenge them.

One way to identify core beliefs is through the downward arrow technique. You identify your emotion and the automatic thought that led to it, and then you ask: What does that mean to me?

For example, you are assigned a project for work, you go back to your office and look over your notes and think, "These make no sense." You feel a wave of fear. You ask yourself, "What does that mean to me?" You answer: "I didn't do a good job paying attention to what my boss wanted." Then you ask yourself, "Okay, if it's true that I didn't pay enough attention, what does *that* mean?" You answer: "I'm a lousy employee." You've now spotted an intermediate belief—an assumption that amounts to: "If I don't do a good job on a project, that means I'm a lousy employee."

Now you can go deeper and hunt for a core belief by asking: what does that mean *about* me? You might answer: "That I'm not good enough. That I'm incompetent."[42]


## Retraining

When you've identified your core and intermediate beliefs, and your coping strategies for dealing with the emotions they generate, that puts you in a position to change your beliefs and your actions. Not through sheer willpower, but through further thinking and action.

Cognitive behavioral therapists have developed dozens of tools to help in this process.[43] The most effective ones I've seen and used are in David D. Burns's *Feeling Great*. But, for a flavor: you might start by identifying the evidence for and against your core belief, and the evidence for and against a more accurate, new core belief. Or you can think of extreme examples to use as a contrast: Who are the people you regard as truly incompetent, and how do they compare to you? Or you can investigate the historical reasons you developed the core belief as a child: for instance, that your parents didn't make realistic demands of you but *impossible* demands that no child could live up to. You can speak to that child and help them reach a more accurate conclusion about their adequacy. As your new belief becomes more plausible to you, you can start to take actions to reinforce it and to weaken your old belief.

This is what mental management looks like when it comes to emotions. Instead of passively reacting to your emotions, you have the power to identify them, question them, and deliberate about your actions. That is the power of exercising your free will. That is what it means to think rather than to drift and evade. That is how you exert fundamental control over your emotions.

# You Control Your Life

From the time you're born, you're engaged in active self-creation. You teach yourself to crawl, then to walk, then to speak. You explore your environment, seeking out things that are interesting and rewarding. You test reality to distinguish what's firm and absolute from what's in flux and open to your will. You push the plate off your high chair and it crashes to the ground. Mommy puts it back and you knock it off. Does it fall again or not? Slowly, you adapt yourself to your environment, devising strategies for getting what you want and avoiding what you don't want.

If you are fortunate, this process of growth and maturity is aided by adults. They encourage you to explore. They respect your independence and nurture your desire for an increasing understanding of the world and mastery over the world. They fill your environment with potential values and introduce you to new challenges and adventures. When they see that you're bored with the toy kitchen set, they bring you into a real kitchen so you can learn to cook. When they see that you're bored with picture books, they introduce you to chapter books. They don't order you about but help you grasp the long-range consequences of your actions. Not "take a bath because I say so," but "if you bathe, you'll feel fresh and clean." You learn to project the longer-range consequences of your actions and to take responsibility for your choices.

Time passes and your sense of independence and autonomy increases. You start thinking at greater and greater levels of abstraction. You start projecting goals that reach further and further into the future. You're no longer making discrete choices about what to eat or what sports to play. You're taking on weighty decisions about what kind of person you want to become and what kind of life you want to lead.

All too often, this process of growth and maturity is not aided but impeded by adults. Sometimes they ignore and neglect you—not necessarily to the point of abuse, but they deprive you of the love, acceptance, and encouragement that provide a solid foundation for independent exploration of the world. In other cases, adults actively discourage your autonomy. They demand obedience. You retain your sovereignty, but your desire for self-direction is no longer an untempered source of joy and pride, but a source of pain and conflict. Your desire to understand, experiment, and enjoy life opens you up to threats, disapproval, punishment, and even violence. In the name of peace and safety, you can kill your soul before it is fully born. You can surrender your autonomy and come to fear it, clinging to the security of obedience. Or you can plow ahead, telling yourself that the adults around you are *wrong* and that, someday, you will be in charge of your own life.

Whatever your circumstances, whatever path you choose, the fact that you are self-made is an ineradicable part of human nature. You are not clay that can be molded (though you can allow yourself to be molded if you choose to surrender your mind). You are free and sovereign. You can be imprisoned, enslaved, or destroyed, but you cannot be controlled. Not without your consent.

And yet it does not always seem like you are in control of your life. You can feel trapped by your circumstances, blindsided by external events, suffocated by your boss or partner or children, overburdened by the demands of life.

To say that human beings have free will leaves unanswered one crucial question: *What does it mean to control your life in a world where so much is outside of your control?* If, psychologically, human agency consists of the ability to control your mind, what does it consist of existentially?

The first thing to say is: a lot of things *are* outside of your control. You can't control the nature of nature. You can't wish away the law of gravity, you can't wish away the fact that life is finite, you can't wish away the fact that you must exert effort to get what you want and that success is never guaranteed. These facts are not subject to your control—they are the conditions under which you exercise your control. "Nature, to be commanded, must be obeyed," Bacon said. Human capability is not the power to wish facts into or out of existence—it is the power to understand what exists and rearrange what exists to achieve your purposes.

Take COVID-19. That disease was a fact—not something we could wish out of existence. Some people did try to wish it out of existence, arguing in defiance of facts that it was not a serious threat, trivializing a rising body count, mocking anyone who took sensible precautions to avoid getting sick. Others accepted the fact of COVID-19—most especially the scientists who worked to understand its nature. They used that knowledge to engineer the vaccines and treatments that helped end the pandemic. They obeyed the facts of reality—and were able to command nature on a grand scale.

Human choice is a limited power but an awesome power. We cannot wish disease out of existence—but we can create vaccines. We cannot will ourselves to fly—but we can create airplanes. We cannot pray our way to nourishment—but we can create farms, factories, and grocery stores.

Just as the nature of nature is outside of your control, so are the choices of other people. You cannot make someone think what you think or want what you want. You cannot will someone to love you or to give you a job. But here, too, you are not powerless. You have the tool of persuasion. You have the power to make yourself worthy of love or worthy of employment. And, if you cannot persuade a potential lover or employer, you have the power to go your own way and explore new romantic or career opportunities.

The Serenity Prayer got it right: life requires serenely accepting what you cannot change, courageously changing what you can, and acquiring the wisdom to know the difference. *That* is what it means to take control of your life.[44]

Too many people *don't* take control of their lives. They cheat themselves by *not* trying to control what they can. Think of the people who resign themselves to flaws in their character with the excuse, "That's just the way I am." Think of the people who resign themselves to poverty because "I wasn't born rich." Think of the people who go to school because "I have to" or who stay in a loveless marriage because "I have to" or who stay in a joyless job because "I have to" or who go to church because "I have to." Think of anyone who refuses to question tradition, or convention, or what their parents want, or what some authority says, and blames others for their problems.

As a human being, there's nothing you *have to* do except obey (or futilely rebel against) reality. Everything else is a choice. This fact is crucial to keep in mind because it will allow you to distinguish between *duties*—suffering you endure because you think you're supposed to—and *values*, which always require effort, and which often require struggle, frustration, and hardship. There are no duties in life. There are no unchosen obligations. The only time you should accept the unpleasant is when it's necessary to get what you want. And by the same token, if you surrender what you want because you're not willing to pay the price to get it, then you're selling out your life—and you have no excuse. The only thing stopping you is you.

There's one partial exception here: when others try to *impose* duties on you by the use of physical force. Here the issue is simple. Whereas you should never rebel against reality, you must rebel against coercion in whatever form is open to you. That may mean advocating freedom and voting for candidates who support freedom. It may mean fleeing a dictatorship or taking up arms against it. In the worst case, rebellion may mean reminding yourself, as you're trapped inside a tyrant's prison, that your punishment is unjust and that you deserve to be free.

The tragedy is how many people who *are* free rob themselves of happiness by refusing to control what they can. They don't engage their minds, they don't choose goals, they don't work to achieve them, and so they surrender control over their lives. They tell themselves that success comes from good luck and that they are the helpless victim of bad luck. Such people *do* become deterministic puppets whose life course is the product of chance. But they made themselves into puppets. They could have been human beings.

The reality is that free will doesn't give you total control over your life—it gives you *fundamental* control. It gives you the power to set long-range goals, accumulate knowledge relevant to your goals, and move purposefully toward your goals, even in the face of obstacles. You can try to predict and prepare for chance events. When you encounter good luck, you can act to capitalize on it. When you encounter bad luck, you can search for another route to your goal, sometimes even turning negatives into positives. Free will is your ongoing ability to set (and change) your life course, and to continually engage in learning so you can develop new and better strategies for moving from where you are to where you want to be.

For example, when I started working as a freelance writer, I had no illusions that my success was under my total control. I couldn't control the economy, I couldn't control whether other people would pay me for my services, I couldn't control whether competitors would try to undercut me on price. But I didn't feel as though I were playing the lottery because I wasn't. I was able to take an active role in creating the future I wanted.

I was able to reach out to potential clients, and when I received rejections, to mine those for lessons: Was I going after the wrong market? Had I priced my services too high? Had I failed because my sales skills were lousy? And when I did win clients, I was in control of how I performed, and by meeting and surpassing their expectations I could ask for referrals and further expand my client base. That's what agency looks like.

The circumstances you find yourself in and the chance events that come your way don't control you—they provide a context for your choices. They present you with challenges and opportunities, and it's your choices that determine whether you overcome your challenges and whether you capitalize on your opportunities.

You control your life, and if you want to make the most of that life, you have one job: to take charge. To focus, to think, to open your eyes. That is the path to happiness.

# Lesson 3

# Pursue Happiness

## You Need a Guide for Happiness

The most personal question you can ask someone is, "Are you happy?" To answer that question honestly means confessing every secret: the state of your psychology, the state of your sex life, the state of your moral character. Happiness is a verdict on how your life is going. It is, in Ayn Rand's definition, "that state of consciousness which proceeds from the achievement of one's values."[45]

Happiness is your highest spiritual state—and your most demanding. It's not a string of transitory pleasures that comes from satisfying short-range desires. It takes precious little experience and reflection to see that a life made up of nothing but vacations, massages, and Netflix binging is not a life worth living. Pizza is delicious, but it won't cure misery.

This has led some to declare that satisfying your desires is irrelevant to happiness. Under the influence of Eastern philosophy and Stoicism, much of today's conversation about happiness equates it with *absence* of desire. On this view, desire leads to frustration, and happiness is really about avoiding frustration and other negatives. Stop wanting anything and you'll have everything you want. As Ryan Holiday, a champion of Stoicism, puts it:

> The key to happiness, to success, to power—any of these things— is not to want them really bad. It's not putting what you're after on a pedestal. The key to happiness and success is realizing at a granular level that the things most people desire actually suck.
>
> That being rich isn't that great. That getting lots of attention is a chore. That being in love is also a lot of work. That the prettiest view in the world still has mosquitos or a biting chill or it's hot as hell.[46]

There's another word for people who think that life has little to offer: *depressed*. The view that life is suffering and desire is suffering and happiness is to be found in becoming someone who cares for nothing can't lead to happiness. It means *giving up* on happiness.

Achieving desires, if they are rational, is vital to happiness. They aren't empty, they don't suck, they are that great. Your goal should be to value deeply, passionately, and rationally—not squelch your desires. Your aim should be to care so much for your values that you will live for them and, if necessary, die for them—not to turn yourself into an empty vessel who experiences meeting the love of your life and watching the love of your life murdered with the same equanimity.

Happiness is *not* "not giving a shit." It's an enduring form of joy that comes from achieving your values and being on the road to achieving even greater values. Externally, it means being engaged with life, tackling meaningful goals, and realizing them over time. Internally, it means being proud, confident, and serene. You feel good about who you are, sure of what you can do, worthy of what you achieve. Happiness is *love of being alive*.

You can see that state, or the precursor to it, in children, who typically face life with a sense of eagerness, wonder, playfulness, and delight. Their attitude amounts to: *the world is here for my fun and enjoyment*. At the adult level, I like to think of the attitude projected by famed scientist Richard Feynman, who conveyed a childlike zest for life, that same passionate playfulness, but encompassing a much wider and deeper sense of the fun and enjoyment that life offers. And I also think of people I know who are quiet and serious. Their happiness doesn't leap out at you, but you can sense it if you pay attention— it's a calm but unmistakable radiance that comes across as an ease in living, an unself-conscious pride, an air of dignity earned through virtue. Happiness comes in varieties, and it whispers as much as it yells, but its indelible mark is peace and passion.

A common mistake is to view happiness as a sense of finality, where the work of living is done. Social scientist Arthur Brooks commits this error when he equates happiness with satisfaction and observes that no matter what you achieve, you're never truly satisfied. He recounts a conversation with his teenage daughter:

> As we wind our way through life, I explained, satisfaction—the joy from fulfillment of our wishes or expectations—is evanescent. No matter what we achieve, see, acquire, or do, it seems to slip from our grasp. . . . Satisfaction, I told my daughter, is the greatest paradox of human life. We crave it, we believe we can get it, we glimpse it and maybe even experience it for a brief moment, and then it vanishes.[47]

There is no great paradox here. The reason no single value can satisfy you for eternity is because the work of living is never done. Happiness is a perspective on the ongoing life process. It's not about achieving one goal and then living happily ever after; it's about being the kind of person who continually sets goals, achieves them, and sets still further goals. You can and must satisfy your desires—but you will never satisfy *desire*. What would be the point of living if you could?

This, then, is what it means to commit yourself to happiness: to draw a line in the sand and say, "I'm going to do everything in my power to make the external and internal conditions of my life as good as possible. I'm going to settle for nothing less than the best life I can create."

Not everyone does that. Not everyone makes the commitment to be happy. Everyone may wish to be richer than they are or feel better about themselves than they do. But all too often people tolerate failure, frustration, and fear. Forget about what they wish and judge them by their actions: their lives don't matter to them.

Happiness is a goal you have to embrace by *choice*.

To pursue happiness, you must conceive and achieve a life you want to live. You have to formulate a vision of the particular values that will constitute *your* life—and then take responsibility for everything that's required to achieve those values. To quote a Spanish proverb Ayn Rand was fond of: "God said: Take what you want and pay for it."[48]

Happiness *is* about getting what you want. But reality and human nature impose limits on the kind of wants that *can* be achieved. You cannot achieve the impossible: success without effort, self-esteem without virtue, love without self-esteem. Attaining happiness requires choosing a life that is attainable. Nor can you achieve contradictory goals, since the fulfillment of one aim will frustrate your other aims. If you desire health and fitness, you cannot also eat and drink whatever you feel like. If you desire to save adequately for your future, you cannot also buy whatever you want whenever you want. If you desire a fulfilling romantic relationship, you cannot also jump into bed with any attractive person you meet. To achieve happiness, you need to conceive of a life where all your goals and the actions required to achieve them fit together into a harmonious whole. Only then can you realize "that state of consciousness which proceeds from the achievement of one's values." Rand elaborates:

> Happiness is not to be achieved at the command of emotional whims. Happiness is not the satisfaction of whatever irrational wishes you might blindly attempt to indulge. Happiness is a state of non-contradictory joy—a joy without penalty or guilt, a joy that

does not clash with any of your values and does not work for your own destruction, not the joy of escaping from your mind, but of using your mind's fullest power, not the joy of faking reality, but of achieving values that are real, not the joy of a drunkard, but of a producer. Happiness is possible only to a rational man, the man who desires nothing but rational goals, seeks nothing but rational values and finds his joy in nothing but rational actions.[49]

What are rational goals, rational values, and rational actions? How do you know what sorts of aims and actions can form a rewarding, achievable, non-contradictory whole worthy of your striving? The science that answers these questions is ethics, or, the study of moral principles. Morality is the subject that helps you conceive and achieve a life filled with joy.

That is the purpose of this lesson. To define a *morality of happiness* to guide your choices to that you can build a self and a life that you love.

Many of the goals and actions that will constitute your life will be particular to you. Morality doesn't tell you whom to marry, where to live, or what kind of work to do. Instead, it takes a mountaintop perspective on human life and identifies the broad categories of needs, goals, and activities that constitute the human way of life. It gives you an abstract summary of what human flourishing consists of, and then leaves open to you the particular ends and means that fit your unique context.

You can think of morality as a travel guide. It doesn't dictate your vacation. Instead, it lays out for you all the desirable places you might wish to go (and how to get there) and warns you about the dangerous places you should avoid. It's up to you to choose from among those options based on what you want.

This isn't how we're taught to think of morality. We're taught to think of morality as a set of rules and prohibitions keeping us from doing what we want and commanding us to sacrifice ourselves. It's not that we're taught this conception of morality is true, and other conceptions of morality are false. What's drummed into our heads since birth is that morality *means* giving up what we want. This amounts to equating the *subject* of morality with a particular conception of morality we've inherited from Christianity. Morality simply *is* something that places limits on what we want. What we want? That has nothing to do with morality. That is mere prudence and practicality. Morality is about setting aside prudence and practicality in order to obey God's plan or serve other people or do our duty because it is our duty.

But most people do want to live and enjoy their life here on earth. They yearn for guidance. But what the culture has offered them, tragically, is a false alternative: happiness without morality—and morality without happiness.

## Happiness Without Morality

"Do what makes you happy."

If you're under the age of 50, you've probably heard that message all your life. From your parents, your teachers, your friends, the media, popular entertainment. Maybe you've even heard it at church. Sure, you'll also be told to share your toys, to love your enemies, to serve a cause greater than yourself, to think of others first. But declaring that you want to be happy will not exactly send shockwaves through your community and transform you into a counter-cultural rebel. It won't even get you canceled on social media.

Probably.

What is true is that the pursuit of happiness is not seen as a moral quest, and the advice offered to help you achieve happiness is not moral advice. Happiness is seen as a perfectly fine thing to want, but that has to do with the practical side of life. The side that involves getting a job, making money, seeking out pleasure and fun. And the people we turn to for such advice aren't moral philosophers. More often than not, we turn to the self-help industry.

Self-help can definitely be helpful. My own shelves are filled with books by Tim Ferriss, Robert Greene, and Brian Tracy. And if we extend "self-help" to include success advice more generally, then I sometimes wonder where I would be without Cal Newport's productivity advice, Dan Kennedy's marketing advice, or John Gottman's relationship advice.

The problem is not that the success field is unhelpful. It's that it's hit or miss. Take today's most successful self-help author, Tony Robbins. For every good idea about goal setting or breaking out of self-destructive patterns there are an equal or greater number of ideas that are pure junk science—from his obsession with "neuro-linguistic programming" to advice from one of his early books to eat nothing but fruit for the first half of the day because something something alkaline.

Even books that aren't filled with bad advice are generally superficial. I mentioned goal setting, which shows up not just in Tony Robbins's work but in probably 50 percent of the self-help literature. I'm a fan of goal setting, but these books almost never answer vital question like: What goals should I set? What is truly worth going after in life? What kind of goals are achievable and how can I select goals that fit together so that I can build a life worth living? Answering these questions is left to the reader—yet *these* are the hard questions. Yes, it is difficult to get what you want. But knowing what you want, and knowing that it's worth wanting? That is life's most daunting challenge.

Given the shortcomings of the self-help genre, more and more people are turning to psychology for guidance. Positive psychologists like Martin Seligman concluded that psychology had focused for too long on helping people escape negatives like depression, anxiety, and addiction. Didn't it have advice for people who simply wanted to be happier?

Unlike self-help books, psychology promises a scientific approach to happiness. Psychologists use "happiness studies" to attempt to understand the sources of happiness and unhappiness. That seems sensible enough, but the results have been underwhelming.

Happiness studies try to establish a science of happiness basically through polling and statistical regressions. What traits are associated with people who report being happy—and what traits are associated with people who report being unhappy?

Some of these polls literally just ask people how happy they are. Others try to break happiness into components. Here, for example, is the Oxford Happiness Questionnaire, which is typical. People are asked to rate themselves 1–6 on each of these, with 6 being strongly agree and 1 being strongly disagree.[50]

### Oxford Happiness Questionnaire

1. I don't feel particularly pleased with the way I am.
2. I am intensely interested in other people.
3. I feel that life is very rewarding.
4. I have very warm feelings towards almost everyone.
5. I rarely wake up feeling rested.
6. I am not particularly optimistic about the future.
7. I find most things amusing.
8. I am always committed and involved.
9. Life is good.
10. I do not think that the world is a good place.
11. I laugh a lot.
12. I am well satisfied about everything in my life.
13. I don't think I look attractive.
14. There is a gap between what I would like to do and what I have done.
15. I am very happy.
16. I find beauty in some things.
17. I always have a cheerful effect on others.
18. I can fit in (find time for) everything I want to.
19. I feel that I am not especially in control of my life.
20. I feel able to take anything on.

21. I feel fully mentally alert.

22. I often experience joy and elation.

23. I don't find it easy to make decisions.

24. I don't have a particular sense of meaning and purpose in my life.

25. I feel I have a great deal of energy.

26. I usually have a good influence on events.

27. I don't have fun with other people.

28. I don't feel particularly healthy.

29. I don't have particularly happy memories of the past.

The problem? A lot of these questions are irrelevant to happiness ("I laugh a lot," "I can fit in (find time for) everything I want to"), some of them are arguably negatively correlated with genuine happiness ("I have very warm feelings toward almost everyone," "I find most things amusing"), and if you take into account the way that people rationalize immorality, roleplay to themselves and to others, and poorly introspect then you would conclude that this whole approach to understanding happiness is hopeless. It's worth noting, in this regard, that the Oxford Happiness Questionnaire wasn't developed to study happiness: it was, according to its authors, originally "designed for clinical application with the purpose of diagnosing manic and depressive states of mind."[51]

To teach us anything about happiness, psychological studies have to decide how to define and measure happiness. But how to define happiness is a philosophic question. For example, is happiness the avoidance of pain? Or is it the achievement of joy? Is happiness temporary jolts of positive emotion? Or is it an enduring state? Is it easy to know whether one is happy? Or does it take an ability for introspection and self-honesty that most people lack?

Here is one example that illustrates why trying to understand happiness while ignoring philosophy can lead psychologists to produce extremely misleading results. A research team led by Katherine

Nelson-Coffey performed an experiment where they divided partici-pants into four groups. Group 1 was asked to perform "random acts of kindness" for themselves (for example, going shopping); Group 2 was asked to perform "random acts of kindness" for other people (for example, visiting an elderly family member); Group 3 was asked to perform acts of kindness to improve the world (for example, donate to charity); Group 4, the control group, was asked simply to track their daily activities. Can you guess the results? Groups 2 and 3 rated higher on a happiness questionnaire given to them in the weeks following the experiment, while Group 1's results were indistinguishable from the control group.[52]

Studies like this one have led many psychologists to conclude that serving and sacrificing for others is part of the formula of happiness. What nonsense. For one thing, being kind to other people is definitely *not* the same thing as serving and sacrificing for them. Even charity need not be a sacrifice: part of how we pursue our interests is by help-ing the people and causes we care about. It's as if you observed that people who owned guns were happier than people who didn't and con-cluded that murder leads to happiness.

But there's also a subtler problem. We live in a culture where peo-ple have been taught since birth that serving and sacrificing for others makes you a good person. Most people base their self-esteem, at least in part, on that idea. So should we be surprised that when they see them-selves as acting unselfishly, this leaves them feeling good, at least for a while? *That is precisely what an advocate of self-interest would predict.*

The question is not whether something makes you feel good for a few days or a few weeks, but whether something *is* good for you in the full context of your whole life. Think of a man whose sense of self-worth is based on the idea that "I'm good because women desire me." He may very well bask in the glow of his latest conquest for a while, but that only masks the deeper sense of inadequacy he's trying to compensate for. Altruistic acts perform a similar role for people without a secure foundation of self-esteem, only it's more powerful because the whole culture tells them that self-sacrifice really does make them good. It's as if the seducer lived in a society of pick-up artists, where every notch in his bedpost won him lavish praise from his community. Would his positive affect prove that promiscuity was a pillar of happiness?

Emotions, we've seen, emerge from your values, and if you achieve something you value, you will experience that as an emotional positive, regardless of whether it's genuinely good for you. This means that it is a fundamental error to try to establish what you *should* value by asking, "What makes you feel good?" The answer will be: *whatever you happen to value.*[53] Irrational values do leave a mark: a positive feeling one day will be followed by a hangover the next; momentary relief from suffering will be followed by worse suffering in the future; the satisfaction of one desire will conflict with other desires. But those second- and third-order effects won't be captured by a psychologist's survey. Could happiness studies have any value? Maybe. But their value would depend on first reaching a philosophic understanding of what happiness is and the fundamental values it requires.

The clearest evidence that our conventional approach to happiness doesn't work is that it *hasn't worked.* In a world saturated by bestsellers promising happiness without morality, what we've seen is sky-high rates of addiction, depression, loneliness, anxiety, *unhappiness.*

This has led a growing number of voices to proclaim that we've been pursuing the wrong thing. The pursuit of happiness has failed, they argue, because concern with your own personal happiness is the wrong goal. The reason people are so unhappy is because they're trying to be happy. Instead, they should try to be moral.

The most eloquent spokesman for this view is *New York Times* columnist David Brooks. A moral person, says Brooks in his bestseller *The Road to Character,* "wants to love intimately, to sacrifice self in the service of others, to live in obedience to some transcendent truth, to have a cohesive inner soul that honors creation and one's own possibilities."[54] Instead, most of us are "career-oriented, ambitious."[55] We want to "build, create, produce, discover things."[56] And the tragedy is that our culture has encouraged this ambitious, creative self-assertiveness at the expense of a moral concern with self-sacrifice.

> As I looked around the popular culture I kept finding the same messages everywhere: You are special. Trust yourself. Be true to yourself. Movies from Pixar and Disney are constantly telling children how wonderful they are. Commencement speeches are larded with the same clichés: Follow your passion. Don't accept limits. Chart your own course. You have a responsibility to do great things because you are so great. This is the gospel of self-trust.[57]

The result, Brooks says, is a culture that turns people into shrewd, crafty, fame-hungry narcissists who lead shallow, lonely, empty lives.

Is he right? Is the cause of our unhappiness seeking happiness? And is a morality that preaches selflessness and self-sacrifice the cure?

## Morality Without Happiness

One of the laziest, and most common, rhetorical techniques is to offer your audience a choice between false alternatives. When President Obama was promoting the Affordable Care Act, he would often say that his opponents thought the status quo in healthcare was fine, and anyone troubled by problems with the existing healthcare system should support his plan. The possibility that some of his critics recognized the very real problems in American healthcare but thought the ACA would make them worse? Inconceivable.

David Brooks and other crusaders for sacrifice play the same game. You can either lead an empty life of self-interest, which consists of accumulating money, power, and status by any means necessary—or you can recognize that there are things more valuable than money, power, and status and embrace selflessness and self-sacrifice.

To drive home this alternative, Brooks tells the story of two football players: Johnny Unitas and Joe Namath. "Unitas grew up in the old culture of self-effacement and self-defeat," says Brooks. As a result, he was "unflamboyant and understated," an "honest workman doing an honest job."[58]

Namath, by contrast, "lived in a different moral universe" that celebrated the individual, and he embodied this new ethos. Namath was brash and braggadocios, viewing himself as "bigger than the team." The man titled his autobiography *I Can't Wait Until Tomorrow 'Cause I Get Better Looking Every Day.*

> Without a reticent bone in his body, he'd bring reporters along as he worked his way through bottles of scotch the night before games. He openly bragged about what a great athlete he was, how good-looking he was. He cultivated a brashly honest style. "Joe! Joe! You're the most beautiful thing in the world!" he shouted to himself in the bathroom mirror of the Copacabana one night in 1966.[59]

Who do you admire more? Who do you want to emulate? Brooks, of course, intends the answer to be self-evident. And maybe it is. But it leaves out a third alternative: a conception of self-interest that *doesn't* involve the amoral pursuit of money, power, and status. A conception of self-interest that takes morality seriously. A conception of self-interest that doesn't counsel hiding your insecurity behind a mask of false confidence, but which teaches you how to achieve true self-confidence—the kind that doesn't need to announce itself because it comes from the conviction not that "I'm better than others," but that "I'm good."

That is the concept of self-interest I'll be presenting in the rest of this book. Before we turn to that, however, I want to make clear what it is the opponents of happiness advocate as the alternative to self-interest. Because just as they give us a distorted picture of what it means to pursue your own interests, they paint a distorted picture of what it means to altruistically sacrifice your own interests. When they speak of altruism, they call to mind a vision of people who are warm, joyful, caring, benevolent, helpful. People whose lives are rich in meaning and whose strong moral character challenges and inspires us. Nothing could be further from the truth. What the advocates of morality without happiness are selling is poison. It has nothing positive to offer you.

Even though we're taught to equate altruism with caring about others or helping others, that's not how the term is used in practice. Consider this: who is more celebrated for their altruism—Moderna or Mother Teresa? Thanks to its COVID-19 vaccine, Moderna has saved millions of lives. And yet no one calls it altruistic. Why not? Because it profited by helping others. In fact, *The Intercept* named Moderna and BioNTech executives the *worst* Americans of 2021 because . . . their revolutionary life-saving vaccines made them billionaires.[60] Mother Teresa, by contrast, is the symbol of altruism. Not because of how helpful she was to the world's poor, but because of how much she *sacrificed* for the world's poor.

Take a simpler example. Who would get the most moral credit? A billionaire who gave away a hundred million dollars to charity—or someone who gave his entire $50,000 life savings to charity? The person who helped the most—or the person who sacrificed the most?

And it's not just about moral credit. What about moral blame? In late 2021, YouTuber Jimmy Donaldson, better known as MrBeast, created a real-life contest modeled after the show *Squid Game*, and the video quickly gained more than 100 million views. MrBeast, in case you don't know, is famous for videos in which he gives away enormous amounts of cash (and for charity drives that regularly raise tens of millions of dollars). In his first viral video, for example, he gave away $10,000 to a homeless person. What was the response to his Squid Game video?

> WTF? Your bio says "i wan to make the world a better place before i die" but you are wasting money and resources on building some random SQUID game??? You could give millions of dollars to everyone so no one is poor but instead you waste it on this stupid game.[61]

The backlash was so widespread even the media covered it. "You-Tube Star MrBeast Criticised for $3.5 Million Real-Life 'Squid Game'" read one headline.[62] The message was clear. It doesn't matter if you give away tens of millions of dollars: if you do *anything* that benefits yourself, you're selfish and immoral.

Altruism is not a synonym for "nice." It means, as one dictionary reports, "the belief in or practice of disinterested and selfless concern for the well-being of others."[63] The term was coined by the positivist philosopher Auguste Comte. "Thus the expression, *Live for Others*, is the simplest summary of the whole moral code of Positivism," he wrote.[64] Comte is largely forgotten today, but he was highly influential in the 19th century. Even many of his critics happily embraced his moral ideal, which was seen as a substitute for Christian ethics at a time when religion was a waning influence among the era's thought leaders. Religionists warned that the death of God would mean the death of morality. The altruists said not to worry: instead of serving God, we can simply serve humanity. Indeed, altruists claimed to be morally superior to Christians, who selfishly demanded personal immortality as a reward for virtue. A truly virtuous person, said Comte's follower John Bridges, believes that "Our duty is to annihilate ourselves if need be for the service of Humanity."[65]

Though people today are seldom that explicit about the meaning of altruism, it is Comte who they are echoing when they condemn Moderna and MrBeast. Ayn Rand summarizes the doctrine this way:

What is the moral code of altruism? The basic principle of altruism is that man has no right to exist for his own sake, that service to others is the only justification of his existence, and that self-sacrifice is his highest moral duty, virtue and value.

Do not confuse altruism with kindness, good will or respect for the rights of others. These are not primaries, but consequences, which, in fact, altruism makes impossible. The irreducible primary of altruism, the basic absolute, is *self-sacrifice*—which means: self-immolation, self-abnegation, self-denial, self-destruction—

which means: the *self* as a standard of evil, the *selfless* as a standard of the good.

Do not hide behind such superficialities as whether you should or should not give a dime to a beggar. That is not the issue. The issue is whether you *do* or do *not* have the right to exist *without* giving him that dime. The issue is whether you must keep buying your life, dime by dime, from any beggar who might choose to approach you. The issue is whether or not the need of others is the first mortgage on your life and the moral purpose of your existence. The issue is whether man is to be regarded as a sacrificial animal. Any man of self-esteem will answer: *"No."* Altruism says: *"Yes."*[66]

What makes it hard to pin down the meaning of altruism is that few people today explicitly advocate it. Not because they don't believe it—but because *everyone* believes it. It's the same reason why you won't find many Southerners defending racism in the early 1800s. There was no one to defend it against. One person who does publicly champion altruism today is Peter Singer, who *The New Yorker* has called "the most influential living philosopher" and who was named by *Time* as one of the "100 most influential people in the world."[67] His argument is precisely that everyone believes altruism to be true, but almost no one seriously tries to live up to its demands—no one except the burgeoning movement of Effective Altruists.

In his popular book, *The Most Good You Can Do: How Effective Altruism Is Changing Ideas About Living Ethically,* Singer describes some of the activities that characterize Effective Altruism, a movement that encourages people to "do the most good we can."[68]

Effective altruists do things like the following:
- Living modestly and donating a large part of their income—often much more than the traditional tenth, or tithe—to the most effective charities;
- Researching and discussing with others which charities are the most effective or drawing on research done by other

independent evaluators;

- Choosing the career in which they can earn most, not in order to be able to live affluently but so that they can do more good;

- Talking to others, in person or online, about giving, so that the idea of effective altruism will spread;

- Giving part of their body—blood, bone marrow, or even a kidney—to a stranger.[69]

By way of illustration, he tells the story of a promising philosophy student who abandons a career in philosophy to work on Wall Street so he would have more money to give away.[70] He tells the story of Zell Kravinsky, who gave away most of his $45 million fortune and, convinced he had not sacrificed enough, donated a kidney to a stranger.[71] He tells us about a young woman named Julia Wise, who struggled with the decision of whether to have children: "she felt so strongly that her choice to donate or not donate meant the difference between someone else living or dying that she decided it would be immoral for her to have children. They would take too much of her time and money."[72] (Singer reassuringly says altruism is compatible with having children since they too might grow up to be altruists.[73])

What altruism requires of us is not the occasional donation to the Make-a-Wish Foundation. Indeed, Singer thinks it's morally dubious to give money to make dying children happy when that same money could be used to stop other children from dying.[74] But his main point is that altruism demands radical sacrifice. To take altruism seriously, you don't need to give up everything—but you should give up virtually everything.

[I]n 1972, when I was a junior lecturer at University College, Oxford, I wrote an article called "Famine, Affluence and Morality" in which I argued that, given the great suffering that occurs during famines and similar disasters, we ought to give large proportions of our income to disaster relief funds. How much? There is no logical stopping place, I suggested, until we reach the point of marginal utility—that is, the point at which by giving more, one would cause oneself and one's family to lose as much as the recipients of one's aid would gain.[75]

What could possibly justify this moral outlook? Why should you treat your career, your wealth, your children, your internal organs, your *life* as nothing more than a means to the ends of others? Don't *you* matter? In his earlier book *The Life You Can Save*, Singer claims his radical conclusions follow from moral premises everyone accepts. Here's his argument:

> First premise: Suffering and death from lack of food, shelter, and medical care are bad.
> Second premise: If it is in your power to prevent something bad from happening, without sacrificing something nearly as important, it is wrong not to do so.
> Third premise: By donating to aid agencies, you can prevent suffering and death from lack of food, shelter, and medical care, without sacrificing anything nearly as important.[76]

Conclusion?

> [Y]ou must keep cutting back on unnecessary spending, and donating what you save, until you have reduced yourself to the point where if you give any more, you will be sacrificing something nearly as important as preventing malaria—like giving so much that you can no longer afford an adequate education for your own children.[77]

How, asks Singer, can a nice house, outfits that make you feel attractive, romantic meals at fancy restaurants, a hard-won vacation to Telluride, or even a savings account large enough to provide enduring financial security be more important than the lives you could save by giving away that money? How can you justify living a middle-class lifestyle when your income could prevent the poorest people on earth from dying?

Singer's conclusion makes many people uncomfortable, but they can't spot any flaws in his reasoning. The trick is hidden in his second premise. Singer claims, "If it is in your power to prevent something bad from happening, without sacrificing something nearly as important, it is wrong not to do so." The question is: more important *to whom?* Isn't *my life* and *my happiness* more important *to me* than the life and happiness of a stranger I'll never meet?

Singer's basic assumption is that I should *not* value my own life more than the lives of other people. But why not? Placing priority on my own life doesn't mean I regard other people as servants or resources I can exploit. On the contrary, to assert my right to exist for my own sake is to recognize that other people have a right to exist for *their* own sake. On that view, I won't sacrifice for other people for the same reason I don't expect them to sacrifice for me.

To the extent Singer's second premise is plausible it's because we take it to mean: if you can help someone in an emergency situation without great cost or risk to yourself, you should. And that's true. Other human beings are values to us. Even strangers are fellow human beings, and absent evidence to the contrary, we see them as potential allies in the quest for happiness. We want them to thrive and to succeed. We don't want them to suffer. If I see a child drowning and I'm in a position to save him, I will. Not from some sense of duty, not because some professor will castigate me for not helping, but from my love of my own life.

When you love your life, you love human potential and seek to encourage and honor that in action. To save a drowning child when there's no significant danger to yourself *is not a sacrifice.* But that doesn't mean you follow the kid home, and assume responsibility for his food, his housing, his education. It doesn't mean that you abandon your career and travel around the world in search of drowning children.[78]

Singer is pulling a bait and switch. He brings to mind situations where helping is not a sacrifice and then asks us to draw a moral principle that demands total sacrifice. Here is the correct principle: be loyal to your values, never sacrificing a greater value to a lower value. This may very well mean helping someone in an emergency, but it can't mean treating human suffering and misfortune as such as a claim on your life.

The reason to help others is precisely because emergencies are rare and exceptional. You can provide aid in emergencies without diverting yourself from pursuing your own happiness. Most people, most of the time, to the extent a country is free, have the power to support their own lives. And they should. They should not surrender their own lives to us—and we shouldn't surrender our lives to them.

For all their focus on global poverty, Effective Altruists rarely talk about the cause of that poverty. The reason that a billion people continue to live in extreme poverty is *not* because we've given too little to charity: it's because they *don't* live in free countries. If you truly wanted to do "the most good you can," you wouldn't promote Effective Altruism. You would promote freedom.

All that said, the practitioners of Effective Altruism are in a sense an aberration. They try to faithfully implement altruism's demand for sacrifice. But altruism really isn't intended to be practiced. The best way to understand it is not as a code of morality, but as a psychological weapon. When people invoke altruism, it's usually not because they genuinely want to help others—it's because they want to control and exploit you. And the point isn't that they're misusing altruism—it's that this is what altruism is designed for.

Consider this: no one—not even Peter Singer—demands that you sacrifice yourself consistently. To practice altruism consistently would entail suicide, since every bite of food you take is needed more by someone else. A consistent altruist would be a dead altruist.

Altruists will let you get away with living most of the time. But when they want your wealth or your obedience? That's when they'll demand that you sacrifice. They will rely on your guilt. You don't want to be selfish, do you? Who are you to object to my demands? You're no moral paragon. You've been out there enjoying your life while others suffer—now it's time to serve.

I recently spoke to a young woman whose sick father is insisting that she place her life on hold to take care of him. Doesn't she realize that's her moral duty to the family? *That* is what altruism looks like. A truly moral person may ask for help. But to demand it as a duty? That is depraved, and yet it's precisely what altruism preaches. If you are in need, other people are your servants.

You might wonder: Aren't those demanding others serve them being selfish? And isn't that inconsistent with altruism? Economist Thomas Sowell once posed the puzzle this way: "I have never understood why it is 'greed' to want to keep the money you have earned but not greed to want to take somebody else's money."[79] In other words, if the good is the "non-good for me," doesn't that mean that we all should sacrifice—and that *no one* should be able to collect on those sacrifices? Isn't altruism self-contradictory since you're supposed to serve others, but from their own standpoint, they aren't "others"? They are people bound by the same moral code, which says that the good is non-them? Rand puts the paradox this way:

> Why is it moral to serve the happiness of others, but not your own? If enjoyment is a value, why is it moral when experienced by others, but immoral when experienced by you? If the sensation of eating a cake is a value, why is it an immoral indulgence in your stomach, but a moral goal for you to achieve in the stomach of others? Why is it immoral for you to desire, but moral for others to do so? Why is it immoral to produce a value and keep it, but moral to give it away? And if it is not moral for you to keep a value, why is it moral for others to accept it? If you are selfless and virtuous when you give it, are they not selfish and vicious when they take it? Does virtue consist of serving vice? Is the moral purpose of those who are good, self-immolation for the sake of those who are evil?[80]

But, Rand goes on to point out, this is only a paradox—not a contradiction. The morality of altruism allows you to collect sacrifices and gain values—provided you don't *earn* them. If you're a producer, you don't have a right to what you produce. That's greedy. But if you're a parasite who produces nothing? That is precisely what gives you a moral right to what others produce. "It is immoral to earn, but moral to mooch—it is the parasites who are the moral justification for the existence of the producers, but the existence of the parasites is an end in itself."[81]

According to altruism, if you earn values, you have to give them up. What entitles you to values? The fact you didn't earn them. A *need* you're unable or *unwilling* to satisfy is what entitles you to have your needs fulfilled by other people's efforts and at other people's expense. A lazy bum who makes excuses for his failures is morally superior to the affluent relatives he mooches off of—he is a needy victim while they are selfish and greedy for only sacrificing a small portion of their wealth for him. This is the actual meaning of "From each according to his ability, to each according to his need."

When altruists say they are champions of "the good of others" what they really mean is, "the worst people get to demand to have their wishes satisfied by the sacrifices of the best people."

This is the dead end of morality without happiness. It has nothing positive to offer, nothing uplifting to sell.

You *do* need morality—but not a morality that teaches you to throw your life away.

# Embrace Morality

We need to rethink morality.

What morality can and should offer us is an *ideal*—the highest vision of what is possible to us as human beings. An inspiring vision that renders life not a meaningless series of disconnected days, but a meaningful, adventurous, exalted sum.

Not morality without happiness or happiness without morality but *a morality of happiness.*

In my view, the most robust morality of happiness was developed by Ayn Rand. In the popular culture, Rand's moral views have been to "be selfish," which in turn gets translated into: "Screw other people, get rich, and brag about your Lambo." But Rand's conception of what a person's interests consist of is radically different from, and far richer than, the straw man her critics love to dismiss, attack, and mock.

Her conception is, at root, about selfishness of soul—about cultivating a reverence for your own life through a commitment to demanding virtues and deep, meaningful, material and spiritual values. "My philosophy, in essence," she wrote, "is the concept of man as a heroic being, with his own happiness as the moral purpose of his life, with productive achievement as his noblest activity, and reason as his only absolute."[82]

The symbols of Rand's theory are not Gordon Gekko and Donald Trump but the intransigence of a Frederick Douglass and the curiosity of a Richard Feynman and the passion of a Steve Jobs and the courage of a Jackie Robinson and the adventurousness of an Ernest Shackleton and the independence of an Alexander Hamilton and the creative intelligence of a Maria Montessori and the ambition of a Jeff Bezos. It is, for those who have read Rand's novels, Dagny Taggart, Howard Roark, Francisco d'Anconia, Hank Rearden, and John Galt.

## Embrace Man's Life as Your Standard of Value

Happiness sets the purpose of ethics: it is your ultimate value or ultimate goal. But a goal is not yet a guide. To translate that goal into actionable advice you need a *standard of value* to help gauge what will lead to happiness and what won't.

Any time you're pursuing a goal, you're relying on some more or less well-defined standard of value. For example, when Domino's Pizza launched, its motto was: "Fresh hot pizza delivered in 30 minutes or less, guaranteed." Every business decision was made in light of the question: Will this slow down or speed up the delivery of our pizza? The pizza's taste and cost were secondary considerations. *Speed of delivery* was its standard of value.

Coming up with a standard of value for morality is challenging because it has to be general enough to encompass all the fundamental components of a happy life, but it can't be so general that it's devoid of content. "Do what makes you happy" isn't a standard—it's a bumper sticker.

Happiness, moreover, is an emotional state. As we've seen, emotions depend on our values. To say, "Do what makes you happy" amounts to saying, "You should value whatever you happen to value." That's not guidance—it's a declaration that you don't need guidance.

So what's the solution? It's to realize that happiness is intimately connected to *successful living*. Pleasure and pain, joy and suffering, are signals calling attention to the life-and-death stakes of our actions. We feel good when life is going well—when our needs are met or when we're on the way to meeting them. "He's so alive" we say of the happy person. By contrast, pain and suffering warn us that our life is going in the wrong direction, that we're failing to meet crucial needs, that we're heading toward death. "My life's a mess," we tell our therapist. Human beings are biological organisms and happiness is a biological signal. It is what the experience of pursuing and achieving *life-sustaining values* consists of. As Rand explains:

> The maintenance of life and the pursuit of happiness are not two separate issues. To hold one's own life as one's ultimate value, and one's own happiness as one's highest purpose are two aspects of the same achievement. Existentially, the activity of pursuing rational goals is the activity of maintaining one's life; psychologically, its result, reward and concomitant is an emotional state of happiness. It is by experiencing happiness that one lives one's life, in any hour, year or the whole of it.[83]

To seek your own happiness as your ultimate value is to treat your own *life* as your ultimate value. This means much more than that you don't want to die. It means that you seek the best possible state for your life: materially, mentally, emotionally. Just as a healthy marriage isn't one that barely avoids divorce court, a healthy life isn't one that barely avoids the morgue. It's a life where you're satisfying your most important needs and strengthening your capacities to meet tomorrow's challenges. To treat your life as your ultimate value means being committed to growth and achievement in every aspect of your life and throughout your time on earth.

In grasping the connection between happiness and successful living, we now have an objective way to assess potential values: Does this further or undermine my life? And this, in turn, points us toward an objective *standard of value* for morality. We simply have to ask: Is there some basic thing human beings need to do in order to live? We already know the answer to that. As we discussed in Lesson 2, our basic means of survival is *reason.*

*If* you want to live, *then* you must live by reason.

Rand calls the moral standard reflecting this fact "man's life," or "that which is required for man's survival qua man."[84] It means "the terms, methods, conditions and goals required for the survival of a rational being through the whole of his lifespan—in all those aspects of existence which are open to his choice."[85] She elaborates:

> The Objectivist ethics holds man's life as the *standard* of value—and *his own life* as the ethical *purpose* of every individual man.
>
> The difference between "standard" and "purpose" in this context is as follows: a "standard" is an abstract principle that serves as a measurement or gauge to guide a man's choices in the achievement of a concrete, specific purpose. "That which is required for the survival of man qua man" is an abstract principle that applies to every individual man. The task of applying this principle to a concrete, specific purpose—the purpose of living a life proper to a rational being—belongs to every individual man, and the life he

has to live is his own.

Man must choose his actions, values and goals by the standard of that which is proper to man—in order to achieve, maintain, fulfill and enjoy that ultimate value, that end in itself, which is his own life.[86]

If man's life is our moral standard, then what is the nature of the good? The good is anything and everything that is proper to the life of a being who survives by reason. What is the evil? Anything that opposes or harms the life of a rational being.[87]

This standard will help us identify the human way of life, and so enable us to select a particular way of life that will add up to our own, unique, individual happiness.

## The Supreme and Ruling Values: Reason, Purpose, Self-Esteem

If *man's life* names "the terms, methods, conditions and goals required for the survival of a rational being through the whole of his lifespan," then what are those terms, methods, conditions, and goals?

Altruists like David Brooks often *define* "self-interest" as the pursuit of money, status, and power.[88] Their understanding of the values life requires is on par with primitive doctors who thought health came from balancing bile, blood, and phlegm.

Rand names three cardinal values "which, together, are the means to and the realization of one's ultimate value, one's own life": not money, power, and status, but *reason, purpose*, and *self-esteem*.[89]

Reason, as his only tool of knowledge—Purpose, as his choice of the happiness which that tool must proceed to achieve—Self-esteem, as his inviolate certainty that his mind is competent to think and his person is worthy of happiness, which means: is worthy of living.[90]

Like all values, reason, purpose, and self-esteem are both means and ends. As ends, they are the realization of a human life—to live is to nurture reason, to act with purpose, to have self-confidence and self-worth. As means, they make possible everything else that you value, from your career to your relationships to your ability to put food on the table. If the goal of morality is to give you an ideal at which to aim, then a life of reason, purpose, and self-esteem *is* that ideal.[91]

## Reason

To value reason is to value your survival faculty. We often hear how important it is to value your health and to treat your body like a temple. To value reason is to treat your mind like a temple. It's to recognize that everything you want and everything you care about comes from your ability to think, and so to devote yourself to the cultivation and maintenance of your mind.

Philosopher Onkar Ghate has analogized valuing reason to the attitude of a frontiersman or a soldier toward his gun. He knows that without his gun, he's finished—and so he treats his gun with an almost sacred respect. Recall the mantra recited by the soldiers in *Full Metal Jacket*: "This is my rifle. There are many others like it, but this one is mine. My rifle is my best friend. It is my life. I must master it as I must master my life. Without me, my rifle is useless. Without my rifle, I am useless." That is the attitude a valuer has toward his rational faculty. Your mind is your best friend. It is your life. You must master it as you master your life.

In the next lesson, we'll look in detail at *how* one gains and keeps the value of reason. Here we can simply say that to value reason requires not taking it for granted. Your capacity to think is given to you—but the development and maintenance of that capacity is a matter of choice. If you choose to live, then you have to work to understand what reason is, what its proper functioning requires, and then to devote yourself to the use and development of that faculty. To love your life requires loving your mind.

## Purpose

To value purpose is to value the exercise of your free will. Whereas animals are programmed to pursue life-sustaining values automatically, human beings are not. Setting aside automatic biological functions like respiration and circulation, your actions are volitional and your default state is one of passivity. Valuing purpose means a commitment to act to gain and keep a state of full focused awareness across your lifespan. It means exercising the effort to conceive of the values that will sustain you across a lifetime and working to realize those values across a lifetime. As philosopher Leonard Peikoff explains in his book *Objectivism: The Philosophy of Ayn Rand*:

> The principle of purpose means conscious goal-directedness in every aspect of one's existence where choice applies. The man of purpose defines explicitly his abstract values and then, in every area, the specific objects he seeks to gain and the means by which to gain them. Whether in regard to work or friends, love or art, entertainment or vacations, he knows what he likes and why, then goes after it. Using Aristotelian terminology, Ayn Rand often says that this kind of man acts not by efficient causation (mere reaction to stimuli), but by final causation ("fines" is Latin for "end"). He is the person with a passionate ambition for *values* who wants every moment and step of his life to count in their service. Such a person does not resent the effort which purpose imposes. He enjoys the fact that the objects he desires are not given to him, but must be achieved. In his eyes, purpose is not drudgery or duty, but something good. The process of pursuing values is itself a value.[92]

Valuing purpose starts with rejecting passivity. It means embracing the goal-directed activity life requires. That doesn't entail ceaseless frantic activity. Rest is a vital component of an active life. It *is* purposeful, when used as rejuvenation. It is only when rest becomes an escape from value pursuit that it represents a default on purpose.

Purpose isn't about stress or struggle (though it can sometimes entail these for short bursts). It's about knowing what you want and taking responsibility for getting it. Take something as simple as being invited to a party. To act without purpose is to act on impulse. You say yes without thinking about competing obligations or what you want to get out of the party. You show up, wander around in a daze, carelessly stuffing your mouth with food or a few too many drinks.

Someone who values purpose, by contrast, doesn't have to be a stiff who stays home or shows up with a party "to do" list. But before she says yes, she asks herself: What do I want to get out of this party? Will it give me a chance to unwind after a hard week at work? Will it give me the chance to have stimulating conversations with interesting people? If there is a potential value at stake, she'll ask herself: Is this the best use I can make of my time?

When she arrives, she knows what she wants and goes after it. If she's wants to meet new people, she won't cling to the friends she knows, but will approach strangers. She might relax with a glass or two of wine, but she won't get sloshed. Nor will she compulsively check her phone for work emails. She's all-in on what she came for. She can be fully present because she knows why she's there and has no divided loyalties.

## Self-esteem

To value self-esteem is to value *yourself*. Your need for self-esteem is rooted in the fact that you have free will. Because you shape your character and your life—and because on some level you *know it*—you can't help but pass a verdict on whether you're fit to live in this world—on whether you're able to live and are worthy of happiness. That is self-esteem. To value self-esteem is to aim at a state of confidence and cleanness. Confidence is crucial motivation to pursue values; clean-ness is what allows you to enjoy the values you do achieve.

To value self-esteem is to work to achieve self-confidence—not the localized self-confidence of being able to achieve some specific value, but a generalized self-confidence that comes from being able to deal with reality as such. Such generalized self-confidence can only come one source: confidence in your tool for dealing with reality, i.e., your mind. You build confidence by developing and exercising your basic tool of survival in the quest for values. You nourish self-esteem by nurturing the values of reason and purpose.

If you characteristically choose to think, you gain a sense of effi-cacy and control over your life. You learn that if you set your mind to the task of getting what you want, you can get what you want. Nor-mally, this leads naturally to the sense that you are *worthy* of getting what you want. A farmer who plants and tends his crops doesn't won-der, "Yeah, but do I deserve them?" He put in the work, he made the crops possible, they are *his*.

But this attitude toward life isn't inevitable. You can accept wrong standards of self-worth. You can measure your worth, not by the extent to which you choose to think and take responsibility for getting what you want, but by things outside of your control. I'm worthy if I make the team; I'm worthy if people think I'm attractive; I'm worthy if I never make mistakes; I'm worthy if I never show vulnerability; I'm worthy if I'm richer than my neighbors; I'm worthy if I outperform my col-leagues. Most damaging of all, you could embrace standards of worth that are at odds with personal happiness: I'm worthy if I set aside what I think and I want and do what God says; I'm worthy if I treat other people's lives as more important than mine; I'm worthy if I'm selfless.

This is one reason why having an explicit, rational code of moral-ity is so important. A rational code of morality puts the good on the side of your personal happiness, and it demands of you only what is possible to you. As we'll see in detail in the next lesson, what moral-ity demands is ultimately one thing and one thing only: rationality.

Your choice to think does not simply make you able to live—it is that choice that makes you worthy of happiness.

## Personal values

Reason, purpose, and self-esteem are the supreme and ruling moral values life requires—but they are far from the only values life requires.

Moral values are fundamental, universal values that apply to every human being and pervade a person's life. They are what shape your life and how you approach all of your other values. But many of your values will be concrete, specific, particular. Consider three of the most important personal values.

*Career.* Morality tells you that you need a career—a *central* productive purpose to organize your life around. But it doesn't tell you which career to choose. That choice is up to you, given the unique context of your interests, abilities, and life situation.

*Romantic love.* Morality tells you that romantic love is a vital component of happiness and it tells you about some of the broad conditions of romantic love (for example, that it be based on mutual admiration, not codependency). But it doesn't tell you which partner to choose. It doesn't tell you whether they will be a man or a woman. It doesn't tell you what body shapes are desirable or which sex acts are fulfilling. These are personal matters.

*Art.* Morality tells you that you need art to keep your spirit alive—but it doesn't dictate what art should fill your life. Music or literature (or both)? Tool or Tchaikovsky (or both)? J. K. Rowling or Ayn Rand (or both)? These are personal choices that will flow from your deepest core beliefs.

As we'll see in later lessons, morality is not silent on *how* you choose and pursue your personal values. It demands certain virtues—above all, rationality—that will shape how you make *every* choice. The point here is (1) you can't deduce your personal values from morality, and (2) the fact that a value is personal does *not* mean that it is unimportant. Your life *is* your values, including your personal values. And your highest personal values can be so crucial to your happiness that you're willing to die to protect them. I have two children, and I would not hesitate to throw myself in front of a car to save their lives. *Not* because I value them *more* than my life—but because my life *is* in crucial part the life of Livi and Landon's father. My interests are bound up in theirs, and watching them perish if I were in a position to save them would empty my life of much of what makes it worth living.

What emerges from a morality that upholds man's life as the standard of value is not a list of ethical rules but an integrated *way of life*: a harmonious constellation of values and virtues based in reason that work together to sustain you.

Existentially, this way of life keeps you in existence—psychologically, it leads to happiness, which is the result, reward, and fuel for living by a rational code of ethics. "Happiness is the successful state of life, pain is an agent of death. Happiness is that state of consciousness which proceeds from the achievement of one's values."[93]

In defining a code of values to guide your actions toward life and happiness, Rand's ethics unapologetically urges you to pursue your self-interest. This is not an "anything goes" approach to self-interest. It is not a predatory form of self-interest. It is not a misanthropic form of self-interest. It is, instead, a principled conception of egoism, which holds that your life matters and you have the right to make the most of it. You don't exist to serve others, just as they don't exist to serve you.

We now have our agenda for the rest of the book. In Lesson 4, we'll look more carefully at the value of reason, and some of the virtues that living by reason requires. In Lesson 5, we'll look at the value of purpose, and see how to choose and achieve a central productive purpose that fills your life with meaning. In Lesson 6, we'll look at the value of self-esteem, and why it requires proudly embracing and practicing an ethic of Effective Egoism. Finally, in Lesson 7, we'll see how an Effective Egoist can extract every ounce of joy possible from life.

## Lesson 4

# Follow Reason

## Cultivate Virtue

When philosophy severs happiness and morality, the moral and the practical, what's good and what's good for you, it teaches that happiness can be achieved by the seat of your pants. You don't need guidance to get what you want (or to decide what you should want). But it's *not* obvious how to get what you want—not when your values stretch across a lifetime and encompass every aspect of life.

It's obvious, for example, that lying on a job application could help you get the job. It's not obvious that you've injected into your life a quiet but pervasive sense of anxiety, as every sideways look or hushed conversation makes you worry you've been found out. It's not obvious that your willingness to lie on the job application makes other lies easier, and that you may be setting yourself on a course that will wreck your marriage, career, or reputation a decade later.

One of the most compelling examples of what happens when someone tries to live by the seat of their pants, without moral guidance, comes in Don Winslow's novel *The Force*, which tells the story of a dirty cop. The protagonist Denny Malone didn't start out corrupt. He started out idealistic, wanting to do good. "How did you get here?" he asks himself at the end of the novel, as his lies have spiraled and his life has fallen apart. Then he answers. "A step at a time," starting with accepting small, seemingly harmless favors and bribes.

> Thought it was a joke when they warned you at the Academy about the slippery slope. *A cup of coffee, a sandwich, it leads to other things.* No, you thought, a cup of coffee was a cup of coffee and a sandwich was a sandwich.

But that first step down the slope of bribery and corruption? It makes it easier for Malone to take—and rationalize—the next step.

> Plainclothes is where it really started.
> You and Russo walked into a stash house, the skels took off and there it is—money on the fucking floor. Not a lot, a couple grand, but still, you had a mortgage, diapers, maybe you wanted to take your wife out someplace that had tablecloths.
> Russo and you looked at each other and scooped it up.
> Never said anything about it.
> But a line was crossed.
> You didn't know there were other lines.
> But there were other lines. First, targets of opportunity. You don't seek it, you just take it if it's there and rationalize it away, "Because what harm did it do?" But those rationalizations help you take the next step and the next.
> You knew you'd make the transition from scavenger to hunter.
> You became a predator.
> An out-and-out criminal.
> Told yourself it was different because you were robbing drug dealers instead of banks.
> Told yourself you'd never kill anyone to make a rip.
> The last lie, the last line.[94]

Malone thought he was taking actions that were good for his life, but ended up destroying his life, step by imperceptible step. He could see the obvious consequences of his choices—a little money that no one would miss, then a lot of money no one would miss—but he couldn't see the full range of consequences of those choices, the impact those choices would have on his life long range and full context. But that's precisely what he *needed* to see.

If we want to live, we need to conceive of a self-sustaining *way of life*. We need to be able to determine which kinds of goals and actions move us forward—and which weigh us down. Which will enhance our life—and which will harm it.

I want a Coke. Okay, simple enough. I go to the fridge and grab a Coke. But I want far more than a Coke. I want a successful career. I want a fulfilling, enduring romantic relationship. I want passion and adventure and joy. I want self-esteem. How the hell do I get *that*? How can I figure out how the actions I take today will impact me today, next week, next month, or decades in the future? How can I figure out how a given choice will redound across every element of my life—across all my values, my relationships, my character, my mind?

Well, notice that it's at root a *knowledge problem*. I'm trying to grasp a causal relationship between my actions and their impact on my life. In the physical sciences, you start out with simple observations—balls roll, objects fall—and work over time to grasp fundamental *principles* that explain motion in general. *Virtues* are the causal principles of human flourishing. "'Value' is that which one acts to gain and keep," writes Rand, "'virtue' is the action by which one gains and keeps it."[95]

There is a crucial difference between moral virtues and the principles of physics. Moral principles can only govern your chosen actions, and your choices aren't the only factor involved in the achievement of your values. Virtues don't guarantee you'll achieve your values, the way Newton's laws guarantee a dropped brick will fall. Virtues, instead, are the necessary conditions for the achievement of values: they guarantee you'll achieve your values *over time* and *barring accident*—and they guar-antee that you *cannot* achieve your values any other way.

How do you discover what virtues *do* make up the human way of life? By taking stock of crucial facts about human nature in light of the choice to embrace life as your ultimate value. *If* you want to live, you must take the actions human life requires.

In essence, there is only one fact that underlies all of human vir-tue—the key fact about human life: reason is your basic means of sur-vival. *If* you want to live, then you *must* live by reason.

## Rationality Is Your Key to Flourishing

"The virtue of *Rationality*," in Rand's definition, "means the recog-nition and acceptance of reason as one's only source of knowledge, one's only judge of values and one's only guide to action."[96] Happiness comes from being a thinker—from following reason all the time, on every issue, in thought and action, no matter what. Everything else there is to say about virtue is only an elaboration of this basic principle.

### Rationality entails choosing to think and never evading

In the last lesson we saw that to value reason is to value your survival faculty. But what does that mean? If your rational faculty is a vital organ that has to be cultivated and maintained, how do you cultivate and maintain it?

First and foremost, you have to use it. You have to put reason in charge by exercising your basic power of choice and *focus*. The virtue of rationality urges you to focus, not on occasion, not when it suits your emotions, but as a way of life.

When you focus you bring a higher level of awareness to every aspect of life. You understand your environment—the world around you and the people that inhabit it. You can see more clearly what's possible to you, what's impossible, and what among the possible is worth striving for.

When you focus, you can make informed decisions about what you want and devise intelligent strategies for getting it. When you encounter obstacles or changing conditions you haven't anticipated, you can adapt and find new and better ways to reach your goals.

When you focus, you can also understand your inner world. Rather than be deluded about what you know and what you don't, or what you desire and what you don't, or what you're capable of and what you aren't, you are in touch with the reality of your self and your soul. You are in a position to know what you're doing and why you're doing it, since your motivations are no longer vague and mysterious. You're in a position to be moved by values rather than by fears because you're not passively and blindly reacting to whatever urges bubble up from your subconscious.

The opposite policy is evasion—deliberately turning away from reality, lowering your level of awareness, struggling not to see what you see and know what you know. When you evade, you say, in effect, I'm unwilling to live in reality, which means: I'm unable to live in reality and I'm unworthy of living in reality. But there's no other place to live. Evasion means choosing to make death, rather than life, your goal.

If you do choose to think, the goal and the result is an ever-expanding sum of knowledge. To be rational is to revel in the pursuit of knowledge—not as an end in itself, but in the conviction that understanding reality gives you power in reality. The more you understand, the more you can achieve. Rationality encourages you to be curious, to seek out connections, to constantly integrate your knowledge so that your control over your life continually deepens and makes possible continually expanding ambitions.

In *The Beginning of Infinity*, David Deutsch makes this point startlingly vivid when he notes that anything not barred by the laws of nature is achievable—"given the right knowledge."[97] With the right knowledge, Deutsch argues, human beings could in principle make even the farthest reaches of intergalactic space habitable.

> No human today knows how. For instance, one would first have to transmute some of the hydrogen into other elements. Collecting it from such a diffuse source would be far beyond us at the present. And, although some types of transmutation are already routine in the nuclear industry, we do not know how to transmute hydrogen into other elements on an industrial scale. Even a simple nuclear-fusion reactor is currently beyond our technology. But physicists are confident that it is not forbidden by any laws of physics, in which case, as always, it can only be a matter of knowing how.[98]

Coming back down to earth, the only thing that keeps you from achieving *any* goal you want to reach—health, prosperity, love, joy—is lack of knowledge. And the only thing required to remedy that lack is thinking.

"[T]he process of *thinking*," observes Rand, "is the process of defining *identity* and discovering *causal connections*."[99] Rationality encourages you to be a disciple of causality. Not just to relentlessly seek out cause and effect relationships, but to build your life around them.

Being a disciple of causality means never seeking effects without causes: if you want something, you accept full responsibility for doing what's required to achieve it. If you want to be a writer, then you study the principles of writing and sit down every day at your desk. If you want to make a fortune, then you study the principles of business and create something of value. If you want to have a great sex life, then you make yourself worthy of love, find a partner you admire, and make love with wild abandon.

Being a disciple of causality also means never enacting a cause without assuming responsibility for all of its effects. You don't have kids and abandon them, or get married and ignore your partner's needs, or take on a project at work then pass the buck when it fails. You expect the rewards for your achievements, and so you willingly pay the costs—and willingly accept the penalties for your failures. You do not try to "get away" with anything.

Being a disciple of causality means, finally, never attempting to *reverse* cause and effect: to treat an effect as proof you possess the cause. You do not treat money, gained through fraud, as proof of your ability. You do not treat sex, gained by negging a drunk girl into bed, as proof of your attractiveness and personal value. You do not treat admiration, gained through a phony image you project to the world, as proof of your virtue.

Every form of irrationality involves evading the fact that reality is what it is and pretending your whims and delusions control what is. Rationality is the opposite: it is the policy of never placing an "I wish" above an "It is."

## Rationality means harmonizing reason and emotion

Conventional wisdom equates rationality with non-emotion. To be rational is to be like Spock, operating as if emotions didn't exist. But that is neither possible nor desirable. Emotions are the voice of your values. You cannot pursue what you want unless you know what you want. To be rational isn't to ignore your emotions—it's to understand and assess them.

An emotionalist's error is not that he experiences emotions or pays attention to them. It's that he treats his emotions as a substitute for reason and acts on them blindly. Often when you ask children why they did something dumb and impulsive their answer is, "I don't know." And that's an honest answer. But adults can act with that same lack of self-awareness (often accompanied by rationalizations to pretend they aren't acting blindly). They jump back into an unhealthy relationship because they feel that this time it will be different. They spend more than they can afford on the latest iPhone because they feel that they have to have it. They go to church because they feel that going to church is what good people do. But an emotion, as we've seen, is an evaluation; that evaluation may be true or it may be false. Rationality consists of never acting on an emotion or desire whose source you do not understand and have not validated.

Consider the realm of romance. To pursue romance rationally doesn't mean conjuring up some list of sensible traits a lover should have and checking off boxes. The more common pattern is that you meet someone who attracts you, who fascinates you, who takes your breath away—often for reasons that aren't easy to pin down. To be rational is not to ignore that evidence *or to follow it blindly*. To be rational is to ask yourself: Why do I feel what I feel? If the answer is, "This person is so lousy that I feel superior by comparison" then that's a big problem! But if the answer is, "I'm falling in love because they are confident, and witty, and radiantly serene" then your mind and your heart are in harmony, and you can move forward in the relationship without reservation.

Emotions are not your enemy. But they are not a substitute for reason. They are, instead, a vital source of information about what you care about—and the form in which you experience the reality of your values. If you harmonize reason and emotion, then you'll be free of the inner conflicts that pervade most people's lives, and instead be able to give yourself fully to your values. It is this form of deep commitment that allows you to experience the most profound emotions human beings are capable of: joy, worship, exaltation.

## Rationality entails honesty

People don't usually engage in pure evasion. They deploy strategies to assist with evasion. One of the most common is dishonesty. If evasion means denying facts, then dishonesty means creating a fantasy world of facts as a substitute. You find sexually tinged texts on your lover's phone. Your lover doesn't deny the texts exist—but he pretends a friend sent them as a joke.

Dishonesty is the handmaiden of irrationality. Without dishonesty, many other irrationalities could not be indulged in, at least not for long. Imagine trying to be an honest murderer, or an honest thief, or an honest philanderer, or even an honest heroin addict. The destructive effects of your course of action would be too immediately obvious. Dishonesty gives you the illusion you can escape cause and effect. As Sam Harris observes:

> Honesty can force any dysfunction in your life to the surface. Are you in an abusive relationship? A refusal to lie to others—How did you get that bruise?—would oblige you to come to grips with this situation very quickly. Do you have a problem with drugs or alcohol? Lying is the lifeblood of addiction. If we have no recourse to lies, our lives can unravel only so far without others' noticing.[100]

The problem with dishonesty is that you can't escape cause and effect. Your phony reality doesn't wipe out actual reality. On the contrary, when you lie to escape some unpleasant fact, you only add a new set of facts that threaten you, namely, the fact of your lie. Reality is interconnected—every fact is related ultimately to every other fact—and so lies create ripple effects: one lie necessitates more lies, putting you in conflict with more and more facts, and making you more and more vulnerable to discovery.

It's interesting, in this regard, to observe how police interrogations work. Unlike the movies, the police don't start out shining a light in your face and calling you a scumbag until you confess. Instead, they simply ask to hear your side of the story. They want you to commit to a set of facts—as many facts and as specific a set of facts as possible. They'll ask you to repeat your story again and again, forwards and backwards. They know that a liar will inevitably contradict himself or contradict some fact of reality. He'll forget what he said the first time around, or he'll say something the police can prove is untrue. It's at this point the interrogation becomes adversarial, as the cops lean on the contradiction, force the suspect to confess or change his story. Telling the truth is easy—inventing a fantasy world and keeping people from seeing how it clashes with reality is extremely difficult. Ultimately, it's impossible.

Honest people sometimes think that the liar must be filled with guilt, unable to sleep at night. This isn't true. When people lie as a way of life, they don't feel guilty for lying. They can even come to enjoy it. The act of manipulation gives them a feeling of power over others. But this actually makes the liar *more* vulnerable. The liar comes to believe he is smarter than others, more clever, more cunning. This self-delusion leads him to become more brazen in his lies, and his ability to assess the likelihood of getting caught in a lie becomes warped and distorted. Typically, the serial liar gets caught doing something completely reckless.

If it stood in the liar's mind as: "facts are facts, they're out there to detect, and I'm not the smartest person in the world so I can't fully predict how people will detect me," his chances of avoiding detection would be much greater. But, then, if that's how the issue stood in his mind, it would be hard for him to bring himself to lie at all. The liar's pretense at superiority, his feeling that he is a master manipulator, would be replaced with the recognition that his dishonesty made *him* the puppet. As Rand puts it:

> [A]n attempt to gain a value by deceiving the mind of others is an act of raising your victims to a position higher than reality, where you become a pawn of their blindness, a slave of their non-thinking and their evasions, while their intelligence, their rationality, their perceptiveness become the enemies you have to dread and flee. . . . [The liar becomes] a dependent on the stupidity of others . . . a fool whose source of values is the fools he succeeds in fooling.[101]

To be rational is to be fully committed to honesty. If rationality entails devotion to the truth and the whole truth, honesty entails devotion to nothing but the truth.[102] Honesty means the refusal to engage in any form of pretense: in the quest for values, you don't fake reality to yourself or to others. Why not? For the very selfish reason that the unreal is unreal and can have no value. If happiness requires a constellation of values that are achievable and harmonious, seeking the unreal means rejecting happiness as your goal.

It's not simply that lies make you vulnerable to getting caught—it's that dishonesty means subverting your mind. But everything that makes life possible and worth living comes from your mind. To pursue happiness means to come up with a vision of life—of the values you seek and the actions that will help you realize them. A million dollars at the price of a lie is worthless because the actual price *is* throwing out your vision of life. You can live the life of a liar or the life of a thinker—you cannot live both. You can live in harmony with the facts or you can go to war with them—you can't do both. You can make the minds of the people you deal with your ally or your enemy—you can't do both.

Jordan Peterson has noted that to lie is to use "words to manipulate the world into delivering you what you want."[103] Honesty is the recognition that anything worth wanting can't come from manipulating. Love gained through manipulation isn't real love. Admiration gained through manipulation isn't real admiration. Money gained through manipulation may spend just as well as honestly earned cash—but it came at the price of your soul and becomes nothing more than an insignia of your loss. Who would want to be Michael Corleone, sitting alone in his mansion and hating his life?

What, then, about so-called white lies? It's easy to see that being a manipulator and a con man puts you at war with reality and starves your life of values. But what about the small lies people tell to avoid conflict, grease the wheels of social interaction, protect their friends and family from hurt feelings?

Honesty doesn't require telling everyone you meet every thought you have. Indeed, honesty is compatible with outright lying in certain cases. The philosopher Immanuel Kant argued you owe the truth to a killer seeking the location of his victim. But honesty's advice is not to always tell the truth no matter the circumstances: it's to never attempt to gain a value by faking reality. When I refuse to tell the Nazis that Anne Frank is hiding in my attic, I am not the one at war with reality. I am engaging in self-defense, and if I have the moral right to use my fists to protect myself and others, then obviously I have the moral right to use words.

"White lies" can seem like lies of self-defense. But in reality, they are lies aimed at gaining values through pretense. And their consequence is to destroy the values you claim to be seeking. You claim you're lying to protect your friend—in reality, you're harming your friend and your friendship. You're robbing them of feedback they need to improve their lives on the insulting assumption that you know what's best for them and they aren't capable of dealing with reality. Take the standard "do I look fat in this dress?" example. Sam Harris replies compellingly:

> Your friend looks fat in that dress, or any dress, because she is fat. Let's say she is also thirty-five years old and single, and you know that her greatest desire is to get married and start a family. You also believe that many men would be disinclined to date her at her current weight. And, marriage aside, you are confident that she would be happier and healthier, and would feel better about herself, if she got in shape. A white lie is simply a denial of these realities. It is a refusal to offer honest guidance in a storm. Even on so touchy a subject, lying seems a clear failure of friendship.[104]

Rationality demands you place our allegiance with reality. And that requires an allegiance to honesty.

## Rationality requires rational action

Thinking is not an end in itself—it's for the sake of action. Rationality entails taking the mental actions necessary to achieve knowledge and using that knowledge to guide your existential actions. It means having *integrity*.

Socrates thought that to know the good was to do the good. But Aristotle recognized that isn't always the case:

> [W]e speak of knowing in two ways; we ascribe it both to someone who has it without using it and someone who is using it. Hence it will matter whether someone has the knowledge that his action is wrong, without attending to his knowledge, or he both has it and attends to it. For this second case seems extraordinary, but wrong action when he does not attend to his knowledge does not seem extraordinary.[105]

The virtue of integrity tells you to attend to your knowledge when you act: to form principles, apply them to specific instances, and to implement that knowledge in reality. Its root meaning is "intact." Integrity means you are whole, undivided—a union of mind and body. To have integrity is to never allow any breach between thought and action. No matter what you feel, no matter what other people say, you face every choice by asking, "What do I know that's relevant?" And then you act according to your best understanding.

We often think of the man of integrity as putting his principles above his interests. But that's wrong. If your principles are based on reality, if they reflect a clear-headed understanding of what's genuinely in your long-term interests, integrity is the only way to achieve your interests. Remember why we need morality: the values that life and happiness require are not obvious. They consist, not only of food, clothing, and shelter, but of reason, purpose, self-esteem, and much else besides. They stretch across every aspect of life and across the whole of your lifespan. *Without principles, you don't know what your interests actually are.*

There's a pivotal scene in Ayn Rand's novel *The Fountainhead* that drives this point home. The hero, Howard Roark, is an innovative architect, but precisely because his approach is so revolutionary, he finds it difficult to find clients. He has one last chance to secure a commission before he will have to close his office, but the potential client will not hire Roark unless Roark agrees to make changes to his design that Roark thinks will ruin the building.

> [Roark] spoke for a long time. He explained why this structure could not have a Classic motive on its facade. He explained why an honest building, like an honest man, had to be of one piece and one faith; what constituted the life source, the idea in any existing thing or creature, and why—if one smallest part committed treason to that idea—the thing of the creature was dead; and why the good, the high and the noble on earth was only that which kept its integrity.

The client is unmoved and insists that Roark accept the commission with their changes or reject it.

> "Yes or no, Mr. Roark?"
> Roark's head leaned back. He closed his eyes.
> "No," said Roark. . . .
> "I want you. We want your building. You need the commission. Do you have to be quite so fanatical and selfless about it?" . . .
> Roark smiles. He looks down at his drawings and says: "That was the most selfish thing you've ever seen a man do."[106]

Conventional wisdom says that it's self-evidently to Roark's interest to accept a commission, particularly when he's in financial dire straits. What Roark recognizes is that his interests are bound up in a certain kind of life: the life of an architect. "The only thing that matters," he says, "my goal, my reward, my beginning, my end is the work itself. My work done my way."[107] Not only will Roark gain no joy from designing this particular building, but sacrificing his artistic integrity will make it harder for him to achieve the kind of career he wants. He will never find *his* kind of clients—the kind who want a

Roark building—if he starts putting up buildings that compromise his vision. That's what makes his action selfish: he kept alive his knowledge of what was truly valuable to him.

Integrity, then, is the virtue that prevents rationality from being nothing more than mental masturbation. It stresses the need to form reality-based principles and to implement them in practice. It is your reminder that there can be no breach between the moral and the practical.

If you want to live, if you want to achieve happiness, if you want to take control of your life and enjoy the values that constitute a human life—then *rationality*, in all its aspects, is the virtue you have to cultivate.

But to fully cultivate rationality, we need to go deeper because "reason" is one of the most disputed concepts in philosophy. Plato said he was for reason. Aristotle said he was for reason. Aquinas said he was for reason. Descartes, Locke, and Kant said they were for reason. Yet all of these thinkers had wildly different conceptions of what reason is and how it works.

To complete the case for rationality, we need to ask: What is reason and how can we use it to reach reliable knowledge?

# Think Logically

Reason, we've said, is the faculty that takes us from the perceptual level to the conceptual level. It allows us to classify things, to form generalizations, to make judgments, to project the far-off future and analyze the distant past. It is what makes us thinkers.

But just as we're born not knowing how to walk, we're born not knowing how to think. The difference is that everyone eventually learns how to walk. You don't find freshmen rolling down the halls of their high school. You do, however, find plenty of grown men and women uninterested in what's true, or unable to see through lousy arguments and bullshit claims.

Becoming a thinker starts with caring what's true. And here the biggest risk isn't that you'll openly declare, "To hell with the facts, I *want* this to be true." It's that you'll engage in self-deception through *motivated reasoning*. Motivated reasoning isn't true reasoning, but the pretense of reasoning: the goal is not actually to reach the truth, but to prop up your current set of beliefs, defend your self-image, protect yourself from painful emotions, and look good to your peers. You seek out evidence to confirm what you want to believe, ignore evidence that conflicts with what you want to believe, and reinterpret what you can't ignore to avoid changing your mind.

I find that I'm much more prone to this on personal issues than intellectual issues. On intellectual issues, particularly when I know my views are outside the mainstream, my natural inclination is to wonder: Why do I think I'm right and so many intelligent people are wrong? Are they seeing something I'm not? What are the best arguments against my position? What biases do I have that might prejudice me? But on personal issues, I'm much more likely to dig in my heels and become defensive if I'm being criticized. "What do you mean I've been aloof and ignoring your needs? I asked you last Thursday how you were doing!"

Motivated reasoning is such a seductive trap that it's not enough to set genuine reasoning as an intention. You have to actively work to expose and uproot any self-deception. Charles Darwin, for instance, made this an explicit policy as he developed his theory of natural selection.

> I had also, during many years, followed a golden rule, namely that whenever a published fact, a new observation of thought came across me, which was opposed to my general results, to make a memorandum of it without fail and at once; for I had found by experience that such facts and thoughts were far more apt to escape from the memory than favourable ones.[108]

In *The Scout Mindset*, Julia Galef recommends using various thought experiments to push back against motivated reasoning. Whenever you're thinking through an issue or making a decision, you should ask yourself: If my incentives were different, would I reach a different conclusion? If I was an atheist, would I find this argument for God persuasive? If I was in my partner's shoes, would I consider withholding this information a lie? If my peer group held the opposite view, would I still defend my current view? If this study didn't support but contradicted my position, would I still find it persuasive?

Galef says this last question dramatically changed her approach to her book. During her research, she found a paper claiming that motivated reasoning causes people to have more success in life. She was certain it must have major methodological flaws, and sure enough, she found them. "Then, somewhat grudgingly, I did a thought experiment." She asked herself, what if the study had *supported* her thesis? "In that case, I realized, my reaction would have been: 'Exactly as I suspected. I'll have to find a place for this study in my book!'" This realization led her to reexamine all of the studies she was planning to cite with the same rigor she would have used had they contradicted her thesis. "Sadly, this ended up disqualifying most of them."[109]

It's not enough to *feel* that you're being rational. Rationality requires actually being rational. It requires putting in the work to ensure that you're following the evidence wherever it leads rather than stacking the deck in favor of what you want to believe.

Becoming a thinker doesn't just mean caring about what's true in some narrow sphere. It means cultivating a deep curiosity about the world, other people, and yourself. In particular, a thinker is curious about *causality*: he wants to understand *how things work*. Not only to know who won the Battle of Shiloh, but to understand why the American Civil War was fought, why the Union won, why Reconstruction failed, how that impacted black Americans in ways that continue to have effects today.

At a more personal level, let's say you're a student struggling to maintain good grades. Or maybe you're acing your classes but at the expense of any fun or social life. To be a thinker is to ask *why*? Why am I struggling while others succeed? Why am I in the library twelve hours a day while some of my classmates are thriving in class and out of class? Can I do better?

When Cal Newport, now the best-selling author of books such as *Deep Work*, arrived in college, he noticed he was spending hours and hours on his schoolwork, reading and re-reading textbooks and class notes until the information (hopefully) made its way into his head, constantly feeling behind, and pulling no small number of all-nighters.

> It was a truly chaotic existence. But when I looked around, all of my friends seemed to be having the same experience—and none of them seemed willing to question it. This didn't sit right with me. I wasn't content to work in long, painful stretches and then earn only slightly above-average grades for my efforts.[110]

So Cal became curious: how could he become more efficient? He started experimenting and ultimately found a method that allowed him to achieve straight A's while spending less time studying. "By my senior year it got to the point where, during finals periods, I would sometimes *pretend* to be heading off the library just so I wouldn't demoralize my roommates, who were preparing for yet another grim all-nighter."[111]

He didn't stop there. Cal started questioning other students able to perform at a high level while remaining relaxed and engaged with college life, trying to assess what causes they were enacting to achieve these effects. He would go on to write a book on strategies for overcoming procrastination, taking targeted notes, preparing efficiently for exams, and writing standout term papers. Being curious about cause and effect is how we learn—and how we thrive.

But curiosity is itself a skill we can practice and improve. It involves asking questions, and we can learn which kinds of questions are most fruitful to ask. Some of the most important questions a thinker asks include:

- *"What is it?"* This is the question that helps us identify the nature of the things we deal with.
- *"Why?"* This is the question that helps us think causally and allows us to understand the past.
- *"What for?"* This is the question that allows us to project long-range purposes and invent the future.

In the rest of this lesson, we'll probe the kinds of questions and strategies that allow you to gain, validate, and use knowledge. The questions and strategies that will help you distinguish truth from falsehood and integrate what you know into an ever-expanding sum.

## Learn to Conceptualize

Reason operates by concepts. Aside from proper nouns, all words stand for concepts. Dog, cat, computer, neutron, justice—these and countless other concepts reflect our ability not just to see and hear the things in front of us, but to grasp increasingly complex relationships between the things we see and hear (and the complex relationships between things so small, large, or distant that we can never see or hear them).

A full theory of how and when to form concepts is outside the scope of this book. For those interested, I recommend starting with philosopher Harry Binswanger's book *How We Know*. For our purposes, the key idea is that we can't just arbitrarily group things together using concepts. Taking dogs, trash, and sulfur and calling them all "stinkies" is a mental dead end. Almost nothing you learn about a dog will apply to sulfur.

Concepts work by grouping together things that are *essentially similar* so that we can apply what we discover about some of the units to the others. We couldn't grow food if seeds didn't share certain properties. We couldn't generate electricity if turbines didn't share certain properties. If we weren't confident there were essential similarities between airplanes, then no way in hell would we risk stepping aboard a passenger jet.

But the fact that concepts aren't *automatically* valid carries with it an enormous responsibility. We have to do the work to make sure our concepts are valid. Most people don't. Our most disastrous thinking errors often are not the result of fallacies like appeal to authority or begging the question, let alone formal deductive fallacies like affirming the consequent. All too often, our most disastrous thinking errors come from embracing illegitimate concepts.

For a concept to be valid you have to be able to answer the question: "What facts of reality give rise to the need for this concept?" You need to be able to know clearly what the units of the concept are, what they're being distinguished from, and why it's legitimate to treat them as units, i.e., why they are essentially similar. Many concepts don't meet these criteria.[112]

Some concepts don't refer to anything at all. This includes concepts that are mystical in nature ("god," "angel," "afterlife"). It also includes bad philosophic concepts, like Kant's "noumena" and Hegel's "dialectic." And it includes certain scientific concepts, such as "epicycle." The point is not simply that these concepts refer to things we can't perceive. We can't perceive electrons. But we can infer the existence of electrons from what we do perceive. Concepts that lack units refer to things that cannot be connected at all to perceptual reality. (We do have legitimate concepts for imaginary things, like "wookie," but in this case the units are "an alien species in the fictional world of *Star Wars*.")

Far more important are concepts that misclassify things that *do* exist. Sometimes, for example, we treat superficially different things as essentially different. For example, people who argue that gay couples shouldn't be able to marry because marriage "is between a man and a woman" take an essentially similar phenomenon—a legal union of romantic partners committed to building a life together—and insist on an artificial distinction between opposite sex couples and same sex couples. Or take the concept "racism." Some argue that racial minorities cannot be racist—that racism equals prejudice plus power. But this means making an artificial distinction between something that's essentially similar: judging someone based on skin color.[113]

The most common conceptual error, however, is treating *superficially* similar things as *essentially* similar. Rand calls these "package deals." "'Package-Dealing' is the fallacy of failing to discriminate crucial differences. It consists of treating together, as parts of a single conceptual whole or 'package,' elements which differ essentially in nature, truth-status, importance or value."[114]

Package deals are everywhere. "Stakeholder," for example, treats as essentially similar a company's shareholders, employees, customers, local communities, and the government. All of these are people "affected by the business," ignoring a crucial distinction between the owners of a business, who have the right to control and profit from it, and groups whose main choice is whether to voluntarily deal with the company or not. The concept "stakeholders" obliterates that difference in order to strong-arm business owners into surrendering control and profits to non-owners.

Or take the concept "judgmental." This concept treats as essentially similar uninformed, prejudicial judgments about people and informed, rational judgments. It equates someone who says, "Zoomers are lazy and entitled" with someone who thoughtfully concludes, "Lucas is lazy and entitled." The result is that we're taught to view all negative judgments, particularly negative moral judgments, as wrong per se (except the negative moral judgment that someone is judgmental).

Or take the concept "selfishness." People often call two radically different kinds of people selfish—the short-term, predatory huckster, and the virtuous person who seeks his own happiness rationally; an Elizabeth Holmes and a Steve Jobs. The implication of this package deal is that our basic moral choice is either to lie, cheat, and steal without regard for other people—or to sacrifice our own interests for other people. There's no category for the person who pursues his own interests, neither sacrificing himself to others nor others to himself.

The test for package deals is to look at how the concepts are used in practice, to look at the specific concretes the concept is meant to apply to, and ask: do these things really belong together? Or is there some important difference that's being ignored or denied? Is it equating the moral and the immoral, the true and the false, the rational and the irrational, the important and the unimportant?

Bad concepts equal bad thinking. To use a concept is to make a declaration: "*This* is the right way to look at the world." Don't be a conceptual slut. Do not use a concept unless you know exactly what it means and you're rationally convinced it gets reality right.

## Validate and Connect

Your senses give you direct access to reality. Your concepts allow you to go beyond what you perceive, to acquire knowledge that applies to all human beings, all organisms, all matter. You use your concepts to make judgments: this is true, that is good, this is false, that is bad.

Just as your concepts aren't automatically legitimate, the judgments you make with these concepts aren't, either. You need to work to ensure your ideas conform to facts. At the most basic level, this means distinguishing the cognitive from the non-cognitive: drawing a line between what I observe and infer on the one hand—and what I feel and what others say on the other.

Typically, this is what people mean when they talk about objectivity. Being objective means going by the facts—regardless of your (or anyone's) wishes, hopes, fears, or desires. That's a great start, but it's only a start. To truly be objective, you need to self-consciously apply a method that validates your knowledge—a method that *keeps* your ideas connected to facts and that allows you to reliably go from what you perceive to what you don't.

All genuine knowledge consists of what you directly perceive or what you logically infer from what you perceive. But what does it mean to be logical? Traditional logic classes focus on deductive arguments. You start with a general proposition and apply it to a less general case. All men are mortal; Socrates is a man; therefore, Socrates is mortal. At each step you're guided by the basic law of logic: the law of contradiction. Since A is A, the same thing cannot be both A and non-A at the same time and in the same respect. Since contradictions can't exist in reality, they must not exist in thought.

Deductive reasoning is vital, but logic is about far more than deduction. "Logic," in Rand's definition, "is the art of *non-contradictory identification*."[115] It includes both deduction and induction (forming generalizations). And, importantly, logic isn't primarily about evaluating a single argument out of context. To be logical is to seek to integrate *all* your knowledge into a consistent whole—a whole rooted in the world you perceive through your senses. To achieve that goal requires two basic processes: reduction and integration.

### Reason requires reduction

What ties your knowledge to reality? Think of a chain you use to tie your dog to a tree. If you wanted to know with total confidence that your dog wouldn't escape, you'd start at her collar and check each link. You'd go back, link by link, to make sure the chain was strong, until you reached the starting point, the tree.

We learn by building more abstract knowledge on less abstract knowledge. We learn to count. Then we use that knowledge to learn to add and subtract. We use *that* knowledge to learn to multiply and divide. Then algebra. Then calculus.

Conceptual knowledge exists in a hierarchy—more abstract knowledge is built on less abstract knowledge. To validate conceptual knowledge means to reduce it by going back through that hierarchy, working to take less solid knowledge back to more solid knowledge—ultimately to what you can directly perceive.

Think of Darwin. After years as a naturalist, he developed a hypothesis about the origin of species: they evolve through the mechanism of natural selection. But he didn't stop there. He wanted to know: is this *really* true?

After Darwin developed his hypothesis, he spent the next two decades trying to establish whether it was true. To do that, he had to be able to answer questions like, "Why do I believe that there is sufficient natural variation in organisms to allow for natural selection to take place?" He confirmed that in part by spending the better part of a decade studying barnacles and concluded that, yes, you do observe significant variation among specimens.

Or, "Why do I believe that natural processes can account for the global distribution of species?" He wondered whether it was possible for a seed to float large distances across the ocean and take hold in a far-off location. When botanists told Darwin the salt water would kill the seeds, he ran his own observational tests and found that, in fact, seeds could be immersed in salt water and still germinate a month later.

Or, "Why do I believe that the minor variation we see in nature is capable of producing an entirely new species?" One line of evidence came from what he called artificial selection. He found, for example, that selective breeding of pigeons by human beings could produce a new species over the course of only a few centuries.[116]

Whether you're assessing a complex scientific theory, a political policy, or a career change, the key to making sure your ideas are connected to reality is to ask of any idea you hold: "Why do I believe this is true?"[117]

For example, you read an article claiming that we need socialized medicine in the United States, and you find yourself getting angry. You say to yourself: "I disagree with this, but why do I believe that socialized medicine would be bad?"

Let's say you can't come up with any reasons. What you *don't* do is google "why socialized medicine is bad," click on the first study you see, and conclude: ah hah! Socialized medicine is bad because the *Journal of Truth* did a study that shows Canada's system has longer wait times for cancer treatment than the US! That's a prime example of motivated reasoning.

What you're trying to get at is the actual reasons that persuaded you of an idea in the past. If you really can't recapture that, or if you never did go through a thought process where you considered the evidence for and against socialized medicine, then you have no business believing it's bad (or good). You have to file that conclusion as "A plausible idea I need to think more about."

Now, let's say you ask yourself, "Why do I believe socialized medicine would be bad?" and you do come up with an answer: socialized medicine destroys medical progress. Great. Now why do you believe *that*? You think: socialized medicine makes healthcare "free" at the point of purchase. But it still has costs: the medical staff, the medical equipment, the drugs, the hospital, the electricity that powers the hospital. So, you think, what's the impact if a person can use these resources without paying for them?

Just as a "free" restaurant would see its costs skyrocket as everyone ordered steak and lobster, so socialized medicine would cost taxpayers an unsustainable amount as people demanded the best tests and the most expensive treatments. Eventually, the government would have to control costs by rationing care. You'd get huge waiting lists for treatment, as we see in Canada and the United Kingdom. Drug companies and medical-device makers, meanwhile, would have to accept a tiny fraction of what they earn today, meaning they could do less R&D, and certainly wouldn't invest in highly expensive, speculative treatments—say, like mRNA vaccines—since they wouldn't be able to recoup their costs. You might think: this is why most medical innovation happens in the US: precisely because drug prices aren't fixed by the government.

In most contexts, that's a sufficient reduction. You've taken your idea, "socialized medicine is bad," and you've made it more precise, closer to what you can perceive. It's not a full reduction because you're not literally going all the way down to the perceptual level. If you later get into an argument or want to write a book on freedom in healthcare, you might have to do more work to fully reduce the idea. But for now you've done the work to know what you believe and why you believe it.

## Reason requires integration

The most obvious fact about great thinkers is that they see connections no one else has noticed. Maybe the most striking example in history is Newton grasping that the same force that causes objects to fall to the earth causes the motions of planets in the sky. But more relatable examples abound. I always think of a young Steve Jobs helping to explain computers to a world unfamiliar with them as "a bicycle for your mind."

Mental connections are *integrations*. All knowledge involves integration. Concepts integrate percepts. Generalizations integrate observations. Principles integrate generalizations. Philosophy integrates principles into a single, unified, consistent view of the world.

With each step you can see more of reality and see it more clearly. When Newton integrated planetary motion with terrestrial motion, that allowed us to apply what we learned about terrestrial motion to astronomy and vice versa.

Integration doesn't just expand your knowledge—it checks it. Integration is how you discover contradictions among your ideas. As Rand puts it, "No concept man forms is valid unless he integrates it without contradiction into the total sum of his knowledge. To arrive at a contradiction is to confess an error in one's thinking; to maintain a contradiction is to abdicate one's mind and to evict oneself from the realm of reality."[118]

We're all familiar with people trying to trap us in an argument by showing that we're contradicting ourselves. "You believe this. You believe that. But this and that are inconsistent, so you must be wrong about this, that, or both." People pointing out your inconsistencies isn't always fun, but it is a gift. To the extent the contradiction is real, your critic is *helping you integrate*.

But the value of integration in rooting out contradictions goes far beyond intellectual debates. How many times have you been tempted to tell a "white lie" to a friend to protect their feelings? "Oh, no. You haven't gained weight." "That haircut looks great on you." "Bro, some-one needs to call the police because those guns should be illegal." But think about what you're actually doing when you tell these kinds of lies. On the one hand, you want the best for your friend. On the other hand, you're not giving them the information they need to make good decisions. You're treating them as children incapable of handling the fact that their weight is unhealthy, their haircut isn't flattering, their workout regimen isn't panning out. Well, that's a contradiction. "I want the best for my friend" and "I'm lying to my friend" don't integrate.

Integration doesn't happen automatically. It requires volitional effort. You have to *choose* to integrate—you have to actively work to relate your knowledge. What does this mean in practice? Integration doesn't mean that every time you hear an idea you sit down and go through every other thing you know in search of connections and con-tradictions. At the simplest level, it just means asking yourself ques-tions: "What does this remind me of? What other things is this related to? Do I sense that this is connected to anything else I know, and if so, can I make that dim sense more vivid?"

Integration is what makes knowledge useful. An idea discon-nected from the rest of your ideas isn't knowledge. Your intellectual firepower consists of your ability to bring the full sum of what you know to every issue you encounter.

# Follow Evidence

One of the most important thinking skills you can develop is "mental filing." Most people engage in haphazard mental filling. Every idea in their head has the same standing: "Stuff I believe." So whether it's 2+2=4, slavery is evil, Epstein didn't kill himself, matter is made up of atoms, the FDA saves lives, there is life on other planets, or a vegan diet is the healthiest way to eat, they make no cognitive distinctions. Same for when they encounter new ideas: their reaction is binary: "I believe this" or "I don't believe this."

Mental filing means expanding your cognitive vocabulary and then carefully assessing ideas accordingly. For example, it's valuable to have a file for "Interesting things I've heard." These are ideas that are plausible, but where you haven't done the work to assess them. "The world is made out of atoms." You've heard it since you were a kid, but unless you studied at least some of the steps scientists went through to prove it, you don't *know* it.

Another valuable file is, "Things I find confusing." Typically, people treat anything that confuses them as false. Worse, if it comes from an authority they respect, it can get labeled in effect as, "Something I believe but don't understand." Proper mental filing means putting stuff that you don't understand into the "confusing" folder until you eventually come to understand and evaluate it.

Maybe your most important set of folders is for ideas where you have to *assess evidence*.

### Assessing evidence

Some ideas *are* binary: you either know them or you don't. "There's milk in the fridge." There's no collecting of evidence—you just go look in the damn fridge. But many ideas require you to collect and assess evidence over time, and there your knowledge moves through stages. You start out not knowing something. Then you get a little evidence for it—it's *possible*. You get more evidence—it's *probable*. You get sufficient evidence—it's *certain*. Good thinking requires knowing where you are in that progression and filing ideas in the appropriate evidentiary folder.

One of my favorite shows is the History Channel's *Pawn Stars*. It's about a real pawn shop in Las Vegas that specializes in rare, high-end items. In one episode, a guy brings in a guitar he claims was owned by Jimi Hendrix. The question is: Is this really Hendrix's guitar? The pawn stars bring in an expert.

The expert examines the guitar carefully. It's a white '63 Fender Stratocaster, and Hendrix was known to have played that type of guitar. At this point the expert might think: it's *possible* this was Hendrix's guitar. It's the right kind of guitar from the right time period. That constitutes *some* evidence. But it's not sufficient. There were lots of '63 Fender Stratocasters *not* owned by Hendrix.

Next, the expert observes that the guitar has scuff marks on the top of the neck, which indicate that it had been played by a left-hander. The guitar also has a whammy bar that's been straightened, which Hendrix was known to have done. The owner then shows the expert photos of Hendrix playing a guitar that looks exactly like the one in the shop. Now the expert can say: this is *probably* Hendrix's guitar.

Finally, the owner shows the expert documents that explain the guitar's "chain of custody" from Hendrix to intermediaries and finally to him. Once the expert sees that the guitar's serial number matches the serial number listed in the documentation he has sufficient knowledge to conclude: "Yes, this was Jimmy Hendrix's guitar. I'm certain of it."

Notice what the expert is doing. He is taking the idea, "This is Jimmy Hendrix's guitar," which he doesn't yet know to be true, and connecting it to what he does know. He is able to see that everything about this Strat is consistent with the claim it was owned by Hendrix, nothing is inconsistent with the claim it was owned by Hendrix, and there is sufficient evidence to meet the standard of proof used to authenticate memorabilia.

That, in essence, is the process that's involved in assessing evidence:

you define a standard of proof, and then you evaluate the extent to which the evidence you have meets it. If you meet the standard of proof, then there are no longer rational grounds for doubting the conclusion.

Note that it isn't easy to define a standard of proof. It takes real thought and expertise. For example, an authenticator has to know a lot about what can and can't be faked by counterfeiters and formulate the standard of proof in such a way that it mitigates against fakes. Similarly, a scientist can't leap from "the evidence is consistent with my hypothesis" to "therefore the evidence supports only my hypothesis." He has to know enough to be able to say, "This is the range of rational hypotheses, and so this evidence supports my hypothesis and *only* my hypothesis."

## The case for certainty

Certainty has a bad rap today. The one thing you're allowed to be certain of is that no one can be certain of anything. But that's because almost everyone misunderstands what certainty is.

The basic building block of epistemology is the concept "fact." A fact is something that accurately describes the world whether we know it or not. Three hundred years ago, it was a fact that matter was made up of atoms—but it was a fact that nobody knew.

The concept that distinguishes ignorance from our grasp of a fact is "knowledge." Knowledge, as Rand puts it, is "a mental grasp of a fact(s) of reality, reached either by perceptual observation or by a process of reason based on perceptual observation."[119] A scientist who understands the evidence for the atomic theory has knowledge, "Atoms are real."

"Fact," then, is a metaphysical term. "Knowledge" is metaphysical and epistemological. "Certainty" is a purely epistemological term: it says that you've met the standard of proof and are entitled to regard your conclusion as knowledge. It is illogical *not* to believe the conclusion.[120]

But this has an important implication: you can be certain of something—and later discover that your conclusion was imprecise or wrong. "Certainty" doesn't mean you're omniscient or infallible. It means you've gone through the process to achieve knowledge, and there are no longer grounds for doubt.

But human knowledge doesn't stand still. You continue to learn and to expand your knowledge. This can lead you to qualify a past conclusion. For example, Newton discovers the laws governing the behavior of macroscopic objects. Einstein later comes along and qualifies what Newton discovered: his laws only apply under small relative velocities and a weak gravitational field to a certain degree of precision. This new knowledge doesn't overthrow old knowledge—it expands it. Einstein didn't invalidate Newton: he discovered something more than Newton.

But new knowledge can also uncover old *errors*. I served on a jury once in a spine-chilling stalking case. The evidence for the defendant's guilt was overwhelming. He briefly dated the woman in question. Then he started acting strange and aggressive and she broke off the relationship. After that, she started receiving threatening texts— from a disposable cell phone bought with the defendant's credit card. The cell phone company could place the defendant's regular cell at the location where the texts were sent. The victim saw the defendant around her house at odd times. Fliers were plastered around her work calling her a slut and whore—and police confirmed that someone who looked like the defendant was seen passing them out. The defense blamed the defendant's twin brother (who had never met the victim and didn't live in the area), but said they couldn't locate the brother to have him testify. We convicted the defendant.

I regard our conclusion the defendant was guilty as certain. But now suppose years later I learned that there was evidence the twin brother was in the area, and that he hated the defendant and told people he wanted to frame him for a crime. And, let's even say the twin felt remorseful after a decade and confessed that he concocted the whole scheme. I would conclude: I was certain—and I was wrong. I made a mistake based on incomplete information that was apt to mislead.

If it's possible to be certain and wrong, then what good is certainty? Why not just say the best you can do is achieve probability? Well, for starters, you can't assign something a probability if you have no idea what would count as certainty. If you have no clue what it would mean to prove something, then you have no clue whether something counts as evidence, i.e., whether it *tends* to prove a hypothesis.

But, second, you need a concept to distinguish when you have *rational* grounds for doubting a conclusion from when you don't. When you lack sufficient evidence for a hypothesis, you have rational grounds for doubt. In a jury context, this is precisely what counts as reasonable doubt: there's some—maybe a lot—of evidence implicating the defendant. But not enough to meet the standard of proof.

But when you do have sufficient evidence, there are no longer rational grounds for doubt. The only doubts that can be offered are *irrational* "maybes." "I don't have any evidence, but maybe the twin brother did it." "I don't have any evidence, but maybe there will be new evidence that overturns the hypothesis." "I don't have any evidence, but maybe another hypothesis nobody has thought of explains these facts." "I can't point to any errors you've made in reasoning, but maybe you've made one."

"Maybe," Leonard Peikoff has said, is a fighting word. Just as you need grounds to say something is true, so you need grounds to say it *might* be true. Just as you need grounds for belief, so you need grounds for skepticism. Every assertion, no matter how tentative, requires you to have reasons. An assertion—any assertion—made without grounds, without evidence, without reasons is a claim based on emotion. Claims based on emotion aren't possible, they aren't probable, they aren't certain—they're *arbitrary*.

## Beware the arbitrary

An arbitrary claim is devoid of evidence. It's any kind of claim where the person's attitude amounts to, "I can't prove it, but prove it ain't so." The right response to arbitrary claims is to dismiss them without consideration.

Why? Because there's no logical way to consider them. You can't integrate them or reduce them because there's no evidence you can use to relate the idea to reality. They're not possible, not probable, not certain—they're not even false. They're *worse* than false. To conclude that an idea is false is a cognitive assessment: "This contradicts what I know." The arbitrary is something you can't bring into any relation with what you know. You can't evaluate it because there's nothing to evaluate.[121]

Imagine a court proceeding where the arbitrary was allowed.

- "The phone was purchased with the defendant's credit card." "*Maybe* someone stole his card and bought the phone."
- "The defendant was seen passing out the threatening fliers." "*Maybe* it was his twin brother."
- "His twin brother was in China." "*Maybe* he bought a plane ticket under a false identity."
- "The defendant was caught on tape talking about how he was the one who committed the crime." "*Maybe* the tape was doctored."
- "The defendant confessed to the crime." "*Maybe* the confession was coerced."

Any of these "maybes" could be legitimate if evidence was offered for them. But to the extent there is no evidence, there's nothing the jury can do to process them. The proper approach: ignore them. Pretend nothing has been said because, as Peikoff explains, "cognitively speaking, *nothing has been said*."[122] If you make a claim about reality, it's your job to support it.

Not every proponent of the arbitrary openly says, "I have no evidence, prove it ain't so." Often they'll give the appearance of giving reasons. Conspiracists, for example, will bombard you with an overwhelming amount of what can superficially appear to be evidence. Religionists will go through the motions of giving arguments for God's existence. But these aren't cognitive acts. It can take work to *see* that they aren't cognitive acts, and that the arguments and evidence offered up are rationalizations for emotionalism, not part of a quest for truth. But once you see that, then you don't have to examine the one billionth "news story" claiming that Trump actually won the election or the one billionth argument for God's existence. You can reject the entire approach as arbitrary.

Now, you might think: Isn't the fact that we can make mistakes *some* evidence that Watkins got his jury verdict wrong? Isn't the fact that elections can be stolen *some* evidence that Biden stole the election from Trump? No. The evidence for a capacity is not evidence that capacity has been actualized in a particular case. The fact that elections can be stolen is not evidence that this particular election was stolen.

In sum, you need to assess evidence. Once you've formulated a standard of proof and met it, then the conclusion is certain. The only kinds of doubts left are *arbitrary* doubts. But the fact that a conclusion is certain does not mean that you never revisit it, and that you ignore new genuine evidence in order to neurotically protect your conclusion. Logic gives you an *ongoing process* for knowing—not one that eliminates the possibility of error, but one that minimizes and corrects errors over time. (This is one major difference between reason and faith, mysticism, or emotionalism: reason is self-corrective; other alleged sources of knowledge are not.)

Any concept that demands you be omniscient or infallible in order to achieve knowledge is out. Certainty can't mean, "Impossible ever to overturn" because it's only omniscience that would make a conclusion impossible to overturn. The challenge you face in life is not to distinguish conclusions where error is impossible from conclusions where error is possible. It's to distinguish knowledge from non-knowledge *given* your lack of omniscience and capacity for error.

## Learn from Experts

Today it's popular to urge people to "listen to the science." Rarely does this mean: dig into the scientific literature and make up your own mind. Instead, it's taken to mean: accept the conclusions of (some) scientific authorities without question. But blindly listening to scientists is as irrational as blindly listening to the Pope. Scientists, and experts more generally, should be seen as advisors—not infallible authorities.[123]

We need experts. Just as the economic division of labor makes us all far more productive than we would be if we were all self-sufficient farmers, so the intellectual division of labor makes us all far more knowledgeable than we would be if we could only make use of knowledge we ourselves had discovered. But relying on experts doesn't mean blindly accepting what they say.

So how should you go about rationally assessing claims made by experts—claims that you, as a non-expert, often cannot verify independently?

For starters, you need to develop baseline skillsets that allow you to make (relatively) independent judgments about expert claims. Above all, this means having a basic understanding of how to assess data-based claims like the ones that we hear in discussions of health, science, economic, and political issues. "Vaccines cause autism." "Coffee is good for your health/bad for your health." "Inequality hurts economic growth." "Climate change will lead to devastating droughts."

Data-driven claims involve three components: data, data processing, and interpretation. It turns out that though you can't assess data-driven claims the way experts can, you can often spot problems at the data-level (input errors) and the interpretation-level (output errors) without expert-level knowledge. You might not understand the complex statistics that go into the claim that coffee is unhealthy, for instance, but you might be able to figure out that that conclusion was based on a small sample of elderly people. Or, on the output error side, you might find that though the media reported a causal connection—"coffee causes cancer"—the actual study simply reported a correlation between coffee consumption and elevated cancer rates. This kind of assessment isn't enough to reliably draw true conclusions without the aid of experts but is often enough to protect you from many of the false claims you hear on social media. (The best introduction to data analysis skills I've found is Carl Bergstrom and Jevin West's *Calling Bullshit*.)

But while improving your B.S. detector is an invaluable foundation, it still doesn't tell you everything you need to know in order to use experts to help you reach the truth. For that, you need some further steps.

First, you have to judge the state of the field. Some fields have plenty of self-proclaimed experts, but the field itself is illegitimate (think: astrology). In other cases, the field might be at too primitive a state of knowledge to give reliable guidance. I suspect this is true in the field of nutrition, given the complexity of the problem they're trying to solve, and the lack of consensus around even seemingly basic questions like what causes weight gain. In still other cases, the field has become politicized. In the field I'm most familiar with, climate science, funding, publication, and hiring decisions tend to encourage catastrophic predictions about $CO_2$'s climate impact. This doesn't mean that we should totally ignore nutrition and climate experts, but it does mean we have to be wary—especially if they are recommending radical changes like going vegan or rapidly eliminating fossil fuels. (For an outstanding guide to using experts to make sense of energy and environmental issues, see Alex Epstein's book *Fossil Future*.)

Second, you have to judge the supposed expert(s). You need to assess whether they understand the field and whether they're trustworthy. When the COVID-19 pandemic hit, for example, I saw people sending around videos from random general practitioners, based mainly on whether they liked the conclusions the GPs had reached. That's like asking your dentist how to treat your throat cancer. In my case, I happened to be friends with Amesh Adalja, an infectious disease expert at Johns Hopkins who specializes in pandemics.

Amesh not only has expert credentials. He's an expert explainer. Part of what establishes whether an expert is trustworthy is how clearly he can explain things to a layman. That means not only explaining his conclusion, but his reasoning. It means explaining his degree of certainty, explaining how much consensus there is among experts in his field, and why various experts might disagree with his conclusions. It means being able to answer your questions in ways that are clarifying. As a general rule, a trustworthy expert's primary goal isn't to try to convince you that he's right—it's to act as a guide to help you understand an area of knowledge that you cannot assess independently.

What should emerge is a reduction—not a full reduction that gives you a complete picture of an idea's tie to reality, but a reduction based on expert testimony. When you have good reasons to trust the expert, and the expert explains his conclusion and the reasoning behind it in terms you can understand, then you have established an idea's tie to reality to the extent that's relevant given your context and purposes.[124]

Note that you don't need to rely on experts in every field of knowledge. In some fields, you'll have sufficient expertise to reach independent judgments. In particular, *philosophy* does not require experts. Or, rather, we rely on professional philosophers to develop philosophical systems, which takes a lifetime (and genius). But philosophical knowledge doesn't make use of specialized knowledge. It uses only knowledge available to everyone. An ethicist can help you think through a difficult issue by drawing your attention to arguments you had not considered. But there's no specialized knowledge an ethicist has that you lack. You can judge his arguments independently.

Follow reason. Treasure your mind. Use your mind to gain knowledge about the world, other people, and yourself. That is the path to success—and to joy.

# Lesson 5

# Create Values

## Become a Valuer

Many people's lives are ruled by what author John Demartini calls "social idealisms": "socially acceptable ways of thinking and behaving." These are things we "should" do, or "have to" do, or are "supposed to" do, but don't genuinely *want* to do. They aren't chosen values but unchosen duties.[125]

To achieve happiness, Demartini argues, we need to be guided by our *highest values*. Your highest values aren't something imposed on you by an external authority. They are "the very essence of *you*: what you're drawn to, what you inevitably seek out, what you live for."[126]

In Demartini's account, you discover your highest values, not by sitting down and envisioning a life that you think you would be passionate about *ex nihilo*, but by examining your actual life to discover what you genuinely value in practice. To identify your highest values, Demartini recommends asking thirteen questions, and supplying three examples for each:[127]

1. How do you fill your personal and professional space?
2. How do you spend your time?
3. How do you spend your energy?
4. How do you spend your money?
5. Where do you have the most order and organization?
6. Where are you most reliable, disciplined, and focused?
7. What do you think about, and what is your innermost dominant thoughts?
8. What do you visualize and realize?
9. What is your internal dialogue?
10. What do you talk about in social settings?
11. What inspires you?
12. What are the most consistent long-term goals that you have set?
13. What do you love to learn about the most?

According to Demartini, these questions will help elicit the top values in your life—things you already value that you can now purposefully choose to build your life around.

I regard Demartini's advice as extremely useful for helping you discard pointless duties and unearthing what you truly value. But it's not sufficient because even if you throw away external "shoulds," it's all too easy to adopt values that are *inconsistent* and *bad for your life*. In philosophical terms, Demartini replaces intrinsicism (duty) with subjectivism (feelings). Demartini believes that moral codes as such are at odds with personal values, and that the only test that matters is whether you already value something. But the truth is that a rational, pro-life, pro-self moral code is the only way to choose and achieve personal values that lead to happiness.

Pursuing your happiness means focusing on the achievement of pro-life values, and the achievement of pro-life values means practicing the virtue of rationality—it means being a thinker. A thinker goes after what he wants, but he doesn't decide what to want lightly. When selecting his values, he applies three crucial tests over and above answering the kinds of questions Demartini would have us ask: the reality test, the cost test, and the integration test.

(1) *The reality test.* The thinker only pursues goals that are achievable. This doesn't mean easy to achieve. The thinker is ambitious. He wants the *best* possible. But that also means he wants the best *possible.*

In part that means possible to *man*; he has no sympathy for those who yearn for a life free from effort, struggle, failure, or death. In part that means possible to *him.* As a child I wanted to be a professional baseball player. But after it became clear I didn't have the speed, strength, eyesight, or hand-eye coordination to give me even a fighting chance, playing pro ball no longer represented a value to me.

The reality test involves more than working to achieve goals that are realistic—it means valuing *values.* It means that you don't chase after whatever you happen to desire, but you're interested in whether your desires are genuinely good for you—whether they work to *keep* you in reality.

Human beings are capable of pursuing goals that work to our detriment. We can pursue relationships that leave us drained and diminished. We can consume substances that weaken our bodies and subvert our minds. If we do not examine our desires to ask ourselves *why* we want what we want, we can pursue seemingly legitimate values in self-destructive ways: we can want a job, not because we love it, but because it will impress people. We can want a lover, not because we're in love, but because we want others to envy us. Our actions can lead us, not to the achievement of life-promoting positives, but to a hollow collection of trophies displayed in the entryway of an empty house.

Every value is both an end and a means to some further value. The thinker examines every value to see the ultimate ends it is aimed at fulfilling. Are they pro-life—or not? He works to see the full ramifications of what he's after on his life—and will not tolerate anything that will weaken him or subvert his life. Or, to put it positively, he sees every value in its full light, and only endorses those values that brighten his life and his ability to deal with reality.

(2) *The cost test.* If a value is achievable and pro-life, the thinker identifies the means necessary to achieve it. He never embraces a value without assuming responsibility for the effort required to achieve it. If he's considering whether to become an entrepreneur, he will want to know: what's required to become an entrepreneur? And he will ask himself: is that a price I'm willing to pay? For great values, he's willing to pay a great price, embracing the fact that every value requires effort. But if he isn't willing to pay the price, then he will not adopt the value.

(3) *The integration test.* We don't pursue values in isolation. At minimum, time spent in the pursuit of one goal means time taken away from other goals. Happiness is a state of non-contradictory joy, where the achievement of one value doesn't entail the frustration of another. The thinker works to bring his values into harmony. If a potential value cannot be integrated with his other values, then he will not adopt it.

Years ago I saw the documentary *Still Bill*, about the musician Bill Withers, who quit music at the peak of his fame. The most striking aspect of the documentary was Withers' clear, independent sense of *what he was about*. He had a vision of what he wanted from life, and fortune and fame meant nothing to him if it wasn't consistent with that vision.

*That* is what it what it looks like to be a thinker. It's not simply having a few values that you go after; it's building a *life*. It's conceiving of what you want your days to add up to, then saying "yes" to everything that moves you toward that vision and saying "no" to anything that doesn't.

Life and happiness are not the result of achieving a single value, but a *code* of values—a systematic constellation of values that fit together into a self-sustaining whole. Not everyone has a code of values. Not everyone knows what they're about. The values they do have are chiefly held in emotional form, intermingled with duties and compulsions and fears. If they do have clear, crisp values, these are often compartmentalized into the sphere of life where they feel most in control (usually work). But their pursuits don't add up to anything—or don't add up to anything consistent.

In her notes for an early novel she planned but never wrote, Rand describes this mentality:

> Most people lack [the capacity for] *reverence* and *"taking things seriously."* They do not hold anything to be very serious or profound. There is nothing that is sacred or immensely important to them. There is nothing—no idea, object, work, or person—that can inspire them with a profound, intense, and all-absorbing passion that reaches to the roots of their souls. They do not know how to value or desire. They cannot give themselves entirely to anything. There is nothing *absolute* about them. They take all things lightly, easily, pleasantly—almost indifferently, in that they can have it or not, they do not claim it as their absolute necessity.[128]

You cannot be all-in on your values if they aren't clearly defined and integrated into a consistent whole. Instead, your desires become muted, contradictory, and all-too-often self-defeating. The lethargy and bland conventionality and ostentatious shallowness and *unhappiness* you encounter in most people finds its roots here: it is an intellectual failure. They have not made the commitment to being goal-directed, have not *thought* about what they want, and so they "do not know how to value or desire."

The purpose of this lesson is to teach you how to value. It's to teach you how to achieve a truly purpose-driven life—a life rich in meaning, passion, and joy. A life that you love.

## Create Your Value Hierarchy

The basic challenge of integrating your values is arranging your life so that all of your crucial needs get met. Even if your values are rational and fit together in principle, it is all too easy to neglect crucial values in practice. You allow work to rob you of human connection or you allow your family demands to trump self-care. To pursue a life is to treat all of your vital needs as sacred, and, to the extent you can, structure your life so that you can tend to all of your major values.

What that means in practice is establishing a *value hierarchy*. Rand explains:

> A moral code is a set of abstract principles; to practice it, an individual must translate it into the appropriate concretes—he must choose the particular goals and values which he is to pursue. This requires that he define his particular hierarchy of values, in the order of their importance, and that he act accordingly.[129]

A hierarchy of values allows you to make decisions about how to live your day-to-day life because it identifies what's most important to you—and it allows you to see how smaller, even trivial decisions relate to your highest, most long-term goals. For example, a fulfilling marriage is not the result of a single grand, sweeping gesture. It is the result of countless small actions: actively listening while your partner tells you about his day, a meaningful compliment as she leaves for work, sharing a secret, playing a game of Scrabble, a thoughtful birthday gift. These concrete activities are *how* you create a fulfilling marriage, and they are *what* a fulfilling marriage consists of. Someone who claims to love his partner, and yet rushes out the door in the morning and holes up in a man cave at night, who cannot make time for his partner, who cannot make it through a shared meal without checking his work email, *does not actually value his marriage*, whatever he might claim.

To honor your values, you have to identify their relative importance in your life and then translate that into specific concrete actions, never sacrificing a higher value to a lower value.

How exactly do you form a hierarchy of values? A hierarchy of values is, in essence, a time hierarchy. To value something is to spend time on that pursuit. This doesn't always mean that your most important values get the most time, but they do get first claim on your time.

I might, for example, spend more time watching baseball each week than having sex, but sex is a higher value because it gets prioritized over watching the Phillies. In forming a value hierarchy, the question I'm trying to answer: what are my priorities? What has first claim on my time, energy, and resources?

To form a time hierarchy, you can't simply make a list of all the things you value and try to rank them from 1 to 10,000. How would you compare going to the gym to listening to Bach to a new pair of shoes? At that level of analysis, your values are incommensurable. Instead, you need to start by identifying broad *categories* of values that capture all the things you have to achieve to live a secure, fulfilling life. For example, your list might consist of:

- Creation
- Connection
- Recreation
- Self-maintenance

These are the areas in which you have to divide up your time. The fact that creation is more important to you than connection doesn't mean you want to spend all your time creating. Since you have to meet all your important needs to achieve happiness, what it means is that your creative work has the *primary* claim on your time.

Within a given category, then, you can make a ranked list of concrete values. Take the value of connection. You might think: I'm going to devote most of my afternoons this week to connecting with the people I value. And my hierarchy of companions might be: my romantic partner, then my kids, then my best friend, then my other friends. So most of my time is going to go to my girlfriend and kids. Then I'm going to spend Saturday night with my best friend and hop on a Zoom call with an old college buddy on Sunday.

In most value categories, you'll want to identify subcategories before creating ranked lists of concrete values. For example, you might break recreation down into exercise, inspiration, learning, excitement, plea-sure—and then make ranked lists of specific values. Once you've got-ten your hour of exercise for the day, for example, you're not going to use any remaining recreation time to go for a hike—you might watch a documentary or listen to Swan Lake.

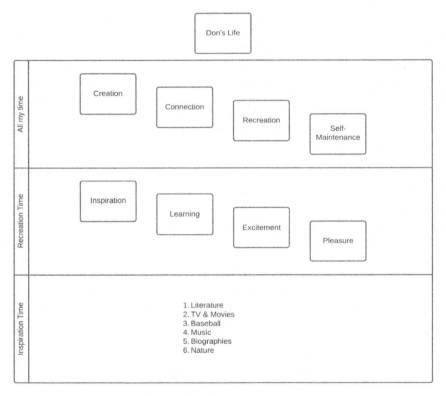

Figure 1

Figure 1 shows a rough sketch of how you might work out part of your value hierarchy.

Your value hierarchy doesn't have to be this formalized and detailed. What's crucial is that you have a general ranking of all your most important values and that when conflicts arise or when you notice some of your needs going unmet, you can step back and clarify for yourself what matters most.

You can think of this as a top-down approach to your value hierarchy. But there's also what you can call a bottom-up approach. When you're contemplating something you want to do or feel you have to do, you might not have a clear sense of where it belongs in your hierarchy of values.

Here it's crucial to remember that all values stand in a means/ends relationship to other values. Right now on my to-do list I have "set up a Health Savings Account." To see where this fits in my value hierarchy, I need to ask, "Why is this a value? What will I gain by doing this or what will I lose by not doing this?" In this case, an HSA will save me money by allowing me to pay my healthcare bills with pre-tax income. That means it belongs under "financial health," which is near the top of my "self-maintenance" hierarchy. When I sit down to focus on my financial health, which I typically do at the end of each month, I'm going to see that making the time to open an HSA is a high-leverage activity: it will take about an hour or two to set up, and yet could save me hundreds or thousands of dollars a year. That's going to take precedence over a lot of other money-saving activities.

One of the benefits of formulating a hierarchy of values and seeing how every activity fits within your hierarchy is that the world becomes value rich. The smallest value takes on an elevated level of meaning and importance because you see its role in serving your highest values.

For example, I spend most of my life in my home office. By seeing my home office as intimately connected to the career that I love, it becomes more than a place to sit down and type. I can see it as a sacred environment where I do what I love. And that encourages me to create the kind of environment that helps me do my work and enjoy my work. In front of me, there's a window which I've fitted with a scarlet curtain (my favorite color) and next to it a portrait of Ayn Rand (my favorite author). On my desk is a soothing water fountain with tea lights. At my feet is a yellow carpet that makes me feel as if I'm stepping into a bright, energized, but relaxed universe every time I enter my office. I'm surrounded by books that make me feel as if I'm living among history's great minds.

That is what it means to fill your life with values. You can turn every area of your life into a slice of personal heaven. You can turn your home into your ideal universe. You can make your wardrobe an expression of soul. You can fill your kitchen with your favorite food and choose a car that serves and expresses your lifestyle. You can—and you should—rearrange the world so that it comes closer to your vision of the ideal world. You can create a stylized universe of your own making—a universe that elevates you, heightens the mundane, and accentuates the exceptional.

When you make your life value rich, something else happens as well. Most of your highest values are long range and abstract. But when you come to see the means to those values as *themselves* being values, you have the continuing experience of successfully achieving values. My most important career value right now is to write this book. But I cannot sit down and "write this book." What I can do is set as my value spending three hours a day writing. Each day that I've invested those three hours is an achievement of one of my values. Contrast that with people whose life is a series of obnoxious duties performed in the hopes that one day far in the future they'll get what they want. You can get what you want *today*—by seeing what you *can* achieve today as serving your long-term vision.

## The Virtue of Productiveness

I've left out one crucial ingredient of a value hierarchy: the purpose at its center. Without a central purpose, you cannot formulate or follow a hierarchy of values. According to Rand:

> A central purpose serves to integrate all the other concerns of a man's life. It establishes the hierarchy, the relative importance, of

his values, it saves him from pointless inner conflicts, it permits him to enjoy life on a wide scale and to carry that enjoyment into any area open to his mind; whereas a man without a purpose is lost in chaos. He does not know what his values are. He does not know how to judge. He cannot tell what is or is not important to him, and, therefore, he drifts helplessly at the mercy of any chance stimulus or any whim of the moment. He can enjoy nothing. He spends his life searching for some value which he will never find.[130]

Only one kind of purpose is fit to be a central purpose: a productive career.

Our need to work is often blamed on capitalism. Absent capitalism's delusions, we would exist in harmony with nature, spending a few hours growing fruit and the rest of the time relaxing with friends and family and playing folk music or whatever. That part is never too clear. What is clear is that, according to capitalism's critics, the time and attention we give to our careers is a disease motivated by an unquenchable desire to consume. "We buy things we don't need with money we don't have to impress people we don't like," Chuck Palahniuk tells us in *Fight Club*.

But it's the critics of work who are delusional. Non-capitalist societies are idealized only by people who don't have to live in them. It's capitalism and the technological innovation it generates that liberated us from endless grueling hours in the sun, the countless dangers of farming, the primitive ignorance of people who had not built universities and the printing press, the nasty, brutish, short lives that people led in prior ages. Capitalism doesn't delude us into working—it liberates us to do the kind of work we want, the way we want to do it, and to live better than kings did a few centuries ago. Capitalism increases the material and spiritual rewards of work. But the need to work? That's built into us.

Biologically, we need material values in order to survive—productive work is how we create them. Human beings can't live "in harmony with nature" the way animals do. Animals are programmed to consume the resources in their environmental niche (with many members of a species dying in the struggle for a fixed supply of resources). Human beings lack that kind of programming. Venture out into to the wilderness without the tools of modern civilization (or just read *Into the Wild*) and you'll quickly find that living "in harmony with nature" really means *dying* in harmony with nature.

We don't consume ready-made material values—we create them through productive work. We look around our environment, figure out how to make the raw material of nature useful to us, then exert the effort to bring new resources and values into existence. We don't just pluck fruit off wild bushes—we plant crops. We don't just hunt animals—we breed them. We don't live in caves—we build houses. We don't scratch words into the dirt—we create the printing press and the internet. We use reason to project a better future and use reason to bring that future into existence. This is why there's no need for the "less fit" members of our species to die off: we don't fight for a fixed sum of resources—we create abundance.

Productive work isn't just one activity human life requires, but the central activity. Life is a process of self-sustaining action. Most human activities—even important ones—consist of consuming values. Visiting the doctor, pursuing a hobby, traveling with friends, taking your partner on a date all involve expending resources. A self-sustaining life requires the continual replenishing of our resources, and only productive work can accomplish that. As a result, when we formulate our hierarchy of values—when we decide how we will apportion our time among the various things we care about—productive work has to have first claim on our time and energy. Our central purpose must be a productive purpose.[131] Productive creation is what makes a human life self-sustaining. It's how we bring new values into existence.

The insignia of productive work's unique place in life is the *pleasure* we take in the process of creating values. Famed educator Maria Montessori observed that this joy in work can be seen even in children. Children, she notes:

don't consider what they do to be play—it is their work. . . . If the mother is making bread, the child is given a little flour and water too, so that he can also make bread; if the mother is sweeping a room, the child has a little brush and helps her. They wash clothes alongside the mother. The child is very, very happy.[132]

But the pleasure of work depends in large measure on the extent to which it uses the full resources of our mind. For an adult, baking bread and washing clothes can be drudgery. We need work that challenges us, that requires us to learn, grow, think creatively. But if we do find such work, then, like children, it can become an all-consuming source of passion and pride.

This is the virtue of productiveness. The essence of a moral life is using your intelligence to create values. This sets your central purpose, and allows you to build a *life*, rather than to drift through a series of disconnected *days*. As Rand puts it:

Productive work is the road of man's unlimited achievement and calls upon the highest attributes of his character: his creative ability, his ambitiousness, his self-assertiveness, his refusal to bear uncontested disasters, his dedication to the goal of reshaping the earth in the image of his values. "Productive work" does not mean the unfocused performance of the motions of some job. It means the consciously chosen pursuit of a productive career, in any line of rational endeavor, great or modest, on any level of ability. It is not the degree of a man's ability nor the scale of his work that is ethically relevant here, but the fullest and most purposeful use of his mind.[133]

The virtue of productiveness tells us that we need to produce in order to live—and that if we want to enjoy life, our work must be a source, not only of wealth, but of joy. As the hero of Rand's novel *The Fountainhead* says, "I have, let's say, sixty years to live. Most of that time will be spent working. I've chosen the work I want to do. If I find no joy in it, then I'm only condemning myself to sixty years of torture."[134]

Too often we settle for a job that pays the bills, a job that makes us lust for Fridays and fear Mondays. That is ghastly. We should not tolerate torture. We should not tolerate one ounce of needless suffering. If our goal is to live and enjoy life, then we need to create for ourselves a career that we love. But how do we do that?

# Build a Career That You Love

When I was six, I wrote a retrospective poem on my life titled "When I was Five." (I can still recall writing the line: "When I was five, I didn't have a Nintendo.") My dad read it and told me it was good—so good he would send it to a friend he had in publishing. He never did get around to helping me launch a career as a poet, but it was nevertheless a powerful experience. This was the first time I can remember feeling *good* at something. My two best friends growing up were natural athletes and so I was always slower, weaker, less coordinated than the people around me. The feeling of efficacy I got from writing was undoubtedly one of the early seeds that would lead me to one day pursue an intellectual career. I had found the way I enjoyed using my mind: putting words on a page.

That's not to say I remained laser-focused on becoming a writer. I went through periods where my obsession was martial arts, or baseball, or music. But writing always lingered in the background. When I discovered philosophy at the age of thirteen, my interests shifted from writing poetry and fiction to nonfiction. I started writing essays on religion, philosophy, and politics just for fun. I wasn't yet on the road to mastery—not self-consciously, anyway. I was just enjoying myself.

The first true step on the road to writerdom came in my senior year of high school, when my journalism teacher, Brooke Nelson—a feisty ex-journalist who loved to cover my drafts in red ink—introduced me to the book *On Writing Well* by William Zinsser. Zinsser's main piece of advice was that good writing isn't fancy and ornate but clear, simple, lean. He advised writers to kill verbal clutter and reach for vivid verbs. This was the first time I can remember self-consciously working to develop a writing skill.

By the time I graduated high school, I knew I wanted to become a writer. But I had no idea how to become one. I had no clue what kinds of jobs existed for young writers and no clue how I could get those jobs. Looking back, I shudder at how passive I was. I didn't ask my writing teachers at college for advice. I didn't hunt down writers online and ask them what I should do. I didn't search for articles or books on how to become a writer. In truth, my desire to write for a living wasn't a goal, but a fantasy. It was something I hoped would happen, but I was doing nothing to make it happen.

That's not quite true. The one thing I was doing was *writing*. I ran a blog, penned a (bad) novel, and later started my own publication for fans of Ayn Rand. I also started taking classes on communication and philosophy from the Ayn Rand Institute. That's what finally led to my break. ARI was looking for a new writer to join their staff and when they asked the writing teacher, Keith Lockitch, who his best student was, my name was at the top of the list. I got an email inviting me to apply for a job and three weeks later, I was driving across the country from Virginia to California to start my career as a pro writer. I was ready to begin my apprenticeship.

When I started at ARI, the first thing I discovered was this: I didn't know as much as I thought I knew. I had been studying Ayn Rand's philosophy for a decade, and yet being around experts like Onkar Ghate, Yaron Brook, and Alex Epstein quickly revealed to me that my understanding of Rand's ideas and how to write about them persuasively was hopelessly primitive. I had arrived in California feeling like a wunderkind and now felt like a novice. At one level, the experience was disheartening. But at another level, I felt inspired by the discovery of a mountain I wanted to climb, and I made the commitment to do whatever it took to climb that mountain.

What it took almost broke me.

For the first two years, virtually nothing I wrote was publishable. I would sit at my computer for hours, carefully crafting two paragraph press releases, only to find them sent back by my editors time and time again. When something eventually would make it through the editing wringer, the final product would reflect only a few of my words—the rest had been rewritten by my colleagues. And that was the easy part. The hard part is that sometimes I would get something through the editorial process and then, at our weekly editorial meeting, our lead intellectual Onkar would explain to me in front of the group why it was wrong and ARI shouldn't have published it.

These were painful, frustrating experiences. But I remember telling myself: pay the price. Eventually, you'll get good. I would spend hours after work reflecting on that day's feedback, struggling to understand why my editors had made the changes they'd made, to understand how Onkar had seen what I hadn't seen. I would read books, listen to lectures, stay up late into the evening trying to sharpen my thinking and improve my prose. I was engaging in what psychologists call "deliberate practice"—the painstaking work of skills development that pushes you outside your comfort zone and subjects you to rigorous feedback. It is how you become good at your work.

One of my biggest assets during this time was my colleague Alex Epstein. Alex would eventually go on to become the world's leading champion of fossil fuels. In those days, he was just getting started, and yet he already seemed to be decades ahead of me. He was able to take complex issues and make them simple. To present ideas with a level of clarity and persuasiveness that no one else could match. He was doing the kind of work I wanted to do the way I wanted to do it, so I started going to him with questions, asking him to critique my work, studying his writing until I felt I understood every word choice and every comma. I even let him use me as a practice dummy for his hobby of Brazilian Jiu-Jitsu, just so I could soak up more knowledge about philosophy and writing. In effect, I was trying to reverse engineer his success, the way that tech companies will try to reverse engineer a competitor's breakthrough product.

Alex was not one of those mentors who couched every criticism between two items of praise. He never attacked me, but if my work was bad, he was blunt and to the point. One evening I had him listen to a radio interview I had done during the financial crisis of 2008. His feedback: "It sounds like this guy"—part of how he made his feedback impersonal was to direct it to "this guy" instead of "you"—"It sounds like this guy is talking out of his ass." And it was true. I was trying to explain why the financial crisis wasn't the result of the free market, and while that much was accurate—the market was highly regulated—I really had no clue how the Federal Reserve worked, how Wall Street worked, how derivatives were regulated, and a lot else besides. Alex stressed that I had to make it a policy never to say anything I didn't fully understand. "This may cause your interviews to be rough at the beginning, but they will be more interesting because the audience will be hearing *you*—not some guy parroting talking points. There's no need to present yourself as an expert on Ayn Rand's philosophy, let alone everything in the world. Just be honest: 'I'm a guy who has thought about a lot of things and knows a lot of things, and although there's a lot I don't know, I'd like to share with you what I do know.'" Pills like these were tough to swallow, but I swallowed them on the premise that "The more you sweat in peace, the less you bleed in war."

But I would be lying if I said that I displayed unwavering grit. There were moments during my first few years at ARI where I felt as though I wasn't making progress. That I simply was not cut out to be a professional writer. I never quite got to the point of giving up, but I did sometimes wonder whether I *should* give up. And yet at the same time, I knew I was getting better. For long stretches I would stay at a plateau, but every six months or so, a bunch of things would click into place and in a matter of weeks I would rise to a higher level of ability. I could think better and write better. The improvements were palpable. The growth was intoxicating and made it easier to endure the long slogs where it felt like I was treading water.

A turning point came when ARI's then-president, Yaron Brook, tasked me to work with him on a book on the morality of capitalism— what would eventually become our national bestseller *Free Market Revolution*. I found the experience of working on a book liberating. Because there wasn't a deadline attached to the project, I felt free to experiment, free to rewrite drafts nine or ten or twenty times in order to get them right. I would spend weeks researching a point and thinking about it to make sure I truly understood it.

My biggest breakthrough came late in the project. Alex had written an essay on the morality of capitalism that I found explosively powerful and persuasive. Meanwhile, another writer I knew wrote a similar essay, only I sensed this one was completely ineffective. I spent hours comparing the two essays side-by-side, and comparing them to the work I was doing on my book. Suddenly, it hit me like a revelation: I could now articulate exactly what distinguished clear and persuasive writing from writing that would leave an audience cold. In particular, I saw that you couldn't write from *your* agenda. You had to start from where the audience was and build a bridge, step-by-step, to where you wanted them to be. I saw how great writing had to anticipate the questions your readers would have and the objections that would occur to them. I saw how to use my philosophy to clarify an issue, rather than use an issue to try to sell people on my philosophy. For the first time, I felt in control of my writing and thinking in a way that had eluded me before.

That was the moment my apprenticeship ended and I started the second phase of my journey: experimentation and refinement. I was now a pro-writer. I knew what I was doing and could reliably turn out publishable work. But I still had holes and blind spots. I hadn't fully formed my own style and approach. I still relied on editors to save me from embarrassing mistakes. I had control over my writing but not *full* control. The best way I can describe it is that I was good but inconsistent, and I didn't have the toolkit to identify and overcome my own flaws.

Over the next six years, that's the space I lived in. I wrote more books, each time pushing myself to be more ambitious and experimental. I continued studying communication and philosophy, but now I was putting more of myself into it. What's *my way* of tackling this issue? What's *my way* of communicating this idea?

I was becoming more creative, but in 2017, I hit a roadblock. My third book, *Equal Is Unfair*, had come out the year before. It was the best thing I had ever written and I had expected it to catapult me into the national spotlight, the way Alex recently had with his book *The Moral Case for Fossil Fuels*. That didn't happen. In part, I blamed my publisher, who had done nothing to market the book; they hadn't even gotten the book into bookstores, which is really the only thing publishers contribute nowadays. But I also knew that ultimately the failure was mine. The book was good—very good—but it wasn't great. And yet I had no clue *how* to make something great. I went through a period of months where I felt deflated and hopeless.

The best way I can explain it is this. In high school, my main passion was guitar. I loved writing music, but I hit a point where my conception of what good music was went beyond my ability to play. My creativity was limited by my toolkit. That essentially led me to give up music. But I wasn't going to give up writing. What could I do to reach the next level? Thankfully for me, that's when Alex reached out with a job offer.

Alex had left ARI a few years earlier and had turned his advocacy of fossil fuels into a thriving business. He wanted me to help him. It would mean leaving ARI, a place that I loved dearly. It also meant stepping back from the spotlight. Instead of writing my books, giving speeches about my ideas, going on radio and TV to discuss my work, I would be behind the scenes helping Alex increase his impact. It would also mean taking a big risk. Alex's venture involved far more uncertainty than working for a nonprofit that had been around for decades.

I took the leap because I was confident that working closely with Alex would give me the skills I needed to reach the next level of my career.

It was the right decision. And it was brutal.

For the first year, I felt like a beginner again. Alex was demanding and the work was fast paced. At ARI I could lock myself in my office for weeks working on an article. With Alex, I'd have to turn around a major project in a day. And still: every word would have to be perfect. To make matters worse, meeting Alex's standards meant hitting a moving target. Alex's standards for "good" keep rising as he improved, and so every step forward I made left me further behind. And you have to remember: we weren't simply writing op-eds for a newspaper. We were creating messaging for energy industry clients paying us five and six figures. If what I did wasn't good, it *mattered*.

What's more, I was no longer just a writer. Alex tasked me with research, marketing, sales—areas where I had minimal experience and minimal aptitude. The challenge, responsibility, and pace of the work was crushing. For the first year or so, I felt terrified I was going to get fired, which is particularly frightening when your only skill is writing about ideas no one agrees with.

And yet, just as had happened at ARI, I started to improve. I learned how to present ideas in a way that was truly persuasive. I learned how judge my own work with a far greater degree of objectivity. I learned how to continually raise my own standards rather than rely on someone else to catch my mistakes. And I also learned the art of intellectual entrepreneurship. I saw how to make my ideas valuable on the market, how to find high-paying opportunities, how to conduct myself when dealing with powerful people. After three years working with Alex, I'd built precisely the skills I had hoped to acquire. I had achieved mastery.

And thank God. Because that's exactly the moment when it all fell apart. In spring of 2020, oil prices crashed and we lost most of our clients overnight. Then came the pandemic and Alex's high-priced speaking gigs dried up. He made the hard decision: I would have to find another job.

Only I didn't. I decided that to have the career I wanted, I would need to roll the dice and go out on my own as a freelance writer and communications coach. But by now I had the knowledge and skills to do it. I was able to make a living—a better living than I had ever made—writing and helping others overcome their communication challenges.

I tell this story at such length because, while the details are unique, the essential contours of the journey aren't. Everyone who achieves a career that they love has gone through some version of the same process: discover what they want to do—and develop the skills to do it well.

That's it. That really is all there is to it.

## What Makes a Career Fulfilling

This lesson is about building a career that you love. But what does it mean to love your work? Just as pursuing happiness requires understanding what happiness is, achieving career success requires understanding what success consists of. Essentially, there are four ingredients that determine how fulfilling your work will be: money, mastery, autonomy, and mission.

### Money

One of the ugliest features of our culture is that it teaches us to disdain money. Or, rather, it teaches us that we ought to disdain money. Since you cannot live without money, the actual result is to prevent you from discovering what a healthy attitude toward money would look like.

Let's start with the obvious: it is deeply unhealthy to treat money as your supreme value. Money is a tool, and the question is always: how can I use this tool to serve my values? It should go without saying that you shouldn't work a job you hate just so you can brag about your paycheck and drive a fancy car.

But if morality is about the pursuit of happiness, then it's good to

141

desire wealth, it's good to earn wealth, and it's good to enjoy the wealth you've earned. Is the problem, then, the desire for "too much" wealth? No such thing. There is no upper limit on how much money a person should pursue. The fact that you have earned a million dollars or a billion dollars does not by itself demonstrate that you have your priorities wrong. J. K. Rowling became a billionaire because millions of people loved her books. If you are doing work that you're passionate about, then all else equal, the more money the better.

And the reverse is true. The fact that your income is modest doesn't prove you have your priorities in order. There are people making $40,000 a year who overvalue money, refusing to take a pay cut to move to a role that is more fulfilling. The question isn't: "How much?" The question is: "What role does money play in your life?" Philosopher Tara Smith puts it this way:

> While there's plenty to lament in contemporary society's prevalent priorities, money is not the fundamental problem. In our eagerness to teach that money is not the most important thing in life, we have swung too far in the opposite direction, denigrating money as if it were worthless. While money and material goods are not inherently good, it is equally mistaken to dismiss them as inherently bad.[135]

That's because, she adds, "Making money (in the literal sense of creating wealth) is the very process of achieving values."[136] Money ought to be the insignia of creating value doing work you love—and it ought to be used in ways that genuinely promote your well-being. You shouldn't sacrifice higher priorities to money, like career satisfaction and your most vital relationships—but nor should you treat your desire for wealth as a shameful secret.

I love money. I love the security it buys me: I don't have to worry about how I'm going to pay my mortgage or feed my children. I love the freedom it buys me: I can fly off to California to celebrate my friend's birthday and turn down work I find tedious and unsatisfying. I love the health that it buys me: I can visit the doctor regularly and hire a personal trainer to help me get in shape. I love the knowledge that it buys me: I can fill my shelves with books and hire brilliant teachers to coach me. I love the pleasure that it buys me: I can fill my home with beautiful art and treat myself to delicious food and relaxing massages. I love the time that it buys me: I can pay someone else to do my taxes and hire an Uber so I can work or sleep while I travel.

But I never forget my hierarchy of values. No amount of money can make up for an unrewarding career and an unfulfilling life. I long ago vowed that, unless I was in a situation where I literally couldn't afford to put a roof over my head or food in my mouth, I would never place financial considerations above career fulfillment. I made the hard-nosed decision to establish a lifestyle that fit my income, instead of striving for an income that would support my lifestyle. For example, in 2017, I moved away from Southern California to a more affordable part of the country in part so that I could take more career risks.

But I don't want to overstate the point. We face tradeoffs between career satisfaction and financial success much less often than people think. If you become good at your work, more often than not, you'll be able to command a healthy income because you'll be creating an enormous amount of value.

That's been my experience. Early in my writing a career I was introduced to someone who worked in my previous field of business proposal writing. He wanted to lure me away and was willing to pay me a six-figure starting salary—far more money than I had ever made. I declined without a second thought. The reason I made that decision is because career enjoyment was more important to me than money. But I also believed that, once I honed my craft, I would eventually make far more money doing what I loved. And that turned out to be true. It took more than a decade, but I eventually reached the point where the major limit on my income was not what people were willing to pay me, but how much time I wanted to spend working with clients versus working on my own material. That's not unusual. That's the logical result of having lots of value to offer.

## Mastery

The best jobs offer two intimately related kinds of spiritual rewards: practice pleasure and performance pleasure.

Think of a musician. Most of a musician's time is spent practicing. Not practicing the way I used to practice guitar, where I'd sit around for hours strumming my favorite songs. No, professionals engage in serious, demanding practice where they push themselves out of their comfort zone in order to acquire new skills. In his deeply insightful book *So Good They Can't Ignore You*, Cal Newport describes the practice regimen of a professional guitarist he met:

> At my request, Jordan laid out his practice regimen for this song. He starts by playing slow enough that he can get the effects he desires: He wants the key notes of the melody to ring while he fills the space in between with runs up and down the fretboard. Then he adds speed—just enough that he can't quite make things work. He repeats this again and again. "It's a physical and mental exercise," he explained. "You're trying to keep track of different melodies and things. In a piano, everything is laid out clearly in front of you; ten fingers never getting in the way of one another. On the guitar, you have to budget your fingers."
>
> He called his work on this song his "technical focus" of the moment. In a typical day, if he's not preparing for a show, he'll practice with this same intensity, always playing just a little faster than he's comfortable, for two or three hours straight. I asked him how long it will take to finally master the new skill. "Probably like a month," he guessed. Then he played through the lick one more time.[137]

This process is pleasurable, but not in the same way as performing on a stage. Performance pleasure is the pleasure of flow—of getting lost in a task that's pushing you to the maximum of your potential without overtaxing your mental resources. It's the pleasure musicians feel when they flawlessly play a song they recently mastered— or when they stand on a stage in front of a capacity crowd. Practice pleasure is more akin to the way you feel after a great workout. The workout itself was uncomfortable and grueling, but it leaves you feeling strong, confident, efficacious. It's the pleasure of making progress and improving.

Bestselling author Daniel Pink calls this element of a fulfilling career *mastery*: the best jobs fulfill our "desire to get better and better at something that matters."[138] It combines our cultivation of rare and valuable skills, achieved through a challenging practice regimen, with the exercise of those skills, which results in flow experiences.

Not every job offers the opportunity to pursue mastery. If you're stuck in a job you don't know how to do, it can be deflating and anxiety inducing. I once was put in charge of implementing some new software for tracking business proposals. As someone who barely knew how to use Microsoft Word, it was one of the most unpleasant work experiences of my life. But by the same token, if a job is too easy, it becomes monotonous and mind-numbing. The best jobs hit the sweet spot: they force us to stretch and grow—but they don't stretch us so much that we break. They give us the opportunity to perform at the peak of our current skillset—not struggle to do things we're utterly incapable of or mindlessly repeat a simple routine.

Note that this is seldom inherent in the job. Whether or not a productive role offers the opportunity for mastery depends as much on us as on the job. This is why you'll often need to change jobs whenever the opportunity for increased mastery vanishes. I spent eleven years at the Ayn Rand Institute. But I reached a point where I noticed my skills plateauing. Even though I loved the work, the organization, and my teammates, I made the hard decision to leave in favor of a role where I'd be in unfamiliar territory and need to develop new skills. In the short-term, the decision was costly. I went from feeling capable to feeling like an incompetent beginner. But in less than three years I had developed a new set of skills that made it possible for me to take the next step in my career: to work for myself. And that turned out to be the most important career move I ever made because it gave me the one thing that had been missing from my career: autonomy.

## Autonomy

That challenging new job I took after I left the Ayn Rand Institute? As I mentioned, I lost it during the 2020 pandemic, just as I was about to close on my first home. I spent several terrified days thinking I might have to find a job doing something other than writing just to make sure my family could make ends meet. Then I got a call from a previous employer. They were eager to rehire me. I turned them down.

Or to be more exact, I made a counteroffer: I would work half the week for them freelance. Looking back, I'm surprised I had the courage to turn down the full-time role. The income from one client would not be enough meet all of my financial commitments and I had no idea whether I'd be able to find more clients, particularly in the midst of the pandemic. But the reason I insisted on a freelance arrangement was simple: I wanted control over my career. I wanted autonomy.

Autonomy is not a matter of whether you're working alone or collaborating with others—it's about the degree to which you are in charge of what you do, when you do it, how you do it, and who you do it with. In my case, what I was most interested in was being able to work whenever I wanted to work, and to say whatever I wanted to say. That's why, despite the risk, I was willing to reject a generous job offer from an organization I admired.

(Full disclosure: during the writing of this book, I returned to ARI to help build a coaching program for their educational institution, Ayn Rand University. I have less freedom than when I worked for myself, but ARI still offers a lot of flexibility and, more importantly, I have a lot of autonomy with respect to how I build the coaching program. I point this out to highlight that autonomy doesn't mandate working for yourself.)

The desire for autonomy is rooted in the fact that you have free will. As psychologists Edward Deci and Richard Ryan put it, "Autonomous motivation involves behaving with a full sense of volition and choice, whereas controlled motivation involves behaving with the experience of pressure and demand toward specific outcomes that comes from forces perceived to be external to the self."[139] The more say you have over your career, the more satisfying your career generally is because it is your own judgment and values that are shaping your life, not externally imposed duties. Even when things are hard, even when you're busy, frustrated, flailing, and failing, you have the sense: I am the master of my own destiny. This is the course *I* chose because I believe it is the best one.

It's easy to undervalue autonomy because control is often taken for granted. "*Of course* I need to have someone tell me when to show up to work and what tasks I need to work on. Isn't that what a job is?" Worse, autonomy is seldom granted—it has to be seized by going into business for yourself, or negotiated for, often at the expense of the more conspicuous benefits of a higher salary. Daniel Pink notes that some of the most apparently successful workers—high-powered attorneys—often suffer emotionally because their jobs are generally extremely low autonomy. "Lawyers often face intense demands but have relatively little 'decision latitude.'"[140]

By contrast, many tech companies recognize the value of employee autonomy to both happiness and productive success. They tend to be more flexible in terms of when employees come to work. Netflix, for example, has no policy telling employees when to show up or how much vacation to take. They're treated as professionals: so long as the work gets done, it doesn't matter when or how they do it. Similarly, Google encourages its engineers to spend 20 percent of their time on a side project of their choice. The result is many of Google's most notable products, including Gmail and Google Translate.

We'll see shortly how to gain autonomy in your career. The point here is simply to underscore the fact that if you want a career you enjoy, it is often not the particular industry you're in that matters most, but the amount of freedom you have to direct your work.

## Mission

Mission is the belief that your career adds up to something—that you're pursuing some larger, positive purpose than meeting this quarter's goals. Many people, including Pink, equate mission with finding "a cause greater and more enduring than themselves."[141] Such sentiments reflect the influence of anti-self moralities—not any reality about what satisfies people at work. Cal Newport's characterization of mission is far superior:

> To have a mission is to have a unifying focus for your career. It's more general than a specific job and can span multiple positions. It provides an answer to the question, What should I do with my life? Missions are powerful because they focus your energy toward a useful goal, and this in turn maximizes your impact on your world—a crucial factor in loving what you do. People who feel like their careers truly matter are more satisfied with their working lives, and they're also more resistant to the strain of hard work. Staying up late to save your corporate litigation client a few extra million dollars can be draining, but staying up late to help cure an ancient disease can leave you more energized than when you started.[142]

Yes, although there are lawyers whose mission is to fight for the often-maligned corporations who spearhead human flourishing and human progress. But the larger point is that mission has nothing whatever to do with looking for something outside of yourself that justifies your life. It is instead about shaping the earth in the image of your values. My own mission is to help people learn, live, and advocate ideas I believe are true. That mission drives me, inspires me, energizes me—and yet it is deeply selfish. I'm working to make the world a better place—a better place according to *my* standards for the sake of me and the kind of people I care about.

Almost any career *can* offer a sense of mission. When I worked with Alex Epstein at the Center for Industrial Progress, one of our goals was to teach members of the fossil fuel industry that their work wasn't a necessary evil, but that in providing the world's best source of low-cost, reliable energy they were promoting human flourishing for billions of people. By helping industry members see the larger purpose their work was aimed at, we empowered them to formulate inspiring personal missions that deepened their enjoyment of their work. We received thousands of messages thanking us and crediting our work for changing their lives. Mission, in other words, isn't something reserved for so-called mission-driven companies.

But by the same token, it does take time, thought, effort, and choice to create a career directed toward a mission that resonates with you and inspires you. As much as I value the fossil fuel industry's work intellectually, it doesn't resonate with me spiritually the way it does for Alex. Working at CIP was valuable because it helped me build the skillset I needed to achieve my personal mission, but it didn't allow me much scope to pursue my personal mission. That's fine. Early on in your career, don't expect to be in a position to formulate your mission. Focus on developing the skills that will lead you to mastery. But once you formulate your mission, fulfillment depends on making that the purpose that will direct your career choices.

How do you formulate a mission? By reflecting on what goals and activities actually energize and motivate you, and working to integrate them into a single, unified whole. I said that my mission is to help people learn, live, and advocate ideas I believe are true. I reached that formulation by noticing that there were a few activities that I found completely enjoyable to do and fully rewarding having done: writing (fiction and nonfiction), public speaking, editing, and mentoring people who shared my interests, convictions, and values. At first, these activities felt scattered. Sometimes I was creating my own content, other times I was helping people create theirs. But once I grasped that the kind of content I most enjoyed creating aimed to help "young versions of me," I realized they were all part of the same mission: to empower those who share my ideas.

That's what it means to build a career you love. It means to achieve a career filled with mastery, autonomy, mission, and enough money that you aren't worried about money. In Pink's words, "The most successful people, the evidence shows, often aren't directly pursuing conventional notions of success. They're working hard and persisting through difficulties because of their internal desire to control their lives, learn about their world, and accomplish something that endures."[143] But how do we do that?

## Follow Your Passion—or Create One

The main career advice we're offered today is to "follow your passion." Even family members who quietly nudge us in more "respectable" and remunerative directions will usually pay lip service to this advice. And it is not always bad advice. I more or less knew I wanted to be a writer from the time I was six, and I knew I wanted to write about philosophy from the time I was fourteen. Many professional athletes and musicians and soldiers have similar stories. If you know what you want to do, do it.

But what if you don't know? Too many people go to college as a default then stumble on a job, asking themselves, "Does this feel like bliss?" And inevitably they're disappointed, because almost no job feels like bliss at the start. Though there's a deep satisfaction that comes from being on the path toward doing what you love, the early years are inevitably filled with tedious work assignments, difficulty, and struggle. I spent the first few years as a professional writer feeling like I had no idea what I was doing, receiving blistering feedback on my work, staring at a computer screen having no idea how to fill it with words worth reading. At several points I found myself questioning my path: maybe I would be happier as a teacher, or a psychologist, or an entrepreneur. It was only after I had mastered my craft, more than a decade later, that I could honestly say without reservation I had chosen the right path.

My experience isn't unique. Cal Newport warns of the dangers of what he calls the "passion hypothesis," the view that we achieve a career we love by first figuring out what we're passionate about and then seeking out a job that matches our passion.

> The more I studied the issue, the more I noticed that the passion hypothesis convinces people that somewhere there's a magic "right" job waiting for them, and that if they find it, they'll immediately recognize that this is the work they were meant to do. The problem, of course, is when they fail to find this certainty, bad things follow, such as chronic job-hopping and crippling self-doubt.[144]

Trying to decide "am I passionate about this?" is a dangerous question early in a career because entry-level positions, "by definition, are not going to be filled with challenging projects and autonomy—these come later."[145]

The passion hypothesis says that your ideal career has been decided for you and your job is merely to find it. Worse, it implies that you don't have to do anything to become worthy of that career: once you discover it, you are entitled to it. Both points are wrong. A career you love isn't something you *find*—it's something you *create*. It is less like stumbling on an abandoned treasure and more like fashioning a stone into a sculpture. You decide the final shape, but not through a mere wish. You have to *work* to make your vision a reality. The difference is that with a career you can start creating it before you know the final form it will take.

How is that possible? Because successful careers all have a similar shape. Their final form will be distinctive, but they universally share one fundamental characteristic: they all consist of value-creating activities. If you live on a self-sustaining farm, you're trading your time and effort for the crops you need to sustain your own life. In a division of labor economy, you're trading what you produce for what others produce, mediated through money. This is the trader principle: to get what you want from other people you must give them something they want.

Newport points out that often people who "follow their passion" fail because they are totally focused on what they want without genuinely thinking about whether they have something valuable to offer in return. They want a high-paying job—but don't think about how to increase their company's profits. They want a successful blog—but don't think about how to give readers valuable content they can't find anywhere else. They want a successful business—but don't think about how they'll be providing superior value to their customers, compared to existing alternatives.

The point is not that you should ignore what you want and fixate on helping other people on the premise that their happiness is more important than yours. No. A trader is not a servant. The point is that you live in a division of labor economy, and if you aren't creating value for other people, then expecting them to provide you with rewards means treating them as *your* servant. It's not billionaire CEOs like Jeff Bezos and Mark Zuckerberg who are exploiters—it is anyone who believes they are entitled to have their needs and desires fulfilled without offering anything of value in return. In Rand's words:

> A trader is a man who earns what he gets and does not give or take the undeserved. He does not treat men as masters or slaves, but as independent equals. He deals with men by means of a free,

voluntary, unforced, uncoerced exchange—an exchange which benefits both parties by their own independent judgment.[146]

The trader principle is the key to creating a career you love. As Newport observes,

> The things that make a great job great, I discovered, are rare and valuable. . . . Basic economic theory tells us that if you want something that's both rare and valuable, you need something rare and valuable to offer in return—this is Supply and Demand 101. It follows that if you want a great job, you need something of great value to offer in return.[147]

This means that *whatever* it is you ultimately want to do, the foundation will be cultivating rare and valuable skills that allow you to offer something compelling in trade. Pick any field you find interesting and ask yourself: if I were world class in this field, would I have any difficulty creating a career that I loved? If I were an elite salesperson, or an elite singer, or an elite chef, or an elite software engineer, or an elite lawyer, wouldn't that virtually guarantee I could design a job that would fill me with joy?

That's the starting point of creating a career you love: developing rare and valuable skills. But which skills should you seek to develop? Even if you don't have an intense career passion, you almost always have abundant career *interests*. There are fields that intrigue you and questions that excite you. Such nascent interests are signals to explore further. And the main thing you should be exploring is: *how do I enjoy using my mind?*

Every productive activity involves a distinctive way of using your mind: writing computer code is different from writing marketing copy. Agriculture is different from sales. Accounting is different from playing in an orchestra. It's not simply that the industries are different, or the outputs are different, but the mental processes involved are different. What you're striving to find are the kinds of processes where you most feel at home.

Harvard University neuropsychologist Howard Gardner has identified eight forms of intelligence.[148] I don't endorse his entire theory, but I find his categories useful for identifying the kind of productive roles that can fill your life with joy.

1. Logical-mathematical (think: software programmer or financier)
2. Linguistic (think: writer or public speaker)
3. Spatial (think: architect or taxi driver)
4. Musical (think: composer or music producer)
5. Bodily-kinesthetic (think: baseball player or construction worker)
6. Intrapersonal (think: poet or psychologist)
7. Interpersonal (think: salesperson or teacher)
8. Naturalistic (think: veterinarian or biologist)

When you're deciding what kind of rare and valuable skills to build, you can be industry agnostic—but you can't be mental process agnostic. Someone who feels most at home introspecting and reflecting on their emotional life (intrapersonal) will likely be unsuccessful and unfulfilled in a career relying primarily on logical-mathematical skills. Someone who feels most at home working out and dancing (bodily-kinesthetic) will likely be unsuccessful and unfilled in a career relying primarily on linguistic skills.

What you have to identify is the way of using your mind that feels most natural—the kinds of mental activities where time vanishes, where you're fully engaged and fully alive. Psychologist Mihály Csíkszentmihályi calls this state "flow" or, a term I much prefer, "optimal experience."

The best moments in our lives, are not the passive, receptive, relaxing times—although such experiences can also be enjoyable, if we have worked hard to attain them. The best moments usually occur when a person's body or mind is stretched to its limits in a voluntary effort to accomplish something difficult and worthwhile. Optimal experience is thus something that we *make* happen. For a child, it could be placing with trembling fingers the last block on a tower she has built, higher than any she has built so far; for a swimmer, it could be trying to beat his own record; for a violinist, mastering an intricate musical passage. For each person there are thousands of opportunities, challenges to expand ourselves.[149]

If you're not sure where to find this kind of satisfaction ask yourself this: What do you do when you don't have to do anything? What do you do when you're supposed to be doing something else? It's possible that your answer will be some form of passive mind-numbing, like frittering away your life on TikTok. But more likely there are activities that absorb you and compel you. Sometimes this will point you directly toward a specific career. For me, I spent every moment I could reading and writing about ideas—and I created a career reading and writing about ideas. More often what you'll find is not a ready-made career path, but insight into the kind of mental work you enjoy.

Once you know how enjoy using your mind, then you can focus on building rare and valuable skills that are centered on using your mind in this way.

## Develop Your Skills

Ira Glass is the creator of NPR's revolutionary radio show *This American Life*. When he talks about his path to success he notes that he, like every creator, started out with a problem: there was a dramatic gap between his taste (his ability to know what good work looked like) and his skills (his ability to create good work). He succeeded because he kept working on his skills until he closed that gap. Most people fail because that gap is so painful and involves so much self-doubt that they give up.

> Everybody I know who does interesting, creative work went through years where they had really good taste and they could tell that what they were making wasn't as good as they wanted it to be. They knew it fell short. Everybody goes through that.
>
> And if you are just starting out or if you are still in this phase, you gotta know it's normal and the most important thing you can do is do a lot of work. Do a huge volume of work. Put yourself on a deadline so that every week or every month you know you're going to finish one story. It is only by going through a volume of work that you're going to catch up and close that gap. And the work you're making will be as good as your ambitions.[150]

For every field, there are foundational skillsets that are the price of entry. To be a musician, you have to be able to play your instrument. To be an accountant you have to understand bookkeeping. To be a real estate agent, you have to understand real estate contracts and the basics of sales.

The first steps on the road to mastery consist of identifying the skills your field requires and acquiring them. You identify them through reverse engineering. You acquire them through deliberate practice.

Reverse engineering means studying how others in your field became great and searching for patterns that you can emulate. It can be tempting to resist this kind of modeling in the name of originality, but originality doesn't come from doing something that's wholly new, but from building on what came before, adding your own spin, adapting what has worked in the past to your own unique context.

My screenwriting teacher, when he was getting started and wanted to improve his style, would copy, word-for-word, screenplays he admired. The idea was that this would help him internalize what it felt like to write lean, gripping dialogue. Cal Newport talks about spending weeks analyzing an important academic paper in his field until he understood it better than anyone else. The best way to do original work is by learning to do good work, and that means focusing not on originality, but on acquiring the skillset possessed by past masters. That's where deliberate practice comes in.

The key word there is "deliberate." I spent years "practicing" guitar, but I stopped improving because I was staying in my comfort zone, playing the same songs over and over again. Repeatedly doing something doesn't lead to improvement, which is why most of us have driven cars for years or decades but aren't elite drivers.

*Deliberate* practice, by contrast, means identifying a new skill you want to acquire or a weakness you want to overcome and then stretching yourself beyond your current comfort zone to build that skill. If I wanted to improve at guitar, I should have committed to learning songs slightly above my level of ability. I should have worked at playing them slowly until I could play every note perfectly. Then, I should have started speeding up, a bit at a time, only increasing the tempo when I could play without mistakes.

The reason I didn't do that is because pushing yourself outside of your comfort zone is *uncomfortable*. You can strum your favorite songs for hours. Deliberate practice involves such intense mental focus, tension, and stress that you can only do it for two or three hours a day before you're depleted.

For deliberate practice to lead to improvement, it must involve feedback: you have to know when you're succeeding and when you've made a mistake—and ideally that feedback should come as rapidly as possible. With a musical instrument, you usually know immediately when you've made a mistake. In other cases, you have to rely on mentors to guide you. A surgeon in training, for example, will have a senior surgeon watching their every move and giving real-time advice. As a writer in training, my task was harder. I usually depended on feedback from editors, which would come hours or even days later.

As you reflect on the skills you need to develop to achieve mastery in your field, think about how you might go about practicing those skills. How can you push yourself outside your comfort zone in a way that involves the feedback necessary to gauge your progress? Then commit to a practice regiment that will supercharge your growth.

This is the foundation of success. The only way to do good work . . . is to work.

# Crash Your Career

A major myth claims that there are "tracks to success," and that you're in constant danger of falling off this track: by not getting that high prestige job straight out of college, by not getting into an Ivy League school, by not graduating at the top of your elite high school, by not getting into the elite pre-school. This is madness.

Success has nothing to do with social status. It has to do with creating a career that you love, and unless your mind, heart, and soul compel you to make partner at a top law firm or work at Goldman Sachs, then anyone who tells you that your future happiness depends on following some pre-determined track is lying to you.

I became obsessed with philosophy when I was fourteen and spent all of high school doing the minimum necessary to get by while I devoured the works of my favorite thinkers. I graduated with mediocre grades, selected a mediocre university, and ended up finishing college at a less-than-mediocre night school. My first adult job wasn't at McKinsey. It was packing boxes in a shipping warehouse. And yet, despite no impressive credentials, by the time I was thirty I was a bestselling author writing about philosophy.

Or take my friend Chad. Chad moved from Iowa to southern California after high school and was working in the mail room of a nonprofit when he met champion bodybuilder Mike Mentzer. Chad studied Mike's unique approach to bodybuilding and used that knowledge to start his own gym in Hollywood.

Or take my friend David. He was a self-described computer geek who was obsessed with swing dancing. By the time he was in his mid-twenties, he had become so prominent in the swing dance community that he was able to make a living teaching people the Lindy Hop and Balboa.

Or take my friend Keith. He dropped out of college to become a serial entrepreneur. His latest venture was as co-founder of a company that creates online science lessons that more than 50 percent of elementary schools in the US use. In 2020, Keith sold the company for $140 million.

Success is not a track someone else paved that you have to walk down. It is an open-ended path you have to carve. You need to view your pursuit of productive passion as an adventure. You don't have to know where to start. You can plunge in anywhere.

But *how* do you get started? How do you launch your career when you can't create much value?

The traditional answer is: earn credentials, submit job applications, go on job interviews. Often this approach is paired with a sense of entitlement: I have a degree; I deserve to make $50,000 a year.

No. You deserve only what other people find it in their self-interest to pay you. To build your career, you have to stop thinking like a bureaucrat checking boxes and start thinking like an entrepreneur. To be an entrepreneur, you know that you're entitled to nothing and that what matters is not your credentials but your ability. Your orientation must be to demonstrate that you can create value.

In almost every case, you won't be able to create much value at first. That's fine. That's a problem your journey toward mastery will solve. Your competitive advantage at the beginning is *your ability to work cheap*. If you don't cost much to employ, you don't have to create much value to be profitable to employ. For those who can afford it, a tried-and-true method to get started in any field is the ability and willingness to work for free.

But just as important as your willingness to work cheap is your eagerness to grow. An employer can typically select among cheap entry-level workers. What will make you stand out, whatever skills you have or lack, is hunger. Ambition is the trait great employers look for in young people—above all, the ambition to learn.

When I watched young writers at the Ayn Rand Institute, I had one rule of thumb for judging them. Did they proactively seek out opportunities to learn? Did they devour the works in our library? Did they come to me or other senior writers with questions and for feedback? Did they implement our advice or look for reasons to dismiss it?

Of course, demonstrating that you're hungry requires getting your foot in the door. Writing "ambitious" on your job application accomplishes nothing. You have to learn to *signal* ambition and ability. In my case, the whole reason I got hired by the Ayn Rand Institute is because I had been blogging about Ayn Rand's philosophy for years. I created a public record, not only of my writing ability, but of my commitment. You can imagine ARI's leadership saying, "If this is what he does in his free time without pay, imagine what he'll do full time for a salary."

You can do the same thing in any field you want to enter. Stop thinking in terms of credentials and start thinking about how you can demonstrate your ability to create value—how to demonstrate that you have the skills, hunger, and salary requirements to be profitable to a company from day one.

Find your path. Take your first step. Then move forward by leveraging your increasing set of rare and valuable skills into increasingly satisfying work.

## Leverage Your Career Capital

You have only one fundamental career bargaining chip: your rare and valuable skills. This is your career capital. As you amass that capital—as you become so good they can't ignore you—people will want to hire you and work with you because you can help them get what they want. But it's this career capital that will allow you to get what *you* want, and a common mistake is to trade away that capital solely for financial rewards.

Often a better approach is to leverage most of your career capital in exchange for more fulfilling work: work that will take you further on the road to mastery, work that will give you more autonomy, work that will bring you closer to the achievement of your mission.

The most straightforward path here is to start your own business. Once you have sufficient career capital to do valuable work, starting your own business puts you in the driver seat of your career. By business, in this context, I'm including everything from working as a freelancer to launching a Silicon Valley startup.

I'm convinced that many more people should go into business for themselves. Too often they overestimate the risks and underestimate the benefits. The risks seem magnified because many who do start businesses don't begin by building the career capital that makes success far more likely: they don't know the industry, they don't know their market, they don't have rare and valuable skills, they don't have a competitive edge—they're going on nothing but hope and a prayer. This rarely works. Even entrepreneurs who are successful at a young age, like Mark Zuckerberg and Bill Gates, have almost always spent years building relevant skills, and typically have seen success before they formally launched their enterprises. Zuckerberg, for instance, started Facebook as a hobby and left Harvard only when the company was growing so fast that making it his full-time career was the only way to keep the company going.

But what if you don't want to work for yourself—at least not yet? You can still pursue mastery, autonomy, and mission. Newport tells the story of Lulu Young, a highly talented software developer. Her first work project after college was in quality assurance. She used what on paper was a boring job with minimal upside to automate the testing process and save her company a bunch of time and money. She continued to innovate and add value to the company, but after a few years

161

she stopped using her career capital to bargain for a promotion or a raise and did something else.

> To regain some autonomy from a succession of micromanaging bosses who had been tormenting her, she demanded a thirty-hour-a-week schedule so she could pursue a part-time degree in philosophy from Tufts. "I would have asked for less time, but thirty was the minimum for which you could still receive full benefits," she explained. If Lulu had tried this during her first year of employment, her bosses would have laughed and probably offered her instead a "zero-hour-a-week schedule," but by the time she had become a senior engineer and was leading their testing automation efforts, they really couldn't say no.[151]

That's the method: build career capital, then bargain for a more fulfilling role at your current company or a new company—a role where you have more opportunities to learn and grow, more control over your work, and more chances to tackle projects aligned with your personal mission.

We've now seen the process that will lead to a career you love. If you discover the way you enjoy using your mind, pursue mastery, and leverage your career capital into roles that enhance your autonomy, creativity, and mission, you won't have "found" your passion—you'll have created it.

## Don't Lose Focus

I've been stressing the central importance of work in life, and the virtue displayed by dedicating yourself to productive achievement. But I know a lot of high achievers who are unhappy and unfulfilled, or at least filled with a vague guilt that they should be achieving even more.

So let me start by distinguishing devotion to career from workaholism. Workaholism isn't primarily a matter of how much time you spend at work, but *why*. Is work, for you, a source of creative joy or is it an escape from personal problems? Do you love the work itself or do you love the image of yourself as a high-powered attorney, a business mover and shaker, an altruistic crusader? Is your standard of success your own enjoyment—or is it comparative: being richer, more powerful, more admired than others? Workaholism is an addiction, and what a person is addicted to is escape from negative feelings—above all, feelings of self-doubt.

In *From Strength to Strength*, Arthur Brooks tells the story of a woman who had achieved enormous success on Wall Street, but who was not particularly happy.

> Her marriage was unsatisfactory, she drank a little too much, and her relationship with her college-age kids was all right . . . but distant. She had few *real* friends. She worked incredibly long hours and felt physically exhausted a lot of the time. Her work was everything to her—she "lived to work"—and now she was terrified that even *that* was starting to slip.[152]

Brooks asked her why she didn't do the obvious thing and cut back on her work. It was, after all, making her miserable. She replied: "Maybe I would prefer to be *special* rather than *happy*. . . . Anyone can do the things it takes to be happy—go on vacation, spend time with friends and family . . . but not everyone can accomplish great things."[153]

The first time I read that line—"I would prefer to be *special* rather than *happy*"—my blood curdled. Because what it means in practice is: "I want to throw my life away so that someone will pat me on the head and tell me I'm important."

Work plays a crucial role in building healthy self-esteem. It's through your work that you take responsibility for your own life, grow your capabilities and confidence, and gain a sense of efficacy. But it's a tragic mistake to tie your self-worth to some conventional image of "success." My admiration for achievement is limitless, but success without happiness doesn't make your life special. It makes it tragic.

Even those who avoid the trap of workaholism can often find

themselves experiencing work as a burden or a source of guilt. Shonda Rhimes gave a commencement speech where she noted that people often express awe at how she manages her life as an in-demand screenwriter and mother of three. "[P]eople are constantly asking me, how do you do it?" Her answer: "I don't."

> Whenever you see me somewhere succeeding in one area of my life, that almost certainly means I am failing in another area of my life. If I am killing it on a *Scandal* script for work, I am probably missing bath and story time at home. If I am at home sewing my kids' Halloween costumes, I'm probably blowing off a rewrite I was supposed to turn in. If I am accepting a prestigious award, I am missing my baby's first swim lesson. If I am at my daughter's debut in her school musical, I am missing Sandra Oh's last scene ever being filmed at *Grey's Anatomy*. If I am succeeding at one, I am inevitably failing at the other. That is the tradeoff. That is the Faustian bargain one makes with the devil that comes with being a powerful working woman who is also a powerful mother. You never feel a hundred percent OK; you never get your sea legs; you are always a little nauseous. Something is always lost. Something is always missing.[154]

I don't think it has to be this way. It all comes down to how you judge yourself. Too often people hold themselves to impossible standards. They judge their performance in one area of life as if it were the only area of life: What kind of mother would I be if I were nothing but a mother? What kind of husband would I be if I were nothing but a husband? What kind of creator would I be if I did nothing but work?

But a standard that's impossible to meet is a bad standard. A mother's responsibility is not to be there for every moment of her child's life. A CEO's responsibility is not to reply to emails twenty-four hours a day. Your responsibility is to envision a whole life; a life that involves work, and connection, and rest, and recreation; to structure your life so that you attend to your most important values; and then, when you *are* at work or you *are* with your children, to be fully present. You will miss things, and that will suck. But it should not be a source of guilt.

That, really, is the lesson I want to leave with you. Work should never be a source of guilt. I love stories of intrepid creators who chain themselves to their desks in pursuit of ambitious goals. I've admiringly told many of those stories in my books. But that is *not* what the virtue of productiveness demands, and you should not feel bad if you work your ass off from 9 to 5 then clock out and attend to your other interests. What productiveness does demand is that you *center* your life around productive achievement, in whatever way and to whatever extent fits your vision of what you want from life. There is no moral obligation to limit your work to forty hours a week if what you want demands far more of your time and attention. But there is also no moral obligation to become a slave to your work.

In fact, the more I've gotten to know high achievers, the more I've been impressed with how many of them jealously protect their non-work time. They work more than the average person, sure. But when they sign off, they *sign off.* No Slack. No email. No one foot in, one foot out. Their self-image isn't wrapped up in pretending to be some machine that does nothing but work. They're out to live—not to impress anyone or prove something about themselves.

And when they are at work? What they strive for is not ceaseless, frantic activity but what Alex Epstein calls *relaxed productivity.* Yes, anyone whose work matters to them will face times of stress and tackle projects that demand long hours and limited rest. But the producers I most admire don't wear such moments as a badge of honor. More often, they view them as a failure: had they planned better and executed better, they wouldn't have *had* to resort to Herculean measures.

So whether you end up working forty hours a week or eighty hours, keep in mind: the measure of your success is not *how much* you work—but how much you *enjoy* your work . . . and your life.

# Master Creativity

Every field of work has its own set of skills that are rare and valuable. But there's one fundamental skill that is always rare and valuable and which you will need if you want to build a career you love: creative thinking. To the extent your work is routine, you will be replaceable. Regardless of how hard you work, you won't add much value if you're merely executing a solved problem. The value of your work comes from your ability to solve *new* problems. To possess rare and valuable skills means to be able to do work that's not repetitive, but creative.

Creativity is your power to rearrange the elements of reality in new and valuable ways. It is usually viewed as the private property of artists, but any time you discover a new idea or create a new product or build a new company or solve a new problem or improve an old process you're engaged in creative thinking. Whatever your field— whether you're a writer or teacher or software programmer or math professor or FBI agent or entrepreneur—this kind of creative thinking is the hallmark of mastery and the key to success. It is not some mystical talent possessed by an elect few. It is an ability we all have the power to cultivate.

## What Creativity Is

The best portrait of creative work I'm aware of comes from Ayn Rand's novel *The Fountainhead*. The novel features two architects as lead characters. Peter Keating graduates from college at the top of his class. Not because he is creative but because he is excellent at following the rules laid down by his teachers. His approach to architecture is not to create, but to copy. He wins accolades because he excels at imitating the kinds of buildings that traditional standards say are good.

But from the start, we see the limits of this approach. Keating is paralyzed whenever he comes to an architectural problem not covered by a teacher's concrete rule. He has no way of judging what's good or bad because he has no reference point for atypical building situations. The person he turns to for advice in such moments is an innovative young architect, Howard Roark.

Roark is not popular. In fact, he gets kicked out of college because he refuses to imitate the architectural styles of the past. His new approach to building stupefies most of the people around him precisely because it is creative rather than imitative. Early in the novel, Roark explains his philosophy of architecture:

> "Here are my rules: what can be done with one substance must never be done with another. No two materials are alike. No two sites on earth are alike. No two buildings have the same purpose. The purpose, the site, the material determine the shape. Nothing can be reasonable or beautiful unless it's made by one central idea, and the idea sets every detail. A building is alive, like a man. Its integrity is to follow its own truth, its one single theme, and to serve its own single purpose. A man doesn't borrow pieces of his body. A building doesn't borrow hunks of its soul. Its maker gives it the soul and every wall, window and stairway to express it."[155]

Here we get some crucial elements of how Roark creates. Every building has a theme or central idea the architect uses to select every detail about the building. This is partly why Roark is not paralyzed when he encounters a new problem with no inherited rule to guide him: he isn't guided by inherited rules but the central idea that "sets every detail." And the central idea—the standard of value—itself is neither inherited nor arbitrary. The architect chooses it in light of the materials available, the site where he intends to build, and the purpose the building is to serve. It's this integration of every element of a building around its central idea that makes it beautiful.

For example, late in the book, Roark is tasked with building a low-income housing project, Cortlandt Homes. Rand describes the final design:

The drawings of Cortlandt Homes presented six buildings, fifteen stories high, each made in the shape of an irregular star with arms extending from a central shaft. The shafts contained elevators, stairways, heating systems and all the utilities. The apartments radiated from the center in the form of extended triangles. The space between the arms allowed light and air from three sides. The ceilings were pre-cast; the inner walls were of plastic tile that required no painting or plastering; all pipes and wires were laid out in metal ducts at the edge of the floors to be opened and replaced, when necessary, without costly demolition; the kitchens and bathrooms were prefabricated as complete units; the inner partitions were of light metal that could be folded into the walls to provide one large room or pulled out to divide it; there were few halls or lobbies to clean, a minimum of cost and labor required for the maintenance of the place. The entire plan was a composition in triangles. The buildings, of poured concrete, were a complex modeling of simple structural features; there was no ornament; none was needed; the shapes had the beauty of sculpture.[156]

Philosopher Gregory Salmieri summarizes Roark's approach this way:

[Roark] must first *understand* the relevant architectural problem by *identifying* the proposed building's function and location and the nature of the available materials, then he must *conceive* some central idea as a specific solution to this problem, and then *select* every detail of the building in accordance with this central idea, thereby *integrating* the building into a harmonious whole.[157]

This, in pattern, is the process creative work follows—not just in architecture, but in every field.

When I wrote my first novel, *I Am Justice*, I started out with a purpose. I wanted to write a thriller that showed how a normal person might realistically evolve into a Jack Reacher-type hero. I needed a central idea that would allow me to achieve that purpose. I knew my lead character had to start out as far from a vigilante hero as possible, so I made her a college student. That raised a question: if a typical college student became entangled with a crime, she wouldn't try to solve it—she would go to the police. So I had to have a strong reason why she couldn't go to the police—why she would have to take responsibility for solving the crime. Well, I thought, what if she was partly responsible for the crime? That led to me to my central ideal: a college student kills a classmate but is terrified when the next morning police discover *three* dead students in what appears to be a gruesome hate crime. To keep her secrets buried, she has to find out the truth about what happened that night. That central idea, then, acted as a standard of value to guide me in selecting everything about the novel: the characters, the plot, every line of dialogue, every word choice.

Architecture and writing fiction are obviously creative tasks. But this same process of creative thinking applies even to seemingly non-creative fields. Take the case of Darwin. On the surface, his work wasn't about creativity but discovery. But look deeper. He started with a rich and messy set of facts about living organisms, including the growing conviction by scientists that species hadn't shown up one day in their final form, but had evolved into their current form over millions of years. What scientists couldn't do was explain evolution. They could not answer the question: by what mechanism do species evolve? Darwin's great insight came from reading the work, not of a biologist, but an economist.

Thomas Malthus had argued that agricultural yields grow arithmetically while human populations grow exponentially. This, thought Malthus, necessitated a struggle for survival by human beings, with large portions of the population dying from starvation. Re-reading Malthus's essay, Darwin made a creative leap. He saw how a similar struggle for survival among animals would mean that those most fit to thrive in their environment would tend to survive and reproduce. Small survival advantages would propagate over time leading to large changes over large stretches of time.

Darwin spent the next two decades taking this revolutionary insight and using it to make sense of a wide set of questions a theory of evolution needed to answer. He had to make sure it fit and could explain the fossil record, the geographical distribution of different species, the degree of natural variation among offspring, the extreme perfection of vital organs, etc., etc.—and that no competing theory could account for all of these facts.

Moving from science to business, consider the case of Steve Jobs and the mental process that produced Apple's numerous breakthrough innovations. When Steve Jobs returned to Apple, his first breakthrough innovation was the iPod MP3 player. But Jobs quickly became aware that the iPod would be irrelevant as soon as a phone maker figured out how to put a quality MP3 player onto a phone. One device beats two. So he conceived of a new idea—a product that combined a phone, a music player, and an internet browser. He and his team then went about figuring out how to build that device, which required solving countless new problems, and making countless new creative decisions. Jobs famously oversaw every detail of the project, making sure that it would give the use the best experience possible.

Though creativity cannot be boiled down to a recipe or a necessary order of steps, we can identify several key elements of the creative process:

- Problem: Creative thinking involves problem solving. Roark aims to design a building given the building's purpose, location, and materials; Darwin aims to explain why species evolve; Jobs aims to forestall a competitive threat to the iPod.
- Solution: Creative thinking involves a central idea that solves the creative problem and acts as a standard of value. Darwin conceives of natural selection as the mechanism of evolution; Jobs conceives of a device that combines the function of a phone, a music player, and an internet browser.
- Integration: Creative thinking involves selecting every detail in accordance with that central idea (or, in the case of a scientific

discovery, checking to see if all of the relevant facts do integrate with the solution).

This is the creative process. But *how* do you identify problems, formulate solutions, and integrate everything around that solution?

## How to Think Creatively

Creative thinking, like all thinking, consists of asking questions and answering them. And when you ask questions and answer them, what you are really doing is *searching* and *judging*. You set out to answer a question, or solve a problem, or achieve some purpose. Then you go about your task by querying your subconscious and your environment for raw materials—and judging the results. True or false? Right or wrong? Good or bad? Am I headed toward my goal or away from it? This process of searching and judging continues until you achieve your goal: a theory, a novel, a painting, an app, a new product, a crucial business decision.

The difference between an amateur and a master is not, at the deepest level, a difference in process—but in the quality of the process. The master conducts more fruitful searches and makes more efficient and refined judgments. And, importantly, this ability is not innate. It is an achievement cultivated through practice.

### Searching

Edgar Allan Poe once explained the process he used to craft his famous poem, "The Raven." In his telling, "no one point in its composition is referable either to accident or intuition—that the work proceeded step by step, to its completion, with the precision and rigid consequence of a mathematical problem."

For example, take the poem's most famous line: "Quoth the Raven 'Nevermore.'" Poe knew he wanted a refrain that would "produce continuously novel effects, by the variation of the application of the refrain—the refrain itself remaining for the most part, unvaried." But what should the refrain be? It must be short, he decided—ideally a single word. But which word?

> The question now arose as to the character of the word. Having made up my mind to a refrain, the division of the poem into stanzas was of course a corollary, the refrain forming the close to each stanza. That such a close, to have force, must be sonorous and susceptible of protracted emphasis, admitted no doubt, and these considerations inevitably led me to the long *o* as the most sonorous vowel in connection with *r* as the most producible consonant.
>
> The sound of the refrain being thus determined, it became necessary to select a word embodying this sound, and at the same time in the fullest possible keeping with that melancholy which I had pre-determined as the tone of the poem. In such a search it would have been absolutely impossible to overlook the word "Nevermore." In fact it was the very first which presented itself.[158]

What Poe describes is a process of explicit reasoning. He consciously worked out, step-by-step, the needs of his poem and the best way to satisfy those needs.

A similar approach was taken by Thomas Edison to the discovery of a usable light bulb. Edison didn't invent the light bulb. Instead, he made it useful and economic by finding an affordable, long-lasting filament. Edison's approach was to brute force his way to a solution by testing out thousands of different materials until he got the idea of trying carbonized materials like cotton, which worked far better than other materials. He carbonized everything from hickory to boxwood to the fibers of tropical plants sent to him by biologists until he found the one that worked best: carbonized bamboo.

What's striking about these examples is how *uncreative* they seem. We typically associate creativity, not with step-by-step reasoning or running a series of trials, but with *creative leaps*. A creator approaches some problem and has a moment of insight that takes him beyond where explicit reasoning would lead.

In his book *Blink*, Malcolm Gladwell opens with a story about a Greek statue that was authenticated by scientists. Yet when a number of art historians looked at it, they instantly judged it to be a fraud. The experts couldn't immediately articulate why they were so sure, but further testing showed that they were right. They didn't reason their way to the correct answer—they leaped to it.

There's no question that creative leaps typically do play a crucial role in creativity. Archimedes sits in the bathtub and screams "Eureka!" as he realizes that he can measure the volume of irregular objects using water displacement. Darwin reads Malthus's essay on human population growth and discovers the principle of natural selection. Mozart scribbles out the overture to *Don Giovanni* the morning of its opening performance. Newton grasps the law of gravity watching an apple fall from a tree.

Creative thinkers make creative leaps. But the reason I started with explicit reasoning is because creative leaps should be understood, not as moments of mystical insight, but as lightning-like *counterparts* to explicit reasoning. They are best thought of as *implicit reasoning*. Looking backwards, a creator can, in principle, reconstruct a reasoning process that would have led to these insights and discoveries. Gladwell's art experts, for example, were ultimately able to reconstruct what facts they had grasped intuitively that had convinced them the Greek statues were fraudulent.[159] Even artists, who seem to make creative leaps that defy explicit reasoning, can often reconstruct why they made the creative choices they did—even if they didn't explicitly reason their way to those choices during the act of creation.[160] What you want to cultivate is the master's ability to skip over many of the steps in order to find solutions.

You already have the ability to take creative leaps in some areas of life. If you've ever watched a movie to TV show and predicted the ending, it probably wasn't because you sat down and reasoned out what would happen. Instead, your mind leaped to an answer based on pattern recognition. Looking back, you could probably reconstruct the implicit reasoning that led you to the answer, but you didn't engage in that reasoning consciously. Your subconscious simply fed you the answer.

This is precisely what masters are able to do in their profession. It's not that they sit down and effortlessly solve a difficult problem or create a flawless masterpiece. But over time they are able to put themselves in a position where they eventually do gain a creative insight (or a whole series of them) that leads to a creative achievement.

Masters typically start by immersing themselves in a problem or task. They don't sit around waiting for inspiration to strike. They create a fertile garden for creation. In Jonah Lehrer's book *Imagine: How Creativity Works,* he starts with the story of how a design firm came up with the idea for the Swiffer—essentially, an improved mop. The team was originally tasked by Procter and Gamble with an open-ended assignment: come up with a new floor cleaner. The team started by watching film of people cleaning their homes. "This is about the most boring footage you can imagine," one of them said. "It's movies of mopping, for God's sake. And we had to watch hundreds of hours of it."[161] Boring, yes. But that process of immersion ultimately led them to the insight that existing mops were unnecessarily messy and burdensome.

Or take the case of Darwin. His creative leap after reading Malthus came only after spending five years on the HMS *Beagle* traveling the world: Paul Johnson notes that "no other scientist had traveled anything like so long as Darwin making studies on the spot or had observed so wide a variety of phenomena on land and ocean."[162] During the voyage, the first germs of his theory took shape as he watched finches on the Galapagos islands and noted in his diary, "Seeing this gradation and diversity of structure in one small, intimately related group of birds, one might really fancy that from an original paucity of birds in this archipelago, one species had been taken and modified for different ends."[163] It would be another three years before this inkling culminated in his creative leap to the theory of natural selection.

Contrast this immersion with the kind of person who says, "I want to start a business. I'm just waiting for an idea." Ideas don't arise in a vacuum. They arise in the context of observing and learning about the world. If you want to start a new business, often the best thing is to go work in one. Not only for the general business skills you'll acquire, but because you'll find specific problems faced by your company or its customers and be in a position to come up with ways to better solve those problems. You'll have the raw materials for thinking.

Once a master has identified a problem, he can begin searching for answers. The foundational skillset here is, surprisingly enough, *remembering*. When you try to remember something, you query your subconscious. For example, in *The Mind's Best Work*, D. N. Perkins asks us to think of ten white things. Now, he says, add more conditions: "Remember and list several things that are characteristically white, and soft and edible." Finally, he asks us, "Remember and list vegetables whose names start with the letter *c*."[164] He concludes:

> Certainly all this identifies some interesting capacities, but what do they have to do with creating? Simply that in creating one often has to think of things satisfying several conditions, and furthermore, the conditions frequently lie on both sides of the boundary between thing and name.[165]

The example Perkins gives is a poet, who strives to say something about reality—yet must choose words in part based on their sounds. But the larger lesson is that when you search for answers, you do so by asking for material from your subconscious that meets one or more conditions. This isn't some foreign skillset masters have. Everyone engages in this kind of remembering day in and day out. Instead, what distinguishes masters is the quality of their queries and the results of those queries.

When I work with young writers, for example, I find that they typically don't know how to judge their piece. They'll write something, reread it wondering, "Is this good?" and if nothing jumps out at them as bad, they're ready to sign off. One of the first things I teach them is a method for judging their own writing, starting with a series of questions, such as, "Who is the audience?," "What is your conclusion?," "What is your argument?" I'm teaching them how to query their own work. Instead of asking, "Is this good?" they learn to break down "good" into components so that their subconscious will start feeding them more useful information. When they ask, "Who is the audience?" they may realize that they are skipping crucial steps their audience needs to understand their argument, while in other cases they are belaboring the obvious. Their queries become more effective. Over time they'll automate the process so that when they write a draft, their subconscious will feed them material that's largely targeted to their audience, that's relevant to their conclusion, and that makes a coherent argument. (That doesn't mean masters turn out perfect drafts. It just means that their drafts are of a far higher quality than a novice's.)

What I've been describing you can think of as "targeted remembering": the goal is for your subconscious to feed you the *right* answer. But sometimes you cannot remember anything that satisfies your conditions, or you're not fully clear on all of the conditions that need to be satisfied. In these cases, what you want to remember is not quality answers, but a large quantity of answers. The master's tool here is brainstorming: generating as many possibilities as possible without pre-judging them. You apply your conditions only *after* you have a wide range of options on the table.

For example, in my novel, *I Am Justice*, there is a crucial scene where the heroine is subjected to torture. The question was: How would she be tortured? My query had several conditions: it had to be original, it had to bring her to the brink of death, but it couldn't incapacitate her for an extended period of time. But nothing great came to mind—presumably because I have little first-hand experience with torture. So instead of trying to come up with *good* ideas I sat down with goal of coming up with a lot of ideas. I filled pages of my journal with every manner of torture I could dredge up from my subconscious then supplemented that with research into unusual torture techniques from history. (Yeah, thriller writers are weird.) Once I had that list, I was able then to assess each item to decide which best met my conditions.

Observe that I supplemented remembering with fresh data. This is an example of another creative skillset: noticing. "Noticing" is searching your environment for solutions to problems. Sometimes this means actively doing research, but it can also happen seemingly by accident. When your mind is focused on solving a creative problem, solutions can jump out at you from surprising places. Think of Darwin reading Malthus's essay. Because Darwin was actively thinking about the mechanism for evolution, he was prepared to notice that Malthus's notion of a struggle for survival held the key to the answer. Same for Newton and his apple. Same for Archimedes and his bath.

Whether it's remembering or noticing, mental leaps tend to come when you're not engaged in concentrated thinking. A master struggles to solve a difficult problem. The problem seems hopeless. The master plows ahead, pushes, but still cannot make progress. And then? Then she goes for a walk, or takes a shower, or takes a nap and suddenly, the solution appears. According to Lehrer, this isn't an accident. It's precisely the act of relaxing our mind that opens us up to such insights:

> Why is a relaxed state of mind so important for creative insights? When our minds are at ease—when those alpha waves are rippling through the brain—we're more likely to direct the spotlight of attention *inward*, toward that stream of remote associations emanating from the right hemisphere. In contrast, when we are diligently focused, our attention tends to be directed *outward*, toward the details of the problems we're trying to solve. While this pattern of attention is necessary when solving problems analytically, it actually prevents us from detecting the connections that lead to insights.[166]

I said earlier that our default mental state is one of drift, in contrast to focus. And I stressed that focus is not the same thing as concentration. Lehrer's point helps us hammer home the crucial difference. Breakthrough thinking rarely takes place when you are concentrating. But it also doesn't take place when you are drifting. Instead, breakthroughs tend to happen in a state Lehrer calls "daydreaming." It's similar to drift in that your subconscious "blends together concepts that are normally filed away in different areas. The result is an ability to notice new connections, to see the overlaps that we normally overlook."[167] The difference is that with drift, you don't maintain sufficient awareness to notice a creative thought when it occurs.[168] Lehrer again:

> The lesson is that productive daydreaming requires a delicate mental balancing act. On the one hand, translating boredom into a relaxed form of thinking leads to a thought process characterized by unexpected connections; a moment of monotony can become a rich source of insights. On the other hand, letting the mind wander so far away that it gets lost isn't useful; even in the midst of an entertaining daydream, you need to maintain a foothold in the real world.[169]

I would put it this way: daydreaming is a state where you're still exercising mental management. Only it is not a state of concentration but mental oversight. You're self-consciously allowing your mind to wander instead of zoning out. You cannot reach breakthrough ideas if you passively drift—but you will often not reach them if you stay stuck in a state of concentration.

I learned this while writing my first book. I found that whenever I got stuck on a hard problem, there was a surefire way for me to solve it. I would define the problem as clearly and precisely as I could and then I would go on a walk and allow my mind to wander. I would find the solution during the walk roughly 80 percent of the time. The walk was crucial, but so was the first part. If the problem was vague or fuzzy, a walk would sometimes help, but often not. The more guidance you can give your subconscious, the better it will perform.

One final point on searching. Often your thinking becomes stuck in a closed loop. To reach an answer, you have to break free of (often hidden) assumptions that are keeping you searching for answers in the wrong place. One way to break out of closed loops is to use what I call "questions of imagination." These are questions designed to help you expand your thinking and come up with creative insights, particularly if your thinking feels narrow and you're hitting dead ends or running in circles. Examples include, "What if this problem were easy to solve?," "What if the opposite were true?," or simply, "What would be a completely different way to think about this issue?"

When I was writing *I Am Justice*, I would regularly prod myself with these kinds of questions, even when I anticipated that they would be fruitless. "I'm assuming this person is my protagonist. What if she were the villain?" "I can't think of a way for my protagonist to defeat the villain. What if she made him an ally?" In most cases, these questions led nowhere. But in a few cases, they dramatically changed the direction of the book and made it far more surprising and original than if I had not self-consciously attempted to break out of my assumptions.

## Judging

Though searching and judging aren't fully distinct processes, we've been focused primarily on searching so far. What, then, can we say about judging?

In *Human, All Too Human*, Nietzsche writes:

Artists have a vested interest in our believing in the flash of revelation, the so-called inspiration . . . shining down from heavens as a ray of grace. In reality, the imagination of the good artist or thinker produces continuously good, mediocre or bad things, but his judgment, trained and sharpened to a fine point, rejects, selects,

connects. . . . All great artists and thinkers are great workers, inde-
fatigable not only in inventing, but also in rejecting, sifting, transforming, ordering.[170]

Searching gives you possibilities and sometimes leads you to
insights that feel like revelations. But the search process cannot be
disentangled from a constant process of judging. You query and you
assess the results of your search. You ask yourself a question and you
evaluate the quality of the answer that occurs to you. You formulate
a hypothesis and then check it against the facts. You type out a few
words and hit the backspace key when they don't convey what you
want to express.

Though we typically think of judgment as coming at the end of a
creative process, Perkins notes that:

> judgment applies not only to close editing of the final product but
> to decisions made much earlier in the course of creating. Is such-
> and-such a problem worth pursuing? Is such-and-such a theo-
> ry worth developing? What initial approaches seem most fruit-
> ful? Questions of these sorts are answered, at least implicitly, at
> the beginnings of a creative effort, and the answers send the mak-
> er down one or another path. Failures of judgment in those early
> decisions therefore constitute just as much of a limit on a maker's
> creating as failures of judgment later on.[171]

Though masters are excellent searchers, the sine qua non of mastery is excellent judgment. A master has clearly defined, demanding standards. We've already seen how in *The Fountainhead*, Howard
Roark holds that a building's shape must be determined by the "purpose, the site, the material," and that "Nothing can be reasonable or
beautiful unless it's made by one central idea, and the idea sets every
detail." When Roark says these words, he is not yet a master.

Shortly thereafter, he seeks out a job with the architect he most admires, Henry Cameron. When he shows Cameron his drawings, Cameron responds:

> "So you think they're good? Well, they're awful. It's unspeakable. It's a crime. Look . . . look at that. What in Christ's name was your idea? What possessed you to indent that plan here? Did you just want to make it pretty, because you had to patch something together? Who do you think you are? Guy Francon, God help you? . . . Look at this building, you fool! You get an idea like this and you don't know what to do with it! You stumble on a magnificent thing and you have to ruin it! Do you know how much you've got to learn?"[172]

What's going on here? Roark knows the basic principles of architecture. He studied the foundational skills in college and understands the basic process of selecting a single theme for a building that will set every detail. What more does he have to learn?

What Roark is missing is all the lower-level architectural premises he needs to implement his architectural principles. Yes, he knows the central idea of a building should set every detail, but he doesn't know how to translate the theme into the countless sub-decisions designing a building involves: for example, whether or not to indent a plan. Without worked-out standards for when to indent a plan, he has to rely on what strikes him as "pretty."[173]

Mastery requires establishing a rich universe of premises of judgment. And it takes time, effort, and practice to develop these premises. By the time I became a professional writer, I understood that every piece had to have a theme—it had to add up to single idea—and that the theme had to be made clear and convincing to the audience. What I couldn't do was assess whether I had achieved the clear communication of a theme to my audience. It took me more than five years of feedback from my editors before I gained competence at assessing my work objectively—before I could say with confidence whether the words would communicate what I wanted to the reader.

In the act of creation a master is constantly judging his progress, but he also knows when and how to judge. Judgment, if not exercised with care, can paralyze the search process. A writer, for instance, learns to separate out drafting and editing. To draft, you need leave your subconscious free to put words on the page—the raw material you later craft into something clear and beautiful. It is only when you turn to editing that you put your conscious, critical mind in charge. Many a writer has been stopped by demanding that every word he put on the page be perfect from the start.

When it does come time to judge, masters rarely self-consciously apply critical criteria. Nor do they blindly and intuitively make choices. Perkins refers to creative judgment as "realizing reasons." A painter looks at her work-in-progress and realizes that the vividness of the blue undermines the emotional tone she is aiming to achieve. A writer reads his manuscript and realizes that his protagonist's actions aren't consistent with that character's values. A teacher realizes that the example she planned to use to illustrate a point is too advanced for her class and hunts for something simpler. These realizations often come to the master automatically, without effort.

Sometimes, however, a master will not be able to immediately identify the reasons for a positive or negative judgment. He's received messages in the form of feelings. Recall Malcolm Gladwell's art experts looking at the Greek statue. Georgios Dontas, head of the Archeological Society in Athens instantly knew the statue was fake because "when he first laid eyes on it, he said, he felt a wave of 'intuitive repulsion.'"[174] Emotions, particularly cognitive emotions such as confusion or boredom, can give the master clues that something is amiss (or that something is working particularly well). These are not infallible, but they are critical hints—they are leads to further thinking.

## The conditions of creativity

Creative thinking, I've stressed, is not some foreign act. It's really about learning to harness familiar mental processes in pursuit of demanding and inventive goals. What, then, stops people from reaching their creative potential?

Above all, fear. In their book *Art & Fear*, David Bayles and Ted Orland describe the kinds of fears that stop artists. Most of what they say is applicable to everyone attempting to engage in creative work.

> [I]f making art gives substance to your sense of self, the corresponding fear is that you're not up to the task—that you can't do it, or can't do it well, or can't do it again; or that you're not a real artist, or not a good artist, or have no talent, or have nothing to say. The line between the artist and his/her work is a fine one at best, and for the artist it feels (quite naturally) like there is no such line. Making art can feel dangerous and revealing. Making art *is* dangerous and revealing. Making art precipitates self-doubt, stirring deep waters that lay between what you know you should be, and what you fear you might be. For many people, that alone is enough to prevent their ever getting started at all—and for those who do, trouble isn't long in coming. Doubts, in fact, soon rise in swarms:
>
> *I'm not an artist—I'm a phony*
> *I have nothing worth saying*
> *I'm not sure what I'm doing*
> *Other people are better than I am*
> *I'm only a [student/physicist/mother/whatever]*
> *I've never had a real exhibit*
> *No one understands my work*
> *No one like say work*
> *I'm no good*[175]

Fear is valuable. It alerts us to threats and helps prevent reckless mistakes. But it can also stop us from taking intelligent risks. It can even cause us to see risks where none exist. When I decided to turn down a job and try to build a career for myself as an independent writer, my then-wife was apprehensive. She understandably wanted the stability of employment. But I argued that stability was illusory. After all, I *had* been employed only to find my job erased when market conditions changed. Self-employment, I noted, actually reduced our risks because now instead of effectively having one customer, I would have many. There is no risk-free career. And yet how many people want to start their own business but cling to a job they dislike because it gives them the illusion of safety?

The reason fear has so much power to stop you from achieving your goals is because you misconstrue how best to deal with it. You believe that to move forward, you first must conquer your fear. But this is like the person who says, "I'll start working out once I'm motivated." More often than not, motivation doesn't precede action—it follows from action. You dread the thought of going to the gym—until you're there, moving your body, building your sense of efficacy and progress. Something similar is true of fear. Fear is not to be conquered—but harnessed.

That's the lesson former Navy SEAL Brandon Webb drives home in his book *Mastering Fear*.

> Far too often, we focus on that awareness of danger, and by focusing on it we magnify it, cause it to expand until it starts filling the space in our heads. We start having the wrong conversation about it. We spin this story and then keep telling and retelling it, like that hamster running on its wheel, over and over. Rather than our mastering fear, fear masters us.[176]

Fear stops you when you lose control of your internal conversation. When you focus on everything that could go wrong, everything that you do not want. You cannot think of anything else. The fear fills your whole world and you will do anything in your power to escape it—usually by surrendering what you want. Fear makes that easy. It feeds you excuses: not to try, not to take chances, not to create.

You master fear by accepting it. By putting it in its proper place.

You tell yourself: "These fears are normal. Their job is to keep me alert as I move forward. But I must move forward—focused, not on the fear, but on my aim." If you're paralyzed by fear, then the solution is simple: start. Move forward. Keep going. Don't quit.

There is one more creativity killer to discuss—one that has become all too common today—and that is: distraction. Creative work is hard. It takes long stretches of unbroken time. And yet how often do we give ourselves those stretches? We're bombarded by email, texts, and Slack messages. At the first hint of boredom or discomfort we reach for stimuli. What are people saying on Twitter? What are people posting on TikTok? Externally and internally, we allow ourselves to be pulled away from our creative task.

Cal Newport calls the process of building and using rare and valuable skills "deep work." One of the biggest lies of the success genre is that the key to productivity is spending long, exhausted hours grinding. To succeed, you supposedly have to optimize every minute. "Shave three seconds off emails by not signing your name! Over the course of the year you could save three hours!" I will grant that some jobs require grinding and that every job probably requires periods of intense, non-stop effort. But busyness isn't what creates value. It's thought—intense, creative thought—that creates value. And that, as Newport notes, requires "a state of unbroken concentration."[177]

Deep work is so demanding that you cannot do it for eight hours a day, let alone ten or twelve. For most people, four hours is the absolute max. But what they can achieve in those four hours is far more valuable than what others can achieve in forty. The key is making those four hours count. And that means eliminating distractions.

You must set aside time for deep work and protect that time. Turn off your phone. Close your email. Close Slack. Immerse yourself in your creative task. Learn to accept boredom and look forward to the mental pressure. You'll be rewarded with ideas that just might change your life.

## Lesson 6

# Honor the Self

## Pursue Your Self-Interest

Every moral code has a conception of what you owe loyalty to. Religion says to be loyal to God. Altruism says to be loyal to the needs and wishes of other people. A morality of happiness says to be loyal to the irreplaceable value of your life.

In Ayn Rand's first novel, *We the Living*, the heroine expresses this attitude: "It's a rare gift, to feel reverence for your own life and to want the best, the greatest, the highest possible, here, now, for your very own. To imagine a heaven and then not to dream of it, but to demand it."[178] In saying that this feeling toward one's own life is "rare," part of what Rand is stressing is that reverence for your own life has to be earned. It is not automatic but the product of your choices.

To honor your self you need to *have* a self. You have to cultivate convictions, values, and strong desires. You have to conceive of a life you have a burning desire to lead—a human life aimed at a hierarchy of pro-life values, including reason, purpose, and self-esteem. You have to build your self-esteem by pursuing that life through virtue, i.e., an unwavering commitment to rationality. It is through thinking—through choosing to turn on the light that is your mind—that you come to form a self and value your own life.

What a pro-happiness morality says is: do it. Create a self and a life that you love, and honor that life. Your life matters. You are an end in yourself, not a means to the ends of others. You have a right to exist for your own sake. You have no duty to serve others, just as they have no duty to serve you.

In this lesson, we'll see that self-interest is not the antithesis of morality, but the heart and soul of morality. It is only your desire to create a self and a life that you love that gives you a reason to be moral—and it is only through your dedication to morality that you can achieve the self-esteem that is the foundation of joy. And, I'll add, the foundation of healthy human relationships.

## The Meaning of Effective Egoism

A pro-happiness morality is one that upholds *Effective Egoism*. It's egoistic in that it says you should live for your own happiness. It is effective in that it says the only way to achieve happiness is through fidelity to rational values and virtues. Values like reason, purpose, and self-esteem. Virtues like rationality, honesty, integrity, and productiveness.

Egoism is the most misunderstood concept in morality. We therefore need to be clear about what it means and what it doesn't.

### Effective Egoism is not psychological egoism

Psychological egoism is the idea that everyone is inherently selfish. There's no point in telling people to be egoistic (or altruistic) because we always do what we most want to do. Mother Teresa was supposedly selfish because she *wanted* to serve the poor. On this view, we have no choice to be anything other than egoistic because we come hardwired to pursue pleasure and avoid pain.

Psychological egoism has an enduring appeal to economists, psychologists, and a surprising number of intelligent laymen. But in philosophy, the position never quite recovered from the critique of David Hume. His pen dripping with sarcasm, Hume describes the ultimate absurdity of psychological egoism:

> By a turn of imagination, by a refinement of reflection, by an enthusiasm of passion, we seem to take part in the interests of others, and imagine ourselves divested of all selfish considerations: but, at bottom, the most generous patriot and most niggardly miser, the bravest hero and most abject coward, have, in every action, an equal regard to their own happiness and welfare.[179]

It is simply not true, Hume thinks, that we can "explain every affection to be self-love, twisted and moulded, by a particular turn of imagination, into a variety of appearances."[180] To claim that Christian ascetics who ate only grass, sentenced themselves to solitary confinement, and castrated themselves were really trying to maximize their own *pleasure* is to empty the word "pleasure" of all meaning.

To argue that we always pursue our own interests because we necessarily act to seek pleasure and avoid pain ignores one crucial issue: *values.* Beyond physical pleasure and pain, which explain almost none of our actions, pleasure and pain are the product of our values, and our values are the product of our choices. And here our free will gives us the power to decide: Am I going to choose my values by my best assessment of what's genuinely good for me—or am I going to choose my values by what some authority tells me to do—or am I going to choose my values by copying what other people care about—or am I going to give the issue no thought, picking up values blindly and at random?

Effective Egoism is about your *ultimate* motivation. To be a principled egoist is to direct all of your choices toward the moral end that is your self-interest. An Effective Egoist selects his values according to what he is rationally convinced will be good for his life, formulates a hierarchy of values, and then strives never to sacrifice a higher value for a lower value. Does everyone do *that?* Most people don't have any self-conscious ultimate motivation. They aren't egoists, they aren't utilitarians, they aren't altruists—they're not seeking to implement any ethical theory. They're still influenced by moral notions and make choices that carry moral weight. But they aren't self-consciously striving to realize any particular moral end.

To be an Effective Egoist is to self-consciously aim at your interests. That requires two things: you need to formulate what your interests are and then aim at them in your actions. You need to conceive of a life based on rational moral principles and then strive to realize it.

Psychological egoism is, in the end, a version of determinism. In reality, though we cannot act without some motivation, *we are the selectors of the values that motivate us*. Those values can either be chosen rationally for the purpose of attaining happiness—or they can be chosen on some other grounds—or we can default entirely, and allow our values (or, more precisely, our whims) to arise by accident.

### Effective Egoism requires valuing other people

Other human beings are obviously of tremendous "practical" benefit. They are sources of knowledge and trade. It is clearly easier to flourish in a free, technological society than on a deserted island. But that is hardly the sole or even the primary benefit we gain from other people. Companionship, friendship, love—these are among the greatest pleasures life has to offer. Near the top of any Effective Egoist's hierarchy of values will be the people who matter most to him.

I'll have more to say about how and why an Effective Egoist should form meaningful human relationships shortly. What I want to stress here is this: to uphold Effective Egoism is to say that you are your own *primary* value—it's *not* to say that you are your *only* value. Every action an Effective Egoist takes should be aimed at the preservation of his life and the achievement of his happiness. He isn't a resource for others to exploit, just as they aren't resources for him to exploit. But other people *matter* to him.

An Effective Egoist has a generalized positive attitude toward others rooted in respect since, like him, they are human beings. Think of the best moments of your life: the morning after you've fallen in love or the evening after a major success at school or work. That joy tends to spill over into a wider feeling of goodwill: you hope that others could experience the happiness you're experiencing. The Effective Egoist, precisely because he loves himself and his life, carries with him a similar feeling throughout his life—not some phony "love for humanity," but a generosity of spirit that expects the best from people and hopes to find it. Other people are seen as spiritual allies—until evidence convinces him that they are not.

But what an Effective Egoist feels for the specific people who matter to him is far more profound. The primary benefit we receive from the people we love is *joy in their existence.* Just as we can become invested in our favorite fictional characters, sharing their joy and sorrow, so we become invested in our favorite people. Their happiness makes us happy. Their interests become, to an important extent, our interests.

The point isn't that an Effective Egoist can care for others as much as a committed altruist. The point is far stronger: *only* an egoist is truly fit for love and friendship. When people are riddled with self-doubt and unhappiness, friendships can become one-sided or co-dependent. Painted on smiles can conceal hidden jealousies. When people view self-sacrifice as a moral duty, they tend to oscillate between resentful service and presumptuous demands (since their friends, too, have a duty to sacrifice). Self-confident, happy people aren't takers: they've created lives of abundance and so they are free to express kindness and generosity. Principled people are solid. You can rely on them. They'll tell you the truth. They'll keep their word. They aren't trying to prove something about themselves, so they can take joy in your joy, and be open and empathetic when you need to share your fears and frustrations.

The key to understanding how an Effective Egoist treats human relationships is to keep firmly in mind what a sacrifice truly is. It is not a sacrifice to help someone you care about. It is not a sacrifice to let your friend choose the movie. It is not a sacrifice to pick up the check, or bear an inconvenience, or lift someone up when they're down. A sacrifice means surrendering what you find personally valuable for what you don't.

One insignia of sacrifice in human relationships is when you act out of guilt. When you let your brother mooch off you after he's made a mess of his life and shows no inclination to fix it, that is a sacrifice. When you stay in a sexless marriage because you don't want to hurt your partner's feelings, never mind how they're torturing yours, that is a sacrifice. When you allow your cousin to use you as a source of free day care, when he could easily afford to pay someone, that is a sacrifice. When you lie to your parents about attending church because you don't want to hurt their feelings by admitting you're an atheist, that is a sacrifice. Whenever you give in to someone else's irrational emotion, that is a sacrifice.

There is a flip side to acting from guilt, a form of sacrifice that's more insidious because it doesn't *feel* like a sacrifice. If your motive for doing something for others is the jolt of self-worth you get from helping them, that is often a sacrifice in disguise. Your internal conversation amounts to: "This isn't what I selfishly want to do, but doing this will make me feel like a good person." This can be difficult to distinguish from the inevitable positive feelings that come from doing someone a favor. Here your only protection is a clearly defined hierarchy of values and careful introspection.

To value others, ultimately, is to respect and aid their own egoism. When my friend and mentor Alex Epstein started his own business and was trying to raise funds for a debate with environmentalist Bill McKibben—a debate that would ultimately launch Alex's career into the stratosphere—I donated $500, which was a ton of money for me at the time.

Alex replied: "Don, if you ever try to start your own one-man army, you'll realize just how rare people like you are. I certainly do. And the difference between rare and none makes all the difference."

I said, "Thank you Alex. But I should say, I regard this as an investment in my future. If you succeed, it will be infinitely easier for me. $500 is a ridiculously small price to pay."

"Well, yes," he said, "I was praising you for being selfish. That's what's rare."

## Ineffective Egoism isn't egoism

If you were truly selfish, wouldn't you steal a million dollars if you knew you'd get away with it? This question and questions like it reflect a deep-seated view that self-interest entails predatory and unprincipled behavior. But nothing could be more utterly *unselfish* than manufacturing human victims.

Let's start by reversing the question: why would you think that it *is* to a person's interest to steal a million dollars? You might point to the things a person could buy with the money. Fine. But that does not answer the question. A person's interests, remember, are defined long range and full context. They consist, not of isolated goods or positive feelings, but of a way of life—a constellation of pro-life values that fit together into a non-contradictory whole so that he can achieve non-contradictory joy, "a joy without penalty or guilt, a joy that does not clash with any of your values and does not work for your own destruction."[181]

The question is not whether you can buy desirable things with stolen money. You can. Nor is the question whether it's *possible* to steal a million dollars and get away with it. It's possible, though baldly asserting that a thief "knows he'll get away with it" is ridiculous. Every thief thinks he can get away his crime, but his guilt *is* a fact, and like all facts it is in principle discoverable. No. The question is whether the life of a criminal or of a creator is to your interest. We don't choose between isolated actions but between *kinds of lives.*

Choosing the life of a creator makes the creative intelligence of other people an asset and the facts of reality your ally. Choosing the life of a criminal means volunteering for people to use their creative intelligence, not to offer you values in trade, but to expose and punish you. It means willingly making *truth* and *intelligence* your enemies instead of your allies.

People don't choose the life of a criminal because they are rationally convinced it is to their interest. We all know in some terms that the human way of life requires thought and production. We understand that a nation of thieves would have nothing to steal and would quickly starve to death. The criminal's whole game is become a hitchhiker on other people's thought and production—on the way of life that *actually* allows human beings to flourish.

Any confusion on this point only comes from pretending that we *don't* have to choose between ways of life. That we can view an action out of context. That there is such a thing as a rational, productive person who steals once in a while. But a person who steals "once in a while" *is* a criminal and is living the criminal way of life. Leonard Peikoff puts it this way:

> The power of the good is enormous, but depends on its consistency. That is why the good has to be an issue of "all or nothing," "black and white," and why evil has to be partial, occasional, "gray." Observe that a "liar" in common parlance is not a man who always, conscientiously, tells falsehoods; there is no such creature; for the term to apply to a person, a few whoppers on his part is enough. Just as a "hypocrite" is not a man who scrupulously betrays every idea he holds. Just as a "burglar" is not a man who steals every item of property he sees. Just as a person is a "killer" if he respects human life 99.9 per cent of the time and hires himself out to the Mafia as an executioner only now and then.[182]

Why isn't it in your interest to steal a million dollars? For the same reason you don't cheat on your lover. It's not because "you might get caught." It's because *that's not what you're after in life.* You want an open, honest, fulfilling marriage, where the love and admiration in your lover's eyes means something. In the same way, the reason you don't go around looking for opportunities to steal isn't fear of ending up in prison. It's that you are focused on a life of reason, purpose, and self-esteem—on living a *human* life. Anything that detracts from that, that threatens that, that undermines that *has no value to you.*

An Effective Egoist, in sum, is committed to pro-life values and the virtues required to achieve them. Morality is not a restriction on self-interest, not a limitation or a constraint. It is *the only way to flourish.*

You might call the conventional view of self-interest "Ineffective Egoism." It's ineffective because what achieving your own interests actually requires is fidelity to a morality of happiness. But, in the final analysis, *it's not even egoism:* the person who "thinks only of himself" and is willing to do anything to anyone to get what he wants doesn't, as we'll soon see, even *desire* the best for himself.

### Cruel and evil people aren't selfish

As human beings, we need to understand the world around us. This has often led us to invent and embrace non-explanations that seem like explanations for things we do not understand. Primitive peoples saw lightning and wove tales of angry gods. Today, we laugh at their ignorance. But when it comes to explaining human behavior, we, too, are stuck with primitive just-so stories. We look at dictators, terrorists, murderers, rapists, thieves, addicts, manipulators, jerks, power-lusters, social climbers, thrill seekers, prickly geniuses, successful investors, and ambitious entrepreneurs and we attribute to all of them the same ruling motive: "selfishness."

A motive that explains everything, explains nothing. There is nothing important that unites a murderer and a jerk, let alone a murderer, a jerk, and an Effective Egoist. Labeling everyone who isn't selfless "selfish" prevents us from answering a difficult but important question: What does explain human cruelty and human evil? If it's not driven by a preoccupation with oneself, what is it driven by?

To understand evil, start with this: have you ever been in a room with someone who is strikingly beautiful and become self-conscious about your weight? Have you ever seen a happy couple and become aware of your relationship failures? Have you ever been angry and the sight of someone else's happiness made you angrier? Other people can make us aware of our perceived flaws and short-comings. For healthy people, these are fleeting moments of pain. More often, the sight of other people's virtues and successes sparks positive feelings: the desire to admire, the desire to emulate, the desire to achieve what they have achieved.

For evil people, it's different. Filled with a perpetual and overwhelming sense of self-doubt and shame, they spend the lion's share of their time and energy trying to quell their feelings of worthlessness. Typically this takes the form of seeking out feelings of *superiority*. I'm tougher than others, I'm sexier than others, I'm richer than others, I'm smarter than others, I'm more powerful than others, I'm more terrifying than others. (Different people will gravitate to different pretenses at superiority based on which pretense seems easiest to obtain or which aspect of life makes them feel most insecure.) They secretly feel like a nobody, and so they become fixated on proving they're a somebody.

What happens when this sort of a person encounters someone who actually possesses the values he *pretends* to possess? Resentment, envy, hatred. The sheer existence of strong, confident, healthy, happy people makes him feel deeply inferior, and his ruling desire becomes the desire to destroy. Ayn Rand called this motive "hatred of the good for being the good."

They do not want to own your fortune, they want you to lose it; they do not want to succeed, they want you to fail; they do not want to live, they want you to die; they desire nothing, they hate existence, and they keep running, each trying not to learn that the object of his hatred is himself . . . . [T]hey are the essence of evil, they, those anti-living objects who seek, by devouring the world, to fill the *self- less* zero of their soul.[183]

This is so ugly a motive that a person cannot admit it—to others and above all to himself. He needs rationalizations. And here conventional morality provides evil people with the two most powerful rationalizations: "I don't hate him because he's good—I hate him because he's selfish"—and, "My destructive acts are moral because my motive isn't my own welfare, but the greater good."

If you've ever seen *Breaking Bad*, the core story is the descent of an average man into pure evil. At every stage of his descent, the anti-hero, Walter White, justifies his actions by saying, "I'm doing this for my family." I'm selling drugs—for my family. I'm lying to everyone I know—for my family. I'm killing anyone who threatens to expose me—for my family. In the final episode, White cannot maintain that rationalization any longer. He admits to his wife: I didn't do it for my family, I did it for myself.

You might think that's a confession that his ruling motive was selfishness. But the show reveals the true meaning of his confession. From the beginning of the show, we see that White feels a deep sense of emptiness and inferiority. He feels pushed around by his cocky brother-in-law, by his overbearing boss, by his naggy wife. He feels resentful toward his former business partner who got rich after White had left the company. His motive wasn't selfishness—it was the attempt to cope with his insecurities and resentments by the cultivation of power and the destruction of anyone and anything that threatened his pretenses.

To move from fiction to real life, think of the Soviet Union or Nazi Germany. Communism and fascism rose to power by preaching that individuals have a moral duty to serve and sacrifice for the greater good: for the proletariat or for the volk. Hitler put it this way:

> This state of mind, which subordinates the interests of the ego to the conservation of the community, is really the first premise of every truly human culture. . . . The basic attitude from which such activity arises, we call—to distinguish it from egoism and selfishness—idealism. By this we understand only the individual's capacity to make sacrifices for the community, for his fellow men.[184]

But these appeals to the greater good were only rationalizations for destruction, which is why, despite years and decades of achieving nothing but destruction, those nations never stopped to reconsider their systems. They never said, "our ideology isn't actually achieving a greater good, we need a better ideology." Because their ideologies and systems were in fact achieving exactly what they were intended to achieve: destruction.

Now ask: Does this motivation have anything in common with someone who desires, not to destroy, but to create? Who builds cars or phones or computers instead of gulags and gas chambers? Who seeks the achievement of personal happiness instead of the quelling of envy and self-hatred? Who is committed to a life of reason, purpose, self-esteem rather than manipulation, fraud, and exploitation? No? Then how disastrous to our moral thinking is it to label both kinds of people "selfish"?

Our conventional notion of "selfishness" is a package deal. It teaches us to equate Bernie Madoff and Steve Jobs, Elizabeth Holmes and Jeff Bezos, Donald Trump and Ayn Rand. Every package deal works by uniting things based on superficial similarities. Here the fact that neither criminals nor creators are out "for the good of others" is used to blur an essential distinction: the distinction between the person who *sacrifices* others and the person who *respects* others in his quest for personal happiness.

Instead of reaching lazily for the term "selfishness" to describe every bad actor, we should cultivate a richer moral and psychological vocabulary. And we should reserve the term "selfishness" for those rare people who take their genuine interests, and the pro-self morality that identifies their interests, seriously.

What, then, does an Effective Egoist morality have to say *positively* about how we should relate to other people? If it's not true that we should sacrifice others in order to amass money, power, and status, how *should* we relate to them?

## The Social Virtues: Independence and Justice

Jordan Peterson famously begins his book *12 Rules for Life* with an extended musing about lobsters. Why lobsters? Because they shed light on the nature of social hierarchies and status games. The strongest lobster gets the sexiest lobster, which I guess is a pretty good prize for a lobster.

I have no doubt that you can make sense of a lot of human behavior by seeing it as a competition for social status. I'm thinking of the men who shake hands like they're trying to break bones and of women who throw shade on the mom who can't afford whatever yoga pants are in fashion this spring. I'm thinking of people who buy things they don't want to impress people they don't like. I'm thinking of parents who shame children for not pursuing "respectable" careers or marrying "respectable" partners.

But human beings aren't lobsters. We don't have to play status games—and we shouldn't. We create values—we don't compete for them. We bond over shared values—we don't fight for the most reproductively fit partners. Status games are games played by losers for prizes not worth winning.

Your means of survival is reason, and to live rationally means having as your primary focus, not other people, but *reality*. It is to practice the virtue of independence.

Independence doesn't mean that you ignore other people, detach yourself from them, refuse to learn from or cooperate with them. It means that you take responsibility for your own thinking and you take responsibility for supporting your own life. You want to know what's true—not what other people think is true. You want to know what's right—not what other people think is right. You want to live by the work of your own mind—not copy a routine created by others, or feed on the crumbs of their handouts, or get rich by defrauding and robbing them of what they've created.

Independence, in this sense, is hard. It requires effort to think for yourself and to support your own life. It requires responsibility: if you're independent and you make an error, there's no one else to blame or to pay for your mistakes. It sometimes means coming into conflict with the opinions and judgments of others—provoking their disapproval or animosity. But independence is hard only in the sense that working out is hard—both involve short-term discomfort that buys massive benefits over the long run. As the saying goes: "Hard choices, easy life. Easy choices, hard life."

One of the most independent people I know is my friend Alex Epstein. In his late twenties, Alex became fascinated by the issue of energy. He had grown up with no particular interest in the subject and shared more or less the conventional view: that fossil fuels were outdated, that solar and wind were the energies of the future, that climate change was very likely going to be a major problem. But once he realized the importance of energy—that it is the industry that powers every other industry—he began questioning the conventional wisdom.

Why is it, he wondered, that we only ever hear negatives about fossil fuels, and we only ever hear positives about solar and wind? Don't we need to take an unbiased look at the positives and the negatives of all the alternatives to make good energy decisions? Why was it that the media covered catastrophic predictions about the future from the same thought leaders who had made failed catastrophic predictions in the past? Maybe they're right this time, but shouldn't their track record at least give us pause? Or why is it that we talk about whether climate change is real rather than whether those changes would be catastrophic? Doesn't making good decisions require precision?

It was this persistent questioning that led Alex to formulate a new environmental philosophy, and eventually write two bestsellers: *The Moral Case for Fossil Fuels* and *Fossil Future*. Later in his career, Alex would sometimes be called a stooge for the fossil fuel industry. But the funny thing is that, when he developed his philosophy, he didn't know anyone from the industry. And even when he did, what he found— and I saw this with my own eyes—was that he was usually far more positive about fossil fuels than people who worked in the industry. They often *accepted* the conventional narrative that fossil fuels were a necessary evil. They didn't shape Alex's thinking—*he* reshaped theirs.

The image that best captures Alex's approach to life came just before the publication of his first book. New York City saw the largest climate march in history. Hundreds of thousands of people stomped down the streets of Manhattan chanting, "Hey, ho, fossil fuels have got to go." And Alex? He stood alone facing the oncoming crowd, quietly holding a giant sign that read: "I Love Fossil Fuels." *That* is independence.

The need for independence is, like every virtue, rooted in the fact that you survive by reason. Reason is an individual faculty. You can't delegate your thinking—not even to people who are more intelligent than you are—because they, like you, are fallible. Intellectually, dependence means: I'm going to follow others on faith, I'm going to obey them—and I have no clue whether they're in contact with reality. Maybe they're right, maybe they're wrong, maybe they're evil, I don't know—but I'm going to follow them rather than my own judgment. Existentially, dependence means: I'm going to put my life at the mercy of other people—of their generosity, their gullibility, their weakness. Dependence, in short, means surrendering control over your own life.

Contrast that with a truly independent person. She's forming her own conclusions about what's true and what's good. As a teenager, she's questioning: Do I agree with my parents' views on religion? Do

I respect the things my peers admire? What do I find sexually attractive? What kind of activities do I find engaging? What kind of career do I want? Is this true? Is this good for me? The independent person is building her own view of the true and the good. She's cultivating a strong sense of responsibility: "I am in control of my mind and my life and therefore I'm *responsible* for my mind and my life." She isn't looking to be handed anything, but to earn what she wants. And, through this process, she's developing a strong sense of self. She knows what she believes—and why. She knows what she values—and why. She forms a self by means of reason—and then sets out to achieve an integrated set of values that will constitute her life.

As the independent person proceeds on her quest for values, she will have to navigate a world of other people. People who have free will. People who can shape their soul into something positive, rational, and creative—or who default on that task. Potential allies in the quest for happiness—and potential threats. Here another virtue is required, one that will guide her in distinguishing the good from the bad, that will help her benefit from the best that people have to offer and protect her from the worst that people have to offer. That virtue is *justice*.

Justice, writes Leonard Peikoff, "is the virtue of judging men's character and conduct objectively and of acting accordingly, granting to each man what he deserves."[185] Today being "judgmental" is stigmatized. You're supposed to be tolerant—not just politically, not just in the sense of respecting someone's *right* to live however they choose, but tolerant *personally* and *morally*. That is suicidal. The people you surround yourself with help shape who you are and how your life goes. To remain agnostic about the character and conduct of those people is the equivalent of drunk driving through life.

What makes non-judgmentalism plausible is equating judgment with irrational prejudice. Yet what justice demands is *rational* judgment. To hire someone based on his skin color, to refuse to hire someone because of her sex, to assume someone is dumb because he has an accent, to assume someone is honest because she is attractive—justice forbids such shortcuts. It says: judge people by rational standards and apply those standards with rigor and care.

And then, justice says: act accordingly. Treat people as they deserve. Admire those worthy of admiration. Ostracize those worthy of being shunned. Praise good deeds and condemn bad ones. Meet the good with rewards—withhold rewards and, where appropriate, dole out punishments to the bad. In Rand's words:

> The basic principle that should guide one's judgment in issues of justice is the law of causality: one should never attempt to evade or to break the connection between cause and effect—one should never attempt to deprive a man of the consequences of his actions, good or evil. (One should not deprive a man of the values or benefits his actions have caused, such as expropriating a man's wealth for somebody's else's benefit; and one should not deflect the disaster which his actions have caused, such as giving relief checks to a lazy, irresponsible loafer.)[186]

Just as justice demands judgment so it bars mercy. Mercy is the view that a person should deny people what they deserve. It is to sanction unearned forgiveness, and thereby reward evil while callously ignoring evil's victims. When atheists praise Christian morality, when Jesus is held to be a moral exemplar, what they ignore is the vile center of Christian ethics: the demand that we turn the other cheek, forgive, and love the evil. To love the evil is to spit in the face of the good.

"No, we don't love the evil. We hate the sin, love the sinner." This means nothing. Man is a being of self-made soul—you *are* what you make yourself. This is precisely what evil people seek to evade. Criminals often say of their crimes, "That wasn't the real me." Christians say: "Yes, you're right." A morality of happiness takes morality seriously—it says, to the rapist, the child molester, the thug, the dictator: "That is the real you—and you deserve to suffer the consequences of your immoral choices."

Does justice allow for forgiveness? Yes. If it's *earned*. To earn forgiveness requires more than an apology. Forgiveness is earned when a person has genuinely changed and proved that he's changed. When he's repaired whatever flaws in his character allowed him to conduct himself in an unworthy manner. For a trivial misdeed, very little is required. For a serious grievance, it may take years or even decades to trust someone again. For serious acts of evil—not only crimes, but even something like long-term, conscious deception—there is no path to forgiveness.

If all of this sounds too harsh, it's because we forget the stakes. Justice is not ultimately about condemning and punishing the evil. It's about praising and rewarding the good. The reason evil cannot be forgiven is out of fidelity and love for its victims. "[M]ercy to the guilty," Adam Smith noted, "is cruelty to the innocent."[187]

The essence of justice, its heart and soul, is this: I'm on a quest for values, and I'm on a quest for those who are on a quest for values. Justice isn't primarily about condemning the wicked. It's about telling your kid you're proud of her when she fesses up to a mistake. It's about standing up for the victim of an online mob and letting him know he's not alone. It's about being an ally to the true and the good.

We have now grasped the essentials of self-interest. Your interests consist of living rationally, creating values, and dealing with others as independent equals. But valuing your own interests—valuing your *life*—does not happen automatically. Like every other value, it must be earned. How do you earn it?

## The Virtue of Loving Virtue

The purpose of morality is to help you achieve happiness. But people don't automatically value their own happiness. To desire the best for your life takes work: the work of achieving and maintaining the last of the three cardinal values Effective Egoism demands: self-esteem.

Emotions carry with them an implicit evaluation of "for me" or "against me." Inherent in those evaluations is an evaluation of the "me" involved.[188] Self-esteem, in other words, shapes your every emotion. If your pleasure/pain mechanism is your body speaking to you about the physical state of your being, then the voice of your soul is your self-esteem.

"Self-esteem (or the lack of it)," Nathaniel Braden writes, "is the reputation a man acquires with himself."[189] It's your core belief about your ability and worth, and it impacts every emotion you feel, and every choice you make.

Think of when you procrastinate. Sometimes it's because the task is unpleasant, like going to the DMV. But often it's because you feel you can't do what you're supposed to do—not that you lack some concrete skill, but that you as a person are incompetent to deal with life's challenges—and so your mind rebels at doing something that feels fruitless. That is your soul lacking confidence. Or think of when a friend or partner mistreats you and you don't speak up or walk out because you don't think you deserve better or can do better. That is your soul lacking worth.

To set ambitious goals, to stick to them in the face of obstacles, and to take joy in their achievement requires self-esteem. It requires self-confidence and self-respect. Without such self-esteem, you'll lower your sights, give up on your values, and, if you do achieve them, self-sabotage to restore a sense of proportion between what you have and what you feel worthy of having.

Where does self-esteem come from? It doesn't come from people telling you that you're perfect. It doesn't come from deluding yourself about your own abilities or blinding yourself to your own flaws. Self-esteem has to be *earned*: you develop your core beliefs about your ability and worth through the choices you make.

Your self-judgment is both a metaphysical judgment and a moral judgment you pass on your choices. Metaphysically, the more you choose to think, the more confident you grow in your ability to deal with the challenges of life. The more you shun the responsibility of thinking and act blindly on your emotions, the more out of control and incompetent you'll feel. Morally, to the extent you live up to your ideals, you'll feel worthy of respect, love, and happiness. To the extent you betray your ideals, you'll feel guilt, self-loathing, even self-hatred.

But as with any emotion, self-esteem isn't automatically in touch with reality. You have no choice about reaching some evaluation of your ability and worth—but you do have a choice about the standards you use to measure your ability and worth.

For example, some people judge their ability, not by the degree to which they choose to think, but by their competence at some specific skill: "I'm good because I'm a great programmer," "I'm good because I know how to fight." But self-esteem isn't about any specific ability you've cultivated; it's about your general ability to navigate reality.

Other people judge their ability by impossible standards of perfection: "I'm good if I don't make mistakes." But measuring your self-esteem by unattainable standards constitutes a profound contradiction: your need for self-esteem comes from the fact that you are the author of your choices, and so assessing yourself by a standard that is not open to your choice means saying, "I couldn't have done better but I should have done better."

Or take worth. Some people judge their worth, not by whether they live honestly and with integrity, but by some external or comparative standard: "I'm good because I'm smarter than other people," "I'm good because I'm more beautiful than other people," "I'm good because people like me." But self-esteem is internal: it's about your own estimate of your relationship to reality and morality. To base it on other people in any way is to make it vulnerable and self-defeating: you can't seek self-esteem if you're crawling on your knees or sneering down at inferiors.

Other people judge their worth by self-sacrificial moral standards: "I'm good because I put others before myself," "I'm good because I'm not selfish." But this, too, represents a contradiction: "I'm worthy of happiness because I recognize that other people's happiness is more important than mine." Healthy self-esteem requires that you dedicate yourself to moral principles aimed at human flourishing, not self-effacement.

Judging yourself by wrong metaphysical and moral standards is damaging. Sometimes such mistakes *are* mistakes. It's understandable that a person could confuse his need for competence with a need for unachievable flawlessness. It's understandable that a person who has been taught that morality consists in selflessness would judge herself by the degree to which she's set aside her values for the sake of others.

But for people who are characteristically irrational, wrong standards of self-esteem are more insidious. Precisely because self-esteem *is* a need, they are driven to pursue a substitute—pseudo-self-esteem. Pseudo-self-esteem isn't merely self-esteem gauged by a mistaken standard. It is an attempt to fake self-esteem rather than acknowledge that you lack it. It's a pretense of self-esteem. Branden observes:

> A man's pseudo-self-esteem is maintained by two means, essentially: by evading, repressing, rationalizing, and otherwise denying ideas and feelings that could affect his self-appraisal adversely; and by seeking to derive his sense of efficacy and worth from something *other than* rationality, some *alternative* value or virtue which he experiences as less demanding or more easily attainable, such as "doing one's duty," or being stoical or altruistic or financially successful or sexually attractive.[190]

Just as a fraud who counterfeits money has to twist himself in knots to conceal the truth, thereby making the truth his enemy, so the person trying to counterfeit self-esteem faces constant threats to his pretense. A pretense is hollow. There is an underlying tension that never leaves, amounting to the constant fear: "The clock is ticking. Someday, the truth about me will come out." When you see someone become triggered by something seemingly innocuous—the tiniest slight, the mildest criticism, the faint scent of rejection—you are seeing someone whose pretense at self-esteem has been threatened.

Genuine self-esteem, on the other hand, is *solid*: it is based on the clearest perception possible of the truth about yourself, including your flaws and failings. You *want* to become aware of your flaws so that you can seek to improve them.

If self-esteem is something you earn by making moral choices, the virtue that encourages you to make good choices and form the best possible moral character is *pride*. Pride, in this context, is not the *feeling* of achievement, but the quest for achievement—the achievement of a healthy soul. Ayn Rand describes the virtue of pride this way:

> Pride is the recognition of the fact that you are your own highest value and, like all of man's values, it has to be earned—that of any achievements open to you, the one that makes all others possible is the creation of your own character—that your character, your actions, your desires, your emotions are the products of the premises held by your mind—that as man must produce the physical values he needs to sustain his life, so he must acquire the values of character that make his life worth sustaining—that as man is a being of self-made wealth, so he is a being of self-made soul—that to live requires a sense of self-value, but man, who has no automatic values, has no automatic sense of self-esteem and must earn it by shaping his soul in the image of his moral ideal, in the image of Man, the rational being he is born able to create, but must create by choice—that the first precondition of self-esteem is that radiant selfishness of soul which desires the best in all things, in values of matter and spirit, a soul that seeks above all else to achieve its own moral perfection, valuing nothing higher than itself.[191]

Pride makes possible self-esteem. But to practice pride requires doing something few people take the time to do: defining a moral ideal to aspire to. To achieve self-esteem requires thinking deeply about what morality *actually* demands of you—and then striving to live up to those demands. To live up to them, not partially or part time but fully.

To practice morality full time and so cultivate the virtue of pride means to exhibit *unbreached rationality*. This doesn't require omniscience. It requires consistently acting with your eyes open. It means never evading your knowledge and constantly striving to expand your knowledge—above all, your moral knowledge. To practice pride is to love morality, to be interested in moral issues, to want to know what's right—not so you can preach it but so that you can *practice* it. Pride is the desire to cultivate a virtuous *character* and so achieve, in Peikoff's words, "the best possible spiritual state."[192]

In conventional ethical systems, the basic moral challenge is temptation: you know what's right, but you don't want what's right. Living up to morality's demands, on this view, is impossible, but your job is to struggle to achieve the impossible.

But if morality is a guide to happiness, then temptation becomes a real but trivial issue. The challenge is not to desire the good but to *see it*. Imagine that before you made any choice, you were able to watch a movie that showed you the full consequences of each alternative. You could see how overcoming your fear of strangers and walking up to the girl in the library would lead to a passionate romance. You could see how phoning in sick to work so you could go out golfing would lead to you running in to the company CEO and ruining your career. You could see how standing up for your ideals in the face of an online mob would set you on a path of lifelong courage, while cowering and apologizing would cripple your self-esteem and nurture an ever-growing sense of resentment and self-loathing. If you could grasp, with total certainty, the full consequences of your actions, there would be no issue of temptation—what's right and what's desirable would be one and the same.

You cannot see all of the specific consequences of any of your choices. Temptation occurs when you see a situation out of context. You see with vivid clarity some short-term reward—sex with an attractive person, a brownie smothered with ice cream—but only dimly glimpse the long-term cost—divorce, diabetes. Or you see with vivid clarity some short-term cost—the blistering pain of the dentist's drill, the brutal difficulty of a workout—but only dimly glimpse the long-term benefit—dental health, strength and energy.

But while you cannot see all of the specific consequences of your choices, you can project the consequences *in principle*. You know that evading what you know will harm you, even if the fact in question is painful to confront. You know that telling the truth in a difficult situation will benefit you, even if the short-term consequence will be a fight with your spouse or a poor grade in a class. Morality—a pro-happiness morality—gives you the only crystal ball there is. But it is up to your free will whether you use that crystal ball. "The challenge in life," writes Peikoff, "is not to struggle against immoral passions, but to see the facts of reality clearly, in full focus. Once a man has done this in a given situation, there is no further difficulty in regard to him acting on what he sees."[193]

The fact that a pro-happiness morality is practical, that there's no incentive to violate pro-life moral principles, means that you can live up to morality's demands. Fully, consistently, without exception.

Morality, remember, is a guide for your choices. As a result, morality can't require of you anything that's outside your ability to choose. It can't require you to make a certain amount of money or experience certain emotions or know what's unknowable. It can only tell you to do what is under your direct volitional control. Rand puts it this way:

> Learn to distinguish the difference between errors of knowledge and breaches of morality. An error of knowledge is not a moral flaw, provided you are willing to correct it; only a mystic would judge human beings by the standard of an impossible, automatic omniscience. But a breach of morality is the conscious choice of an action you know to be evil, or a willful evasion of knowledge, a suspension of sight and of thought. That which you do not know, is not a moral charge against you; but that which you refuse to know, is an account of infamy growing in your soul.[194]

When morality is about what's good for you, and when it doesn't demand the impossible of you, then there is nothing barring you from doing what's right *without exception.* There is no reason to settle for less than your best because there is nothing to gain from less than your best. There is no reason to engage in willful self-destruction.

Rand calls this attitude "moral ambitiousness." Since morality is good for you, you should strive to understand and practice what's moral. Not because you're supposed to. Not because some authority will send you to Hell if you don't. But because the more moral you are, the more successful and the more happy you'll be.

To say that living a fully moral life is possible is not to say it's easy. It requires effort. It requires accepting short-term discomfort for long-term benefits. Most difficult of all, it often requires overcoming past mistakes and traumas. By the time you are able to self-consciously think about moral issues, you may have developed all sorts of baggage that makes doing what's good for you extremely difficult. You can become invested in psychological defenses—approval seeking, projecting a phony self-image, numbing negative feelings with drugs or sex or frantic busyness—and the anxiety of defying them can seem more terrifying than living a life without happiness. Dedication to happiness takes courage.

In encouraging you to strive for a fully moral life, I'm not saying you should continually ask yourself if you're perfect and flagellate yourself for any shortcomings. That is a recipe for guilt and depression. What I'm really talking about is cultivating a commitment to continual improvement. If you have moral flaws, the question is whether you're committed to eliminating them over time or whether you surrender to them.

If you do violate your moral principles, what should you do? What does moral redemption look like? It requires more than a resolve to do better in the future. Many a person has woken up with a hangover vowing to never drink again, only to crack open a bottle a few weeks (or a few hours) later. A resolution, by itself, isn't enough.

Moral redemption starts with self-honesty. You say to yourself:

*I told that lie. I took that action. I've engrained this negative character trait.* Self-honesty isn't about settling for where you are today or liking where you are today, but about fully acknowledging the reality of where you are today. It means not pretending that "the real me" is different from the "me" who lashed out at my friend, or cheated on the test, or lied about believing in God, or peeked at my partner's private journal. Self-honesty means seeing myself as I am, right now, at this moment.

Next, moral redemption requires fully accepting the *consequences* of my actions. Irrationality, we've said, means seeking to cheat cause and effect. Moral redemption, in essence, is reasserting respect for cause and effect.

If I was seeking effects without causes, then redemption requires taking responsibility for where I am and getting what I want. Even if I *have* been the victim of injustice or bad fortune, it means that I distinguish between fault and responsibility. It may not be my fault that I'm poor, but it's my responsibility to rise out of poverty. It may not be my fault that I'm depressed or anxious, but it's my responsibility to improve my psychological well-being. I must accept where I am today, including the role my choices played in bringing me to this point. Then I must stop blaming others and stop making excuses, knowing that getting what I want is in my own hands.

If I was enacting causes while trying to escape the effects, then moral redemption requires taking responsibility for what I did. If I took credit for a project at work I was hardly involved in, it means saying to my boss, "By the way, Paige really did most of the work on that one." If I stole Ramen from my dormmate, it means fessing up and replacing what I took. If I cheated on a lover, it means not staying in the relationship under false pretenses of fidelity.

If I was seeking to reverse cause and effect, then moral redemption requires taking responsibility for my own desires and motives. To face the truth: I'm sleeping with people to prove I'm worthy of love, I'm pursuing wealth to prove I have ability, I'm a bully who tries to exert power over others to convince myself I'm not powerless. It means accepting that I lack self-esteem and have to rebuild it by pursuing only rational values and practicing virtue.

Then, moral redemption requires striving to *understand* my poor choices and undesirable character traits. Why did I lie to my boss about how far along I was on the project? Was I afraid she'd get angry—and if so, do I have an irrational fear of people's negative emotions? Or is there something deeper at work? Perhaps I feel the need to project an image of myself as a superstar at work, because deep down I feel incompetent. Self-improvement requires getting to the deepest "why" I'm capable of, so that I can make the biggest correction I'm capable of.

Next, moral redemption requires a plan of action. *This* is the only kind of resolution to do better that matters. A plan can mean anticipating future scenarios where I'll experience the temptation to repeat my past mistakes and coming up with a strategy to avoid repeating them. Or it can be a positive series of steps I'm going to take to instill a new habit or character trait. For example, a lot of people find themselves getting into angry arguments on social media. They come away feeling like they were the worst versions of themselves. To improve, they need a plan such as: I'm not allowed to post anything when I'm in an emotionally charged state.

Finally, moral redemption requires action across time. I cannot think my way to a better character without action. It's action that allows me to assimilate and automatize a new set of behaviors. If you've ever quite smoking, you know that the hardest part is dis-integrating the link between smoking and different settings and activities. You go to have your cup of coffee and it feels unsatisfying, like something's missing. It takes time to break the link between coffee and nicotine. Then, after several weeks, you're starting to enjoy being a non-smoker, only to go out to a party. You're overwhelmed by the sense you won't be able to enjoy late night conversations without lighting up. You have to break that connection as well.

For any habit, including moral habits, you cannot short-circuit that process. You will encounter situations where the old desire will re-emerge, and you will have to consciously remind yourself of your new resolve and will yourself to follow your plan of action. But over time, it will become easier. Over time, the new way of acting will become second nature.

This isn't easy. Although it can feel safer in the moment to suffer internally than to confront your fears, your guilt, your shame, it's not true. Negative emotions tell lies. Alcoholism tells you that you can never enjoy life without your crutch. Depression tells you that you will never find enjoyment in life. Anxiety tells you that you will not be able to cope with whatever fear terrifies you. You need to be able to set those feelings and fears to the side and act on your knowledge: that happiness is possible, that life can be amazing, that confronting your worst fears will make you feel better not worse. That is courageous. That is what it means to lead a moral life.

# Seek Pleasure

## The Virtue of Pleasure

Matthew McConaughey is one of the most thoughtful people in Hollywood and leveled what I regard as the most plausible critique of making happiness your goal in life.

> Happiness is an emotional response to an outcome. If I win, I will be happy. If I don't, I won't. It's an if-then, cause-and-effect, quid pro quo standard that we cannot sustain because we immediately raise it every time we attain it. See, happiness demands a certain outcome. It is result reliant. And I say if happiness is what you're after, then you're going to be let down frequently, and you're going to be unhappy much of your time.[195]

There's a lot that's right about this. Happiness *is* about cause-and-effect. It is the emotion that proceeds from achieving your values. And it's also true whenever you achieve a value, you are quickly if not immediately focused on the next challenge, the next goal, the next value. There is often a gap between what you *think* achieving a goal will feel like—and what it actually feels like.

Psychologists refer to this as the hedonic treadmill. You chase after things that will make you happy—and they don't. Not for long. And the problem isn't just the pursuit of "conveniences," like a new car, a new dress, or a new home. The same pattern seems to show itself in your pursuit of your most inspiring goals. Achieving a goal doesn't satisfy you—it merely spurs you to set a more ambitious goal.

In my own case, my driving goal up until the age of twenty-nine was to author a book. For years I would imagine what it would be like to hold a book with my name on it in my hands. When I would visit bookstores, I would often hunt for the place on the shelf where my book would eventually sit. And then it happened, and what I felt was not the ecstasy I had imagined, but only a quiet sense of satisfaction— and the desire to write more books, that would reach more people, and would tackle more ambitious themes.

This phenomenon has led some people to argue that happiness is illusory. You chase goals thinking they'll make you happy—and then discover that they don't. The solution? Focus on something other than happiness, something better than happiness.

It's the wrong conclusion to draw.

Here is the root of the problem. Life is a process—an ongoing process of pursuing, achieving, and maintaining values. Why? So that you can continue pursuing, achieving, and maintaining values. The work of living is never done. You must continually grow or you'll deteriorate. Stasis is precisely what you can't achieve. You're becoming stronger—or you're becoming weaker. You're raising your sights— or you're razing them. You can tread water, but with every kick you're wasting energy and bringing yourself closer to drowning. Thus, your emotional mechanism drives you forward, from one goal to the next, encouraging you to a summit you can never reach.

And, yet, psychologically, you *need* the experience of summiting. You need to experience your life, not only as a process, but as a series of victories. Yes, you can and should enjoy the process of pursuing goals, of growing, of making progress. But if nothing counts as achievement then nothing counts as progress. You need, throughout your life, the experience that now, today, at this moment *life is an end in itself.*

Ayn Rand puts it this way:

> Since a rational man's ambition is unlimited, since his pursuit and achievement of values is a lifelong process—and the higher the values, the harder the struggle—he needs a moment, an hour or some period of time in which he can experience the sense of his completed task, the sense of living in a universe where his values have been successfully achieved. It is like a moment of rest, a moment to gain fuel to move farther.[196]

How can you attain such moments? How is it you can experience life as an end in itself?

One popular answer today is: mindfulness. Mindfulness has as many interpretations as it does advocates. But the basic idea is that you learn to block out the mental tape playing in your head—the one ruminating about past regrets and future worries—and focus on the here and now. To stay in the moment and take joy in the sheer fact of being alive.

Mindfulness practices can be extremely valuable. They can calm you, recharge you, bring you into the present. But to truly experience life as an end in itself, what you need is the experience of *pleasure.*

When you get a massage, or become immersed in your favorite novel, or play with a puppy, or kiss someone you love, it's not because you think those activities will have some further benefit down the road, but because they feel amazing in the moment. They are moments that are worth living through for their own sake. Nathaniel Branden puts it this way: "Through the state of enjoyment, man experiences the value of life, the sense that life is worth living, worth struggling to maintain. In order to live, man must act to achieve values. Pleasure or enjoyment is at once an emotional payment for successful action and an incentive to continue acting."[197]

And not only that. Branden goes on to note that pleasure gives you a sense of your own efficacy. To feel good is to feel that you are able to meet the demands of reality, that you are in control of your life. To feel pain, by contrast, is to feel helpless and impotent. "Thus, in letting man experience, in his own person, the sense that life is a value and that he is a value, pleasure serves as the emotional fuel of man's existence."[198]

The point here is not that anything pleasurable is good. You *can* value things that are bad for you and set your pleasure/pain mechanism in reverse, the way a junkie does, moving yourself toward destruction. If you want to live, you must choose and pursue pro-life values. The point here is that the only reason to pursue pro-life values, the motive and reward for the hard work of living, is *enjoying yourself* in the here and now. Pleasure is the form in which you directly experience the fact that life is an end in itself—that life is a value and you are a value.

Achieving happiness is a long-range endeavor. You err when you trade pleasure today for destruction tomorrow. But you also err if you focus so much on the long term that you never enjoy today. That's a mistake for the very simple reason that all you have is today. Tomorrow is always out there, one step beyond your grasp. It would be a fool's errand to spend your life living for the long term by denying the short term, in the hopes that in the last moments of your life you could look back at your years and get a jolt of orgasmic pleasure. No. So long as you aren't sacrificing your future well-being, then your policy must be to squeeze as much pleasure out of every "today" as you can.

Too often people live life as if someone is watching and giving them a grade: their lover, their parents, God. When I'm ruled by external "shoulds," pleasure can seem like an indulgence. If I'm working out, or learning something, or producing something, then I can feel good about what I'm doing. But if I'm playing video games? Or eating a delicious meal with my best friend? Or taking a warm bath? Or watching my favorite sports team? Those are just my "guilty" pleasures.

Bullshit. If these moments are not escapes from a life that is going nowhere, if they are woven into the fabric of rational, long-term value pursuit, then there is nothing to feel guilty about. This is the stuff of life. Morality isn't about gaining some authority's approval. It is a guide that allows you to achieve as an adult what you probably achieved so effortlessly as a child: pure, unadulterated enjoyment.

Morality gives you a roadmap that helps you build such a life. It keeps you from sacrificing what's important to what's not important. It keeps you from pursuing fool's gold—shiny objects that seem desirable, and yet that leave you unfulfilled, hung over, guilt-ridden. It orients you toward genuine values—the real gold that *can* bring you pure, unadulterated joy.

Of course, morality doesn't do this by giving you some concrete list of values. Morality isn't religion. It doesn't tell you what foods to eat on which days, or whom to sleep with after which ceremonies. It gives you abstract principles that you have to apply to your own life. Unfortunately, we aren't taught how to live by principles. We're taught to ask for permission.

When people are first learning Ayn Rand's morality, it is common for them to ask questions like, "Is it okay to masturbate?" "Is it okay to like rap music?" "Is it okay to do drugs?" The answer to all such questions is: they are bad questions. They all reflect a religious or authoritarian mindset. Your life belongs to you. You don't need anyone's permission to do what you want. The question is not: "Is this okay?" The question is: "What value am I after—and is that value rational?"

Take the question of drugs. Morality doesn't take a position on drug-use per se. What it does tell you is how to assess any activity. It tells you to respect identity and causality. This means asking yourself: What is this drug? What are its properties? What will it do to me? What *might* it do to me? And, with this knowledge in hand, it teaches you to ask: Given these properties, is there a real value to be gained here, and under what conditions?

Let's say the drug under consideration is alcohol. Like all drugs, its potentialities depend on dose. At small quantities, it can relax, calm, energize, heighten social interactions. At higher quantities, it can wipe out your ability to make good decisions, shut down your capacity to think, make you sick, or even kill you. Over time, it can become addictive, with all that implies. To act morally means, first and foremost, that you make the decision with your eyes open—that you *think* about the issue. You don't bow to peer pressure. You don't drink or abstain because that's what people in your culture or your family do. If you decide to drink, you do it to achieve a legitimate value, like relaxation, not to avoid facing reality, which is wrong for the same reason that any form of evasion is wrong. And it means that you do it in a way that's consistent with achieving positive values—that is, you don't get so sloshed or drink so often that you threaten your values.

But what if you're wrong? What if you think there's a potential value to be gained—and discover that actually there wasn't? What if you pursue a potentially rational pleasure, but get carried away and do it to excess? Again, it's the religious view that teaches you to be terrified of making mistakes. It teaches you that the safe path is to just say no. You'll never be blamed for saying "no" to a potential pleasure. But life is not about winning virtue points by saying "no" to things. It's about saying "yes" to values.

Discovering your values often requires experimentation, and experimentation often entails failure, disappointment, and regret. So long as you act with your eyes open, so long as you have good reason to think that an experience might add to your life, so long as you aren't evading or giving in to peer pressure, so long as you aren't being reckless and threatening your long-term values, so long as you're willing to own up to and learn from any mistakes, then go out there and *sample life.*

The world is filled with potential values. Your job, your only job in this world, is to find them and enjoy them. Seek out things that bring you pleasure—big and small, physical and emotional. Fill your days and hours with pleasure. Aim at the long range but stop seeing life as some painful struggle. Life does involve pain and struggle, but that is not what life is about. Life is about moments of delight. Moments when you look back and think: *that* was worth living through.

Happiness, to put it differently, often remains in the background. To truly enjoy your life, you need to regularly bring it to the foreground. You need to experience, viscerally, emotionally, that life is an end in itself. You need to experience the value of your person, the value of this world, the value of life. That is the role of pleasure.

One of the foundational pleasures of life we've already discussed: productive work. When you get lost in creative thinking and time vanishes, you experience the efficacy of your mind and the intense joy of creativity. When you stand back and reflect on your achievements, you feel an intense pride.

But there are two more foundational pleasures we have not discussed: contemplation and connection.

# Refuel Your Spirit

Out of the night that covers me,
Black as the Pit from pole to pole,
I thank whatever gods may be
For my unconquerable soul.
In the fell clutch of circumstance
I have not winced nor cried aloud.
Under the bludgeonings of chance
My head is bloody, but unbowed.
Beyond this place of wrath and tears
Looms but the Horror of the shade,
And yet the menace of the years

Finds, and shall find, me unafraid.
It matters not how strait the gate,
How charged with punishments the scroll.
I am the master of my fate:
I am the captain of my soul.

(William Ernest Henley, "Invictus")

Words. Just words. Hardly more than one hundred of them. And yet think of the power of those words. They helped sustain Nelson Mandela during his imprisonment. Helped sustain American POWs in Vietnam. Helped sustain civil rights heroes as they fought for equality.

Human beings need spiritual fuel. We have no instincts, including no survival instinct. We have to continually stoke the flames of our desire to live and our commitment to taking the actions life requires. Recall Ayn Rand's statement, which I cited in Lesson 1.

> Just as man's physical survival depends on his own effort, so does his psychological survival. Man faces two corollary, interdependent fields of action in which a constant exercise of choice and a constant creative process are demanded of him: the world around him and his own soul (by "soul," I mean his consciousness). Just as he has to produce the material values he needs to sustain his life, so he has to acquire the values of character that enable him to sustain it and that make his life worth living. He is born without the knowledge of either. He has to discover both—and translate them into reality—and survive by shaping the world and himself in the image of his values.[199]

To shape the world and ourselves in the image of our values means to work to create our ideal self and our ideal world. To envision the best possible and to strive to bring it into existence. But how do we envision the ideal? How do we keep it real to ourselves in the midst of our daily trials and tribulations? When we are knocked down by obstacles, how do we summon the desire to get back up and try again? When we are overwhelmed by the ugliness we see in the media, how do we remind ourselves that what really matters in life—what's really important—isn't the latest scandal or the latest tragedy, but achievement, virtue, happiness, love?

We turn to art.

## Man's Search for Meaning

The physical world around us is rich in meaning. Bright color and light represent energy. The outdoors represents freedom. Candy stores represent abundance. An upright posture represents pride and virtue. Across cultures, our emotional language is tied to the physical in predictable ways. To be sad is to feel blue. To experience joy is to feel light. Elation comes from the Latin *elatus*, which means elevated—raised up.

None of this is arbitrary. In her book *Joyful*, Ingrid Fetell Lee writes about the way that everyday places and objects can evoke intense emotions, and how this has its roots in our nature as evolved beings. The bright lights and colors that energize us, she argues, are in nature indications of literal energy in the form of calorie-dense food. Or take our love of harmony and symmetry. Lee writes:

> Putting objects with similar features together taps into a principle of gestalt psychology called similarity, which says that the brain tends to perceive similar objects as a group. The individual feathers or leaves or toys cease to be seen as independent objects. Instead, they become modules in a larger composition. According to gestalt theorists, the brain does this to simplify and make sense of information coming in through the visual system. After all, similar objects often have a practical relationship to one another, not just a visual one. A group of similar leaves likely belongs to the same plant, and it's simpler to look at a forest and see a hundred trees rather than millions of individual leaves. According to

neuroscientist V. S. Ramachandran, the pleasurable "aha!" sensation we feel when we see related objects as a group suggests that the brain's processes for identifying objects may be intrinsically connected to the reward mechanisms in the limbic system. In other words, joy is the brain's natural reward for staying alert to correlations and connections in our surroundings.[200]

As conceptual beings who survive by viewing existents as units— as members of a group of similar members—we experience *pleasure* in viewing things as units. In seeing "like with like," we experience the joy of a well-organized world, which evokes the immeasurable value of a well-organized mind.

Wherever we look, we see what is—but we can also see more than what is. A while back, I was watching a baseball game. My favorite team, the Philadelphia Phillies, was down by one in the final inning of a game against division rivals, the Atlanta Braves. They were down to their last out when a young man stepped to the plate. Luke Williams was playing in his second professional game—the first start of his career. With one man on, and all the pressure in the world on his back, he hit a towering home run to left to win the game.

My reaction—and the reactions of countless other Phillies fans— went far deeper than the joy of winning a single baseball game. Many of us were brought to tears as we witnessed a moment of triumph against great odds. We witnessed a young man live though a moment he had been dreaming about, hoping for, struggling for, his entire life—and we saw the joy on his face, and his teammates' faces, and his family's faces, and we felt: *this is the stuff of life.*

Human beings have the ability to find deeper meaning in the objects and events around us. A home run isn't just a home run but a story about grit and perseverance. A building isn't just shelter but a monument to human ingenuity. A smile isn't just a smile but a testament to innocence, or joy, or seduction. These things and moments crystalize our abstract values, make them tangible and real, bring

them down to earth so that we can experience them with an immediacy that otherwise eludes us. It is one thing to value courage—it is
another thing to watch a lone man in Tiananmen Square confront a
line of oncoming tanks.

Sometimes, as with Luke Williams's home run, the meaning of
a moment hits you over the head. It forces itself on you. You're overcome with emotion and may not even know why. "It's just a baseball
game. Why am I crying?" But you can also prime yourself for such
moments, cultivate them, actively pursue them. You do this through
the act of contemplation.

To contemplate is to pause on something, to seek its deeper meaning. To contemplate is to take the concrete and ask yourself what it
conveys about life. Poet Sylvia Plath eloquently described the act of
contemplation in a diary entry:

> On a relatively unfrequented, stony beach there is a great rock
> which juts out over the sea. After a climb, an ascent from one jag-
> ged foothold to another, a natural shelf is reached where one per-
> son can stretch at length, and stare down into the tide rising and
> falling below, or beyond to the bay, where sails catch light, then
> shadow, then light, as they tack far out near the horizon. The sun
> has burned these rocks, and the great continuous ebb and flow
> of the tide has crumbled the boulders, battered them, worn them
> down to the smooth sun-scalded stones on the beach which rattle
> and shift underfoot as one walks over them. A serene sense of the
> slow inevitability of the gradual changes in the earth's crust comes
> over me; a consuming love, not of a god, but of the clean unbro-
> ken sense that the rocks, which are nameless, the waves which
> are nameless, the ragged grass, which is nameless, are all defined
> momentarily through the consciousness of the being who observes
> them. With the sun burning into rock and flesh, and the wind ruf-
> fling grass and hair, there is an awareness that the blind immense
> unconscious impersonal and neutral forces will endure, and that
> the fragile, miraculously knit organism which interprets them,
> endows them with meaning, will move about for a little, then falter,

fail, and decompose at last into the anonymous soil, voiceless, face-less, without identity.

From this experience I emerged whole and clean, bitten to the bone by sun, washed pure by the icy sharpness of salt water, dried and bleached to the smooth tranquility that comes from dwelling among primal things.[201]

Contemplation is not a wasteful activity. It is a vital one. It serves two purposes—one mental, one emotional. Mentally, you *need* to be able to experience your abstract ideas and values as if they were perceptual concretes. Only concretes exist, and for you to be able to keep your abstractions tied to reality, you need to be able to experience them as if they were concretes. Emotionally, contemplation can give you the experience of *living in your ideal world.* The world where your values are not out there in the future, waiting to be achieved, but where they have been achieved, here and now. Where the work of living *is* done—if only for a moment.

Though you can gain some of these mental and emotional benefits from contemplating objects and events, there is only one field of human endeavor *designed* to concretize your deepest ideas and values and refuel your soul—a field that exists that exists *solely* for the purpose of contemplation: art.

## What Art Is

Think of the difference between Michelangelo's *David* and the hunched-over figure of Rodin's *The Thinker.* Think of the difference between the twisted, deformed *Pieta*s of the Middle Ages and the proud, upright figure of Mary in Bouguereau's *Pieta.* Think of the difference between the stirring, triumphant melody at the climax of the 3rd movement in Tchaikovsky's 6th symphony and the ominous, crashing notes that kick off Beethoven's 5th.

You could say that these works stir very different emotions, and you would not be wrong. But it would be more accurate to say that each conveys a different kind of *world*. An artist builds a unique world, a universe that conveys: "This is life as I see it." An artist recreates reality, but in a very different way than a photograph recreates reality. A photograph *copies* reality—an artist *stylizes* reality. She selects every detail—of a story, a poem, a painting, a sculpture, a song—and says to us: *This* is what's important in life. This is what counts. This is what's possible to human beings and worthy of contemplation.

Our daily lives are swamped by the journalistic, the accidental, the incidental. An artist cuts through the trivial and says: here's what life is *really* about. That is what makes art, art. Because every element is selected, every element carries a meaning—and the meaning is, "This is what man is, this is what the world is, this is what life is."

And this explains the profound emotional reactions we have to art. We fall in love with art when the artist's view of life matches our own. "Yes, that *is* life as I see it." We recoil in horror in disgust when we encounter a work and think, "No! That's not how I see life." All of this happens automatically and subconsciously. It's not primarily an intellectual judgment, but an emotional reaction. It flows instantaneously from our core beliefs. It can take an enormous amount of work to understand and articulate what an artist is saying, and why it resonates or clashes with our own view of ourselves, the world, and man.

As with any act of contemplation, contemplating art fulfills a mental and emotional need. Mentally, Rand explains, art provides "a confirmation of [a man's] view of existence—a confirmation, not in the sense of resolving cognitive doubts, but in the sense of permitting him to contemplate his abstractions outside his own mind, in the form of existential concretes."[202] Emotionally, "the pleasure of contemplating the objectified reality of one's own sense of life is the pleasure of feeling what it would be like to live in one's ideal world."[203]

Start with the mental need art satisfies. If I told you that you should practice the Christian virtues of faith, hope, and charity, you would have only a vague sense of what that means. You would struggle to understand how a person would apply those abstractions to the concretes of his life. But what if I told you the story of Christ and you asked yourself, "What would Jesus do?" Suddenly, your mind would grasp with enormous clarity the relevant virtues and how to apply them.

Similarly for the moral code I have outlined in this book. I have strived to explain what a morality of happiness requires—the values you should pursue and the virtues you should practice. I have strived to give examples to make these concepts vivid and clear. But the truth of the matter is, you can't really understand the guidance this book offers unless you have read Ayn Rand's novels. As Rand herself notes:

> *Art is the indispensable medium for the communication of a moral ideal.*
> . . . This does not mean that art is a substitute for philosophical thought: without a conceptual theory of ethics, an artist would not be able successfully to concretize an image of the ideal. But without the assistance of art, ethics remains in the position of theoretical engineering: art is the model-builder.[204]

Rand's point and mine is not that art exists as a didactic moral guide. No. Art's primary function is not to teach, but to show. It is for the sake of contemplation, not education. And not all art deals with moral issues. What all art does gives us is a view of life—*a concretized philosophy.*

This is what Jordan Peterson is hinting at when he discusses the importance of myth. Stories, he says, are inchoate philosophy. They provide us with a guide, long before we can articulate explicit philosophic principles. But Peterson's view differs from the one I'm outlining in two important respects. Peterson seems to think that the very age of stories—that they have survived—validates them as guides to action, and that we are doomed if we have the hubris to rationally question them. My view is that art doesn't validate—it concretizes. And it complements philosophy—it doesn't replace it.

Art and philosophy go together. Each needs the other. As Leonard Peikoff explains:

An art work does not formulate the metaphysics it represents; it does not (or at least need not) articulate definitions and principles. So art by itself is not enough in this context. But the point is that philosophy is not enough, either. *Philosophy by itself cannot satisfy man's need of philosophy.* Man requires the union of the two: philosophy and art, the broad identifications and their concrete embodiment. Then, in regard to his fundamental, guiding orientation, he combines the power of mind and body, i.e., he combines the range of abstract thought with the irresistible immediacy of sense perception.[205]

What, then, of the emotional need fulfilled by art? The answer should now be clear. We experience our life as a process—a process of shaping the world and our own soul into our image of the ideal. Art gives us an image of this ideal. It allows us to live inside a world where our values have been achieved, where the best possible is realized, where we can look *out* and see what we're trying to build fully finished.

The critics of happiness are wrong. We aren't stuck on a treadmill where each achievement is meaningless because it unleashes our desire for still greater achievement. We can fill our lives with moments where our work is complete and we experience, in the act of contemplation, the fact that life is an end in itself.

## How to Love Art

Art, at least some of it, can be enjoyed without effort. You turn on your favorite record or read your favorite novel or watch your favorite TV show and you're instantly swept away. What took me a long time to discover, what some people never discover, is that you can get more out of art—if you put in the work.

Art can be more than candy to your eyes and ears. It can have a profound impact on your life and soul by exposing you to new worlds and new emotions. You can experience the heights of joy, beauty, and reverence—and the depths of grief, rage, and despair. You can examine the most profound questions of human existence and become transfixed and transformed. But you need to know *how*.

I first discovered this point in 2008 when I went on an art tour in Boston with a guide named Luc Travers. At that point, I had never had a significant emotional reaction to a painting. And not for lack of trying. I had visited the best museums in France, Germany, and Washington, DC. But all I had felt when looking at works by Da Vinci, Vermeer, Dali, and Van Gogh was a faint sense of: "That looks nice." I would read the plaque, stand there for ten seconds, get bored, and move on.

I thought going with a tour guide might be different. Luc could tell me about the history of the painting and share some stories about the artist. That would be interesting. I love history. I love biography. But that's not what Luc did. Not at all. The first thing he told us? Don't look at the plaque. We weren't there for a history lesson. We were there to learn how to see.

We arrived at the museum and despite the fact that it was filled with hundreds or perhaps thousands of paintings, Luc told us we were only going to look at four. "This is going to be a short tour," I thought.

We stopped in front of a painting. Nothing special. Just a man seated next to a woman. "What do you see?" Luc asked. Someone started to brainstorm what the painting meant, but Luc interrupted. "No. I'm not asking you what you think this painting means. I'm asking you just to tell me what you see. Just start naming things."

"The woman has her face pressed against the man's."

"They're both looking down at something he's writing or drawing."

"They're holding hands."

It went on like that for a long time, with no detail too trivial. Sometimes, when an observation was inferential rather than self-evident, Luc would push us to justify our observation. "His face is serious. Hers is peaceful," someone said. "Peaceful?" Luc replied. "Wouldn't it be more peaceful if her mouth was closed?" "No, you're right. Not peaceful. Reverential."

He went on to ask other questions, like:

- "What words would you use to describe the mood of this place?"
- "Did he go over to her to show her something, or did she come over to him to see him working?"
- "Does he want her to be there? Or does he feel like she's disturbing him? Can you find three clues in the body language that suggests he does?"
- "Where is his primary focus? Where is her primary focus?"
- "What is she thinking at this moment?"
- "Can you find five, subtle details that show how much they intimately care for each other?"
- "When have you had a moment like this?"
- "Can you think of any moments from movies, literature, that are similar?"
- "What background music can you imagine fitting the mood?"

As the discussion went on, the painting became richer and richer with meaning. I could see more and more of it, and more and more *in* it. I felt emotions stirring, the same way I would watching a romantic scene in a powerful movie.

Finally, Luc gave his reading of the painting, which I'm going to quote at length because I don't know of any other way to capture the power of that moment:

A young couple sits together in a golden light. They are intimately close, heads touching, holding hands, and her shoulders drawn into his. But they aren't looking at each other. Their eyes are looking down at the large board he has on his knees where he seems to be writing or drawing. Did he come over to show her something? Or did she go over to him to see what he was working on?

I imagine he might have been sitting in this corner by the open window, taking advantage of the sunlight to illuminate the sketches he is working on. Then his beloved walked into the room and over to him, curious about what he was doing and wanting to be close to him. He doesn't put his board down, nor does he tell her not to disturb him. Rather, he draws his legs back so that she can pull up close to him.

He tilts the board towards her, and he takes her hand, inviting her to observe what he is doing. She leans over, barely aware of the touch of his cheek on her brow, or even of his hand as her fingers loosen in his. Her attention is drawn towards what her lover is doing. The intimacy between the two is there, but it's not at the forefront of their awareness. What is she thinking in this moment? It's not so much, "You are wonderful!" but, rather, "I see how you are doing that."

What is he working on that is keeping both of their attention? He might be showing her something that she'd be keenly interested in, like plans for their future home. Or he might be working on a project all his own that she might admire. In either case, he isn't presenting to her a finished gift. He is sharing something perhaps more intimate—he is having her observe his process of creation. This is not a pristinely manicured poem he displays for her, rather; rather, he invites her to see his thoughts come as he paints. . . .

It's hard to imagine a more romantic scene than in this painting: the early-evening sun shining, a secluded home, a cozy corner, the smell of ripe citrus in the air, and a couple who make me think of what Romeo and Juliet might have been in their late 20s. To add to this mood, I like to imagine a Chopin ballade playing in the background. Yet, in this scene imbued with romance, the intimacy between the two is understated—a subterranean river flowing beneath their shared moment. The title of this artwork is *The Painter's Honeymoon*.[206]

What I felt was rapture, and I remember the group walking away from the museum in awed silence.

Luc wasn't there to spoon-feed us: he was teaching us how to have an esthetic experience.

One of the people with me on that tour was my friend Lisa Van-Damme. If Luc Travers taught me to see, Lisa taught me to read.

Of course, I knew how to read in the sense of grasping the meaning of words on a page—just as I had been able to look at the paint on a canvas. But what Lisa showed me was: there is so much more hidden in the pages of a story than I could get merely by looking at the words on the page.

An artist, Lisa said, is saying something. He or she has selected every detail in accordance with this message. To get the most out of literature, you have to become a detective, putting together the clues until you understand the artist's aim and vision. To be a reader is to be an active-minded integrator.

To be active-minded is to seek to understand: Why did the characters act the way they did? What made them tick? What did the story mean? What was the author trying to say? How did every detail support the message? What about that weird scene at the beginning that didn't seem to have anything to do with the plot? Why was that there?

Here is an example from one of my favorite novels, *Les Misérables*. The story starts with a long section about the Bishop of Digne. Victor Hugo spends 60 pages telling us everything about the Bishop we could possibly want to know before introducing the book's main character, Jean Valjean. After a brief encounter with Valjean that kicks off the book, we never hear from the Bishop again. The question is: *Why?* Why would Hugo write what amounted to a novelette about a seemingly minor character? It's a question I had not asked on my first reading of *Les Misérables*. Lisa taught me to ask it.

*Les Misérables* tells the story of a man's redemption. Jean Valjean begins as a criminal and spends the rest of his life on a quest to become a good man. And so Hugo must, at the start of the book, give us an image of what a good man is—of the ideal Jean Valjean will strive to become. (The first book of the novel is called "The Just Man.") Grasping the purpose of the Bishop not only makes the novel more coherent, it makes the novel more enjoyable.

Great art isn't inscrutable. On the contrary, what makes it powerful is that it can be understood—and this understanding deepens and enriches our experience. The more we understand intellectually, the more powerfully we react emotionally. And, what's more: we learn how to take this same method of carefully observing events and extracting meaning from them, and apply it to our own lives. As Lisa explains in her riveting lecture, "Literature and the Quest for Meaning":

> Without great literature, *we* run the risk of living our lives like an indifferent crowd, of looking at things only with the naked eye, of failing to see beyond the surface of our experiences to their spiritual significance. But Hugo, and great artists like him, help us to develop a more penetrating perception.
>
> Great literature *is* a spiritual microscope, that allows us to examine life minutely and marvel at that which had previously gone unobserved; or a telescope that lets us take in grand, new, and distant vistas in a single glance; or a stethoscope that gives us access to the very heart of life and allows us to know its pulses. All of these metaphors work, because art gives us the power to go beyond the barriers of our ordinary perception, and *to see more.* . . . *[T]o see more* means to see within our everyday experiences a connection to high ideals.[207]

That is the power of literature and of art more broadly. Learn how to love it. And if you don't already know how, seek out powerful guides. I am grateful to Luc and Lisa for teaching me how to love art—and I continue to return to them, to help me see more deeply into the universe of visual art, literature, and poetry, and so more deeply into my own life.

Find your guides. Learn to see, to read, to listen. Then enter your ideal world.

# Seek Love

If you want to grasp the gulf between the conventional view of selfishness and the view I've outlined in this book, there is no better illustration than the fact that, on my view, the greatest reward life has to offer the selfish individual is *love*.

Love is inherently selfish, Ayn Rand once told *Playboy* magazine. So-called selfless love:

> would have to mean that you derive no personal pleasure or happiness from the company and the existence of the person you love, and that you are motivated only by self-sacrificial pity for that person's need of you. I don't have to point out to you that no one would be flattered by, nor would accept, a concept of that kind. Love is not self-sacrifice, but the most profound assertion of your own needs and values. It is for your *own* happiness that you need the person you love, and that is the greatest compliment, the greatest tribute you can pay to that person.[208]

To love someone is to care about them, to want the best for them, to take joy in their happiness, and to suffer when they suffer. You love someone, not for what they can do for you in some instrumental sense—not for the promotion they can help you get or the status they can help you acquire. You take pleasure in their sheer existence, and in sharing your life with them. Depending on the nature of their relationship—whether they are friends, or lovers, or children—their interests become co-mingled to a greater or lesser degree with your own.

To the extent altruism has any plausibility, this is the reason: other human beings are enormous values. If you love your life, you want to see others flourish, and want to help them flourish. And if you love another person, you will often do things that superficially seem like sacrifices: you skip that ballgame to tend to your sick spouse, you spend a long day helping your friend move, you forego a new car to help your kids pay for college. But these only seem like sacrifices if you drop the context—the context that what you are doing is nurturing a relationship that means the world to you.

Altruism, though, encourages people to engage in genuine sacrifices. Far from expressing love and nurturing relationships, these sacrifices poison relationships. When a friend or family member takes advantage of me, demands more of my time than I truly want to give, demands more of my money than I can truly afford, and I accede to these demands, that doesn't strengthen the relationship. It only stokes hidden resentments that reveal themselves in avoidance, in angry outbursts, in passive-aggressive remarks.

Sacrifice has no place in human relationships. Relationships should be mutually fulfilling, rooted in a deep spiritual affinity, where neither side exploits the other nor allows themselves to be exploited. I've got your back and you've got mine. We aren't mutual servants but independent equals, coming together to share values and share lives.

The rest of this lesson is about human relationships—about why they are so supremely crucial to our happiness and how to nurture them so they are truly mutually fulfilling.

## Friendship

You're born into a community—a group of people you interact and spend time with. In forming friendships, you build a *chosen* community. You select the people with whom you'll share your life. People vary in how much selectivity they exercise in this regard. Some form friendships in childhood, mostly by happenstance, and those childhood friends remain their only friends. What remains true is that friendship offers you the ability to create your ideal community—to surround yourself with people you enjoy, respect, and admire.

Friendships exist on a spectrum. All of them involve some degree of mutual caring, intimacy, and shared activity—but they can vary wildly in all three respects.

Some friendships are narrow—a bond over a shared activity. The friend you watch baseball with, the friend you play video games with, colleagues at work, and workout buddies at the gym. These friendships may involve little in the way of self-disclosure. Conversations may rarely travel beyond the shared interest. Such friendships represent real bonds, but the values that constitute those bonds are thin. If you move to a new town or give up an old hobby, the relationship moves from present tense to past.

Other friendships have depth. They are friendships of the soul that can have nearly the strength and intimacy of romantic love. Though they may start out with or involve a bond over a shared activity, the connection stretches far beyond that. Your interests may change. Your friend may move away. You may not see each other for months or even years. But the bond remains because it is rooted in love for who your friend is. Your friend is, as Aristotle put it, "another self." They embody your values in a profound way.

To say this is not to say that your friend is just like you. On the contrary, your closest friends often embody those traits that you value and yet are underdeveloped in your own character. I think of the friendship between Thomas Jefferson and James Madison. Jefferson was bold to the point of recklessness and took comfort in the solidity and cautiousness of his best friend Madison. I think of my tendency toward introversion—and my love of friends who electrify a room and energize me with their outward enthusiasm. Such friendships spring from a shared universe of values but are heightened by complementary differences that help round you out and bring out latent facets of your personality.

Why are friendships so valuable? What need are they meeting? It should be abundantly clear that friendship isn't utilitarian. A friendship I cultivate in order to help my career or enhance my social standing is not a friendship at all. To be sure, friends do help friends. Reciprocity is one way that human beings nurture emotional bonds. I help you move. You pay for dinner. But such reciprocity isn't the *purpose* of the friendship. The reason you are my friend is not because you buy me dinner—you buy me dinner because you are my friend.

There are relationships you form for practical, "you scratch my back, I'll scratch yours," reasons, but these aren't friendships—they are alliances. There is nothing wrong when people network to find potential business partners. We need such alliances, and they can sometimes even evolve into friendships. But in a friendship, it is not something *external* to the friendship we are seeking. The value is in the relationship itself.

A crucial part of what you seek from a friendship is *visibility*. Just as art makes your most abstract values perceptually real, so, too, does friendship—but in a crucially different way. A friend embodies the values you care about and the virtues you admire. You see in their flourishing the kind of life and world you want to live in and create.

But this isn't all. Your friend is not simply acting in the world, the way a character acts in a novel. Your friend is *interacting* with you. Listening to you. Responding to you. Showing understanding, care, and affection. With your friend, you don't just see—you are *seen*. When they celebrate your successes, those successes feel more real. When they share your sorrows, you feel understood. When they praise your virtues, you feel appreciated. When they laugh at your jokes, they heighten your joy.

Whereas art allows us to experience our values as perceptual objects, other people, in Nathaniel Branden's words, allow us "to experience ourselves perceptually, as concrete objects 'out there.'"[209] He goes on:

> Our psychology is expressed through behavior, through the things we say and do, and through the ways we say and do them. It is in this sense that our self is an object of perception to others. When others react to us, to their view of us and our behavior, their perception is in turn expressed through *their* behavior, by the way they look at us, by the way they speak to us, by the way they respond, and so forth. If their view of us is consonant with our deepest vision of who we are (which may be different from whom we profess to be), and if their view is transmitted by their behavior, we feel perceived, we feel psychologically visible. We experience a sense of the objectivity of our self and our psychological state of being. We perceive the reflection of our self in their behavior. It is in this

sense that others can be a psychological mirror.[210]

And like an actual mirror, one of the benefits of this visibility is not simply in helping you experience yourself, but in helping you discover yourself. It is through friendship that you come to learn about your blind spots—hidden strengths and hidden weaknesses, virtues you didn't know you had and flaws you didn't know you needed to correct. It was my friends who helped me see that I could be conflict avoidant and childish in the face of disappointment. And it was my friends who helped me see that I am unusually loyal, generous, and funny.

Friendships, finally, help you *create* yourself. It is through friendship that you can be inspired to grow and improve in new ways—when you see virtues in your friends that you want to emulate. My friend Lisa VanDamme has an unusual talent for making people feel appreciated and understood. My friend Yaron Brook has a magic ability to combine deep moral seriousness with a friendly approachability. My friend Doug Peltz is infectiously curious and enthusiastic about the world. These people make me want to be better and have helped me discover new ways to grow.

But all of this presupposes a solid foundation: that you select friends for their virtues. This doesn't necessarily mean perfect people. But it does mean that you deal with people on the basis of their virtues, and that you acknowledge forthrightly any vices. That may mean delimiting the relationship, it may mean encouraging them to do better, but what it certainly means is that you don't surround yourself with people who help you rationalize and evade your own shortcomings. If I find comfort in being around liars because they tolerate my dishonesty, if I find reassurance in being around losers because they won't judge my lack of ambition, if I seek approval from people with low standards because I'm unwilling to hold myself to high standards, I will not achieve the benefits of friendship. I'll simply build for myself a human casket.

# Romantic Love

Religion is theft. It takes our highest concepts and emotions—the sacred, reverence, exaltation, worship—and binds them to a supernatural fantasy world beyond our reach. They are products of the next world—not this profane world; they are what we feel for God—not human beings. What garbage. At root, these concepts and emotions refer to our attitude toward a moral ideal, to an *earthly* ideal, to man at his highest potential, to a potential we have the power to actualize. These emotions belong on earth—and we experience them most powerfully on earth in the form of *romantic love*. We worship in the bedroom.

Romantic love—*sexual* love—is a response to your highest values embodied in another person. This includes morality—the universal values and virtues that should guide human life—but it includes much more than that. You fall in love with someone's core values—not as empty abstractions, but as expressed and embodied in every detail of a person. You fall in love, writes Rand,

> with that essential sum, that fundamental stand or way of facing existence, which is the essence of a personality. One falls in love with the embodiment of the values that formed a person's character, which are reflected in his widest goals or smallest gestures, which create the *style* of his soul—the individual style of a unique, unrepeatable, irreplaceable consciousness.[211]

To say that you fall in love with a person's soul is to say that you fall in love with their *self-made* soul. Romantic love is a testament to free will. If you truly viewed someone as a deterministic robot, a puppet of forces outside their control, you could not love them. What you love in a person is their chosen values—their soul as they have made it, their character as they have crafted it. Even their physical appearance, though shaped by genetics, is an expression of their choices: how they dress, how they move, how well they maintain their body, how they outwardly express their inner self. Absent free will, your lover would be little more than an animated sex doll.

You cannot fully know a person's soul at first glance, but it is amazing how much you can know. Precisely because a person's style of soul *is* contained in their smallest gestures, you can become enraptured with a person the moment you set eyes on them. This is not love, but it's not mere physical attraction. Most of us have had the experience of finding someone physically attractive and losing interest once they open their mouths. No, you're responding to a much richer source of information. Just as an artist can capture their subject's personality in a single, unmoving frame, so you can see a glimpse of a *person* in your first encounter.

But whether it's in that first encounter or something that evolves over time, the first hints of love emerge in a unique *awareness* of the other person. They seize your attention, your curiosity, your fascination. When they're in the room, you have trouble looking away. When they're gone, they dominate your thoughts. You find yourself trying to weave their name into every conversation. You look for opportunities to spend time with them. You want to know about them—anything, everything about them. The most trivial details captivate you. Your life becomes heightened, electrified, buoyant—you feel *alive*.

If the interest is reciprocal, things progress. Often, what's happening remains underneath the surface. The growing attraction is unspoken and takes place in between the lines. A gaze held. Shoulders or legs brushing and neither person pulling away. At one level, what's happening is all too clear. And yet, doubt remains. The doubt is excruciating—and thrilling. Does he? Doesn't he? Does she? Doesn't she?

And then the switch is flipped. You put the cards on the table. The relationship has been happening, but now, for the first time, you talk *about* the relationship. What are we to each other? Where is this going? How do you feel about me? You make a commitment—a more or less clearly articulated agreement to put energy into the relationship, to put time into the relationship, to treat it as a value to be cultivated and not too easily abandoned.

Intimacy increases. Physical intimacy—you share a kiss, then more than a kiss, then the unrivaled intimacy of love-making. But emotional intimacy as well. You begin to reveal hidden parts of yourself. Your private thoughts, secret desires, fragile vulnerabilities.

As the days and weeks and months pass, you let more of yourself be seen and you see more of your partner. You start collecting a shared history—a life lived together. And more: you envision a shared future. A life you'll build together. Not your dreams and my dreams but our dreams. You don't just share your life with them, you *integrate* your lives. You remain independent, and yet in a profound sense you are dependent on them—they become an irreplaceable component of your personal happiness. Their joy is your joy. Their suffering is yours. You inhabit a shared, private universe that others can glimpse, but never truly see.

You then make a full commitment: you intend to build and maintain your shared universe for the whole of your life. That as the easy passion of an early romance fades, you'll do the work of keeping that passion alive, maintaining your commitment through life's ups and downs, that you'll be fully honest about who you are and what you want, that you'll aim to grow together, to make each other better. Your lover has become irreplaceable to you. If you should lose them, yes, you could love again—but there would always be a hole, a part of your happiness that could not be replaced because it would be love, but not *their* love.

At any point, the process can break down. I don't feel the way you feel. I don't want what you want. You are not who I thought you were. I've changed. You've changed. Few things are as painful. But the pain is only an insignia of the far greater rewards love offers. It offers you the ability to see your values made real in another person's character—and the unique experience of someone seeing your character and treasuring it. Romantic love is visibility par excellence. It is the one area of life where you can be fully vulnerable, fully open, and, therefore, fully seen.

But like all values, romantic love has to be earned. And the price of entry is the achievement of self-esteem and the cultivation of a moral character that makes self-esteem possible.

Absent self-esteem, you cannot truly experience love. For the person of low self-esteem, love involves an irreconcilable conflict: the joy of love is rooted in visibility—a person who lacks self-esteem finds this kind of visibility intolerable. Love offers them a mirror—and they can't stand their reflection. Such a person will still usually seek out a relationship, only now that relationship will be aimed, not at reflection, but evasion. They'll seek a partner who doesn't see them, but the phony *image* they want to project. They'll seek a partner who will tolerate their vices because their partner lacks virtue. They'll seek a partner they can exploit in some way—someone who will cater to their neediness, or bow to their domineeringness, or play the role of mommy or daddy, or increase their social standing, or provide them with financial stability. They will form relationships—they have no clue how to love or be loved.

This doesn't mean that love must wait for the day when you achieve a spotless moral character and untainted self-esteem. It does mean that any flaws in you or your partner will be an impediment. If you both are honest about those flaws, if you both work to grow and improve, and if you have a bedrock of virtue, a core of self-esteem, then that is a solid foundation for romantic love.

And this, then, is the most important piece of advice for anyone who desires romance and hasn't found it. Make yourself worthy of love. Build up your own soul. Perfect your character. Fill your life with values and ambition. I say this, not to deny or trivialize the pain of loneliness. I've been there. I remember walking through the streets of Laguna Beach in my mid-twenties, watching the couples wander past, and I can still feel that aching longing that seems like it will never go away. You cannot fully control when you'll meet someone. What you can control is who you'll be when you do meet them. Will you be virtuous, open, optimistic? Will you have built a world they'll want to enter, a life they'll want to share? Or will you have become a stew of resentment and entitlement that will send good people running for the exits? That's your choice.

Searching for love can sometimes feel hopeless, like it will stretch into infinity. But it's not and it won't. Philosopher Harry Binswanger is fond of saying that your emotions are bad predictors of your future emotions. Loneliness carries with it a sense of eternity. Set that out of your mind. Know that it's only temporary. And when you finally meet someone who becomes your whole world, you'll look back and think how small a sliver of your life you spent waiting to meet them.

## Children

With friends, we build a chosen community. With a lover, we build a chosen family. When that family includes children, we choose to bring into the world pieces of ourselves and our partner—who are at the same time unique, distinct, autonomous individuals.

It is hard to write about children without resorting to clichés, because the clichés are all true—and because having children is an experience so unique that you cannot compare it to anything else. There is nothing like looking down at a person you helped create, feeling the inconceivable weight of being responsible for that person's life, and watching them look back at you, smile, and begin a new, unrepeatable life.

And this is what I see as the central value parenthood offers: the opportunity to get to know someone through the whole of their life, to help shape that life, to help them realize their full potential. So much of the reward (and suffering) of parenthood is rooted in the fact that a child is largely unactualized potential. You see in them what they might become. It thrills you—and, at times, it terrifies you.

But you also see what they are right now. Unself-conscious joy, innocence, curiosity, wonder, amazement. You get to marvel in their uniqueness. My daughter: bold, creative, anxious, drawn to art and fashion. My son: intelligent, headstrong, affectionate, drawn to puzzles and technology. Parenting is not molding clay. It is mentoring and discovering—it is helping a child on their way to self-creation, and finding joy in discovering the kind of soul your child is creating.

Traditionally, parents have seen their role in different ways, but a common theme has been that their job is to rein in a child's selfishness. Nothing could be more wrong. Your actual job is to cultivate the child's budding rationality. To help them become thinkers whose lives are rich with values and who can start to think about their interests in more expansive, long-range ways.

I don't have much to offer in the way of parenting advice, but one thing I'm confident in saying is: treat children with respect. To impose your religion *or your philosophy*, to try to make them develop interests because they're your interests, to try to nudge them to pursue the dreams you want them to pursue (or wish you had pursued), is to treat children, not as individuals, but as objects. Children have free will, their lives belong to them, and while it's your job to help them grow, to trespass on their sovereignty is to cripple their ability to grow.

Should you have children? This is such a hard question to answer. In many respects, there is no joy more profound. But there is also no job more demanding. My general view is that you should not have children unless you're certain you want children. And yet I also believe that you cannot really know what's it's like to have children until you do. So I will say this: don't allow yourself to be pressured by outside forces either way. Know that there is a profound, unique, unrivaled adventure to be found in parenthood—but know that it's not an adventure to be taken up lightly. The stakes—for you and for them—are too high.

# Sex

This has been a book about morality and happiness, and so it's appropriate that we end with the most intense form of happiness: the act of sex.

Traditional morality saddles sex with prohibitions. Sex is what tempts us away from morality's demands. It is what drags the religionist down to earth. It's what the saint renounces. We elevate virginity and treat its loss as a *loss*.

If anything, those who defend sex today are worse than those who condemn it. They treat sex as an amoral physical act. They reduce it to an animal urge and tell us to indulge without thought or standards. Men should rack up numbers. Women should rid themselves of their "hang ups," which include not only a sense of guilt for sexual enjoyment, but *sexual standards*.

Both sides are profoundly wrong, and they are wrong in the same way. What they fail to grasp is that sex is the reward for and expression of our most profound, selfish values. Great, passionate, guiltless, meaningful sex is morality's greatest reward. Not the sanitized, neutered sex Christians talk about—the kind aimed primarily at making babies or strengthening a marriage. No. *Sex*. Real, raw sex aimed at intense physical and emotional pleasure, undertaken solely for the sake of that pleasure.

Sex, in Rand's formulation, is "a celebration of yourself and of existence."[212] Recall our discussion of core beliefs in Lesson 2. At the root of your emotional mechanism is a view of yourself and the world. To achieve happiness you must cultivate self-esteem and a benevolent view of the universe—the view that you're able to achieve happiness, worthy of the happiness you achieve, in a universe open to achievement. Sex's special power is bringing these beliefs into full awareness—to allow you to experience them here, now, as fully realized and fully satisfied. If morality is aimed at pursuing happiness, sex is the pinnacle of that pursuit.

Sex, then, isn't just a physical pleasure. All pleasure, for a human being, has a spiritual dimension. It's why you're not content to wolf down food in the back of a taxicab but seek out beautiful restaurants that create a mood. Sex is the ultimate *union* of the physical and the spiritual. Each heightens the other, each is indispensable to the other. It's part of what distinguishes art and sex. Art is the pleasure of contemplation—it is something external to you. You are looking out at a world and forgetting yourself. Sex is a form of *self-awareness*—your awareness of yourself as a total being, mind and body, able to achieve joy in this world.

The spiritual dimension of sex is best revealed by the crucial importance of your partner. You're not content with a sex doll, even if such a doll had the power to recreate or even surpass the physical sensations of a human being. You desire another consciousness. And more than that, a certain kind of consciousness. If you were to sleep with someone and discovered mid-sex that they were an imposter, the physical sensations wouldn't change, but what you would experience wouldn't be pleasure. No, the physical pleasure would intensify your emotional revulsion.[213]

In order for you to experience sex as self-celebration, you need to be with a partner who shares your values, who *embodies* your values. This is why the best sex, the most fulfilling sex, is possible only in the context of romantic love.

But that doesn't mean that anything less than the best is bad. The fact that sex is best in the context of a serious romantic relationship doesn't mean that you should spurn the realm of sex until you fall in love—let alone until you get married. You build a sex life over time, and it may take years before you're able to fully realize what's possible in the bedroom.

Our first inkling of sexual pleasure comes with the discovery of masturbation. Historically, masturbation—maybe more than any other form of sexual pleasure—has been infused with guilt and shame. Why? Precisely because it is so selfish. Its only justification is your own pleasure and happiness. Religionists have condemned it as immoral. Kant secularized this religious hatred, arguing that it amounted to treating yourself, not as a moral being, but as an amusement park. Self-help gurus have commanded us to forego masturbation and "sublimate" our sexual desires so we can be better at making money. Jordan Peterson has said that masturbation weakens us. May they all rot in hell. Masturbation is a vital part of sexual discovery and sexual happiness.

But masturbation is only the first step toward sexual discovery. As you move into adolescence, you have the opportunity to interact with partners. To tell young people to forego sexual experimentation until they are ready for an adult romance is insane and self-defeating. What young people need to be taught is to treat sex with respect, which means: to approach it on the basis of values. Do I know and trust the person I'm with? Am I comfortable with what we're doing or am I being pressured into something I'm not ready for? Am I aiming at enjoyment? Or proving something about myself (that I'm desirable, that I'm manly)? Or achieving some external result (make this guy like me, impress my friends)? As with all pleasure, the question is not: "Is this okay?" The question is: "Do I think there are real values to be gained here—and why?"

All of this applies to adults as well. As an adult, you know more about what you want from a partner and from sex. But you may not be able to find your ideal partner. Again, this does not mean you should forego sex. But you should look for a partner you know, trust, respect, and admire. Not because God said so. Not because some authority figure will disapprove. The reason to reject casual sex is *causality*. The issue is not that you'll be a bad person if you sleep around—it's that you won't actually get the value sex has to offer. In order to experience sex as a value, it has to be based on values.

But within a context of trust and respect, sex should be treated as a guiltless adventure. For consenting adults who do know, trust, and admire each other—anything goes. Whether it's fun sex, rough sex, loving sex, loud sex, imaginative sex, oral sex, anal sex, straight sex, gay sex—whatever brings you and your partner pleasure represents a virtue.

It is, in fact, your reward for virtue.

# A Final Lesson

I don't often think about death, but recently it occurred to me that the conventional wisdom, which says that no one knows what happens after we die, is 100 percent wrong. We have all experienced death. We spent an eternity not existing before we were born. It wasn't painful, it wasn't tragic. There is nothing to fear.

But how many of us have truly experienced life?

That's what frightens me. Not death, but the failure to live. The failure to enjoy my brief time here on earth. That would be the tragedy.

But whether or not I enjoy my life is under my control. And whether or not you enjoy your life is under your control.

You have free will. You have the power to think, to learn, to grow. You have the power to chart your own course. And, armed with a morality of happiness, you have the power to create a self and a life that you love.

Will you do it?

The choice is yours.

# ACKNOWLEDGMENTS

For a book about self-creation, the list of people who were instrumental in making this work possible is long.

I shared an early version of this book with a few dozen of my newsletter subscribers and am grateful for the supportive comments—and, more common, the unapologetic criticisms from Pablo Alvestegui, Maryallene Arsanto, Mary Barbour, Allison Beard, Stephanie Bond, Elly Brus, Zol Cendes, Ginger Clark, Mary Ann DeRaad, Lucid Fitzpatrick, Steve Gedeon, Ian Gilmore, Paula Hall, Louise Heatley, Allison Kunze, Jim Litzinger, David Maltby, Tom Nowak, George Reis, Samuel Russell, Cliff Styles, Will Szent-Miklosy, John Vincent, Michael Webb, and Jaana Woiceshyn.

A major turning point in the writing of this book came courtesy of a workshop organized by Greg Salmieri, where Greg and several other philosophers gave me detailed feedback that helped vastly improve the book, especially by helping me identify more clearly the book's central argument. I owe an enormous debt to Greg, Ben Bayer, Tristan de Liège, Jason Rheins, and Tara Smith. Greg, I must add, has long been one of my foremost intellectual influences and a stalwart supporter—his influence can be seen on almost every page of this book.

Although they did not read the manuscript, I'm thankful to the many friends who helped me mull over the ideas and who expressed enthusiasm for the project. At the risk of leaving off important names, I have to thank Yaron Brook, Jeremiah Cobra, Adam Edmonsond, Steve Henderson, Chad Morris, Amy Nasir, Robert Nasir, Daniel Richards, Kate Sherwood, Nikos Sotirakopoulos, and Lisa VanDamme. I also want to recognize a number of friends with whose work was particularly helpful to me as I thought through the issues in this book: Matt Bateman, Harry Binswanger, Alex Epstein, Ray Girn, Gena Gorlin, Jim Lennox, Robert Mayhew, Cody Mork, Jean Moroney, Peter Schwartz, Tal Tsfany, Luc Travers, and Darryl Wright. I would also be remiss to not mention a man whom I'm not presumptuous enough to call a friend, but who has always been supportive of my work, and whose own work has transformed my life: thank you, Leonard Peikoff.

Thank you to everyone at the Ayn Rand Institute who was involved in bringing this book to completion. Above all, Donna Montrezza helped save me from numerous embarrassing errors with her expert proof-reading, and Tom Bowden oversaw the publication process, offering helpful suggestions and encouraging comments along the way.

Last but most: Onkar Ghate. Onkar is the man who woke me from my dogmatic slumber: who showed me how much I didn't know about philosophy and then helped me learn most of what I now know. I'm tempted to heap praise on Onkar in a futile quest to express my admiration and gratitude. But it would be pointless: to those who don't know, no explanation is possible; to those who do know, no explanation is necessary. So, let me say simply: thank you, Onkar, for lighting the way.

# ENDNOTES

1.  Ayn Rand, "The Goal of My Writing," reprinted in *The Romantic Manifesto* (New York: Signet, 1975), p. 162.

2.  "Putting the 'National' in National Service," *Washington Monthly*, October 1, 2001, https://washingtonmonthly.com/2001/10/01/putting-the-national-in-national-service/.

3.  "Senator Obama's Call to Service," *Wesleyan University Magazine*, June 2008, https://magazine.blogs.wesleyan.edu/2008/06/20/senator-obamas-call-to-service/.

4.  Jean-Luc Bouchard, "Mark Zuckerberg's Full Commencement Address at Harvard, the School He Left to Start Facebook," *Quartz*, May 2017, https://qz.com/992048/mark-zuckerbergs-harvard-speech-a-full-transcript-of-the-facebook-ceos-commencement-address.

5.  "Romney Encourages Graduates to Get Involved," *Global Gazette*, May 2006, https://globegazette.com/news/romney-encourages-graduates-to-get-involved/article_cb4e393e-29e5-5c4d-a676-921c4f52aa4a.html.

6.  insigniam.com/blog/transformational-leadership-being-committed-to-something-bigger-than-yourself/.

7.  R. A. Shweder, Much, N. C., Mahapatra, M., and Park, L., "The

'Big Three' of Morality (Autonomy, Community, Divinity) and the 'Big Three' Explanations of Suffering," in A. M. Brandt & P. Rozin (Eds.), *Morality and Health* (Taylor & Frances/Routledge, 1997), p. 119–169.

8.  "Self Centered", Urban Dictionary, www.urbandictionary.com/ define.php?term=Self-Centered

9.  Jonathan Haidt, *The Happiness Hypothesis* (New York: Basic Books, 2006), p. 249.

10. Allan Bloom, *The Closing of the American Mind* (New York: Simon & Schuster, 1987), p. 67.

11. Tim Lott, "Jordan Peterson: 'The Pursuit of Happiness Is a Pointless Goal,'" *Guardian*, January 2018, www.theguardian.com/global/2018/jan/21/ jordan-peterson-self-help-author-12-steps-interview

12. Ayn Rand, "The Objectivist Ethics," reprinted in *The Virtue of Selfishness* (New York: New American Library, 1964), p. 26.

13. Rick Warren, *The Purpose Driven Life* (Michigan: Zondervan, 2002), p. 21.

14. "What Is Effective Altruism?," *Effective Altruism*, https://www. effectivealtruism.org/articles/introduction-to-effective-altruism.

15. Sam Harris, *Free Will* (New York: Simon & Schuster, 2012), p. 5.

16. Edwin A. Locke, *The Illusion of Determinism* (BookBaby, 2018), p. 95.

17. Harry Binswanger, *How We Know* (New York: TOF Publications, 2014), pp. 344–45.

18. Sam Harris, *Free Will* (New York: Simon & Schuster, 2012), p. 6.

19. Harris, *Free Will*, p. 31.

20. Harris, *Free Will*, p. 32.

21. Harris, *Free Will*, p. 43.

22. Harris, *Free Will*, p. 39.

23. Harris, *Free Will*, p. 37.

24. Sam Harris (Host), "Final Thoughts on Free Will,"

episode 241, *Making Sense Podcast*, https://samharris.org/podcasts/241-final-thoughts-on-free-will/.

25. "Why Sam Harris Is Wrong About Free Will," Ayn Rand Institute, https://www.youtube.com/live/z-rZotA6SMs?feature=share.

26. Kevin J. Mitchell, *Innate: How the Wiring of Our Brains Shapes Who We Are* (New Jersey: Princeton University Press, 2018), p. 265.

27. Harris, *Free Will*, pp. 8–9.

28. Harris, *Free Will*, p. 9.

29. Alfred R. Mele, *Free: Why Science Hasn't Disproved Free Will* (Oxford University Press, 2014). See also Edwin A. Locke, *The Illusion of Determinism* (BookBaby, 2018), pp. 74–83.

30. E. Turkheimer (2011). "Genetics and Human Agency: Comment on Dar-Nimrod and Heine," *Psychological Bulletin*, *137*(5), 825–828. https://doi.org/10.1037/a0024306. See also E. I. Gorlin and Schuur, R. (2019). "Nurturing Our Better Nature: A Proposal for Cognitive Integrity as a Foundation for Autonomous Living," *Behavior Genetics*, Mar;49(2):154–67. https://pubmed.ncbi.nlm.nih.gov/30101395.

31. In his book *Me, Myself, and Us* (Philadelphia: PublicAffairs, 2016), psychologist Brian R. Little notes how human beings regularly act against their personality traits in order to achieve their goals. An introvert, for example, might behave as an extrovert in order to win over clients for his startup. In other words, personality traits themselves, even if they are partly innate, do not determine our behavior. See especially pp. 45–67.

32. Kevin J. Mitchell, *Innate: How the Wiring of Our Brains Shapes Who We Are* (New Jersey: Princeton University Press, 2018), pp. 265–66.

33. Mitchell, *Innate: How the Wiring of Our Brains Shapes Who We Are*, p. 112.

34. Ayn Rand, "The Objectivist Ethics," reprinted in *The Virtue of Selfishness* (New York: New American Library, 1964), p. 20.

35. Harry Binswanger, *How We Know: Epistemology on an Objectivist Foundation* (New York: TOF Publications, 2014), pp. 37–41.

36. Binswanger, *How We Know*, pp. 37–41.

37. Nathaniel Branden, *The Psychology of Self-Esteem* (San Francisco: Jossey-Bass, 2001), p. 67.

38. Judith Beck, *Cognitive Behavior Therapy, Second Edition: Basics and Beyond* (New York: Guilford Press, 2011), p. 35.

39. Beck, *Cognitive Behavior Therapy, Second Edition*, p. 37.

40. Beck, *Cognitive Behavior Therapy, Second Edition*, p. 172.

41. Beck, *Cognitive Behavior Therapy, Second Edition*, p. 32.

42. Beck, *Cognitive Behavior Therapy, Second Edition*, p. 207.

43. CBT isn't the only effective therapeutic approach, and CBT alone may not always be effective. I think of CBT as providing essential foundational skills in introspection and psychological self-maintenance—not as providing a complete understanding of human psychology. Indeed, I'm in profound disagreement with the subjectivism that tends to run through the work of CBT thinkers like Burns. For example, they tend to reject the idea that self-esteem requires actually living up to one's moral standards. They believe, in effect, that we can talk ourselves into self-esteem no matter our actual behavior. Burns himself goes so far as to deny the existence of the "self." Needless to say, I firmly reject that view.

44. Ayn Rand, "The Metaphysical Versus the Man-Made," reprinted in *Philosophy: Who Needs It* (New York: Signet, 1984).

45. Ayn Rand, *Atlas Shrugged* (New York: Plume, 1999), p. 1014.

46. Ryan Holiday, "The Key to Happiness Is Realizing That Everything Sucks," *Thought Catalog*, October 17, 2018, https://thoughtcatalog.com/ryan-holiday/2017/08/the-key-to-happiness-is-realizing-that-everything-sucks/.

47. Arthur C. Brooks, "How to Want Less," *Atlantic*, February 2022, https://www.theatlantic.com/magazine/archive/2022/03/why-we-are-never-satisfied-happiness/621304/.

48. Ayn Rand, "Causality Versus Duty," reprinted in *Philosophy: Who Needs It* (New York: Signet, 1984), p. 136.

49. Ayn Rand, *Atlas Shrugged* (New York: Plume, 1999), p. 1022.

50. Oxford Happiness Survey, https://www.happiness-survey.com/.

51. P. Hills and Argyle, M. (2002). "The Oxford Happiness Questionnaire: A Compact Scale for the Measurement of Psychological Well-Being," *Personality and Individual Differences*, *33*(7), 1071–82, https://doi.org/10.1016/S0191-8869(01)00213-6.

52. Nicole Celestine, "The Science of Happiness in Positive Psychology 101," https://positivepsychology.com/happiness/. Original paper at http://www.katherinenelsoncoffey.com/uploads/2/7/1/7/27172343/nelson_et_al._2016_-_emotion.pdf. To be fair to Nelson-Coffey, her paper does seek to incorporate a philosophic understanding of happiness and the paper itself doesn't draw the conclusion that we should sacrifice for others. Nevertheless, by failing to distinguish between "pro-social" and "sacrifice," and between genuine self-esteem and pseudo-self-esteem, the study does more to mislead than to illuminate.

53. Ayn Rand makes a similar point in the context of criticizing hedonism. Ayn Rand, *The Virtue of Selfishness* (New York: Signet, 1964), pp. 32–33.

54. David Brooks, *The Road to Character* (New York: Random House, 2015), p. xii.

55. Brooks, *The Road to Character*, p. xi.

56. Brooks, *The Road to Character*, p. xii.

57. Brooks, *The Road to Character*, p. 7.

58. Brooks, *The Road to Character*, pp. 240–41.

59. Brooks, *The Road to Character*, pp. 241–42.

60. The Intercept (@theintercept), January 2022, Twitter, https://twitter.com/theintercept/status/1477450403763695623.

61. Stephen Findeisen, "Mr. Beast Hasn't Donated Enough," Coffeezilla, YouTube, December 2021, https://youtu.be/EmJswAKgqD0.

62. Gemma White, "YouTube Star MrBeast Criticised for $3.5 Million Real-Life 'Squid Game,'" *National News*, November 2021, https://www.thenationalnews.com/arts-culture/television/2021/11/25/youtube-star-mrbeast-criticised-for-35-million-real-life-squid-game/.

63. *New Oxford American Dictionary* (Second Edition).

64. Quoted in Thomas Dixon, *The Invention of Altruism: Making Moral Meanings in Victorian Britain* (Oxford: Oxford University Press, 2008), p 41.

65. Thomas Dixon, *The Invention of Altruism: Making Moral Meanings in Victorian Britain* (Oxford: Oxford University Press, 2008), pp. 73, 90.

66. Ayn Rand, "Faith and Force: Destroyers of the Modern World," reprinted in *Philosophy: Who Needs It* (Indiana: Bobbs-Merrill, 1982), p. 74.

67. "The 2005 TIME 100," *Time*, 2005, https://content.time.com/time/specials/packages/completelist/0,29569,1972656,00.html.

68. Peter Singer, *The Most Good You Can Do: How Effective Altruism Is Changing Ideas About Living Ethically* (Connecticut: Yale University Press, 2015), Preface.

69. Singer, *The Most Good You Can Do*, p. 4.

70. Singer, *The Most Good You Can Do*, p. 3.

71. Singer, *The Most Good You Can Do*, p. 14.

72. Singer, *The Most Good You Can Do*, p. 28.

73. Singer, *The Most Good You Can Do*, p. 8.

74. Singer, *The Most Good You Can Do*, p. 6.

75. Singer, *The Most Good You Can Do*, p. 13.

76. Peter Singer, *The Life You Can Save* (New York: Random House, 2009), p. 15.

77. Singer, *The Life You Can Save*, p. 18.

78. Ayn Rand, "The Ethics of Emergencies," reprinted in *The Virtue of Selfishness* (New York: Signet, 1964), p. 55.

79. Thomas Sowell, *Barbarians Inside the Gates and Other Controversial Essays* (Stanford, CA: Hoover Institution Press, 1999), p. 250.

80. Ayn Rand, *Atlas Shrugged* (New York: Plume, 1999), p. 1031.

81. Rand, *Atlas Shrugged*, p. 1031.

82. Rand, *Atlas Shrugged*, "About the Author."

83. Ayn Rand, "The Objectivist Ethics," reprinted in *The Virtue of Selfishness* (New York: Signet, 1964), p. 29.

84. Rand, "The Objectivist Ethics," p. 23.

85. Rand, "The Objectivist Ethics," p. 24.

86. Rand, "The Objectivist Ethics," p. 25.

87. Rand, "The Objectivist Ethics," p. 23.

88. David Brooks, *The Second Mountain* (New York: Random House, 2019), p. 67.

89. Rand, "The Objectivist Ethics," p. 25.

90. Rand, *Atlas Shrugged*, p. 1018.

91. I owe this point to Onkar Ghate.

92. Leonard Peikoff, *Objectivism: The Philosophy of Ayn Rand* (Boston: Dutton, 1991), p. 298.

93. Ayn Rand, *Atlas Shrugged* (New York: Plume, 1999), p. 1014.

94. Don Winslow, *The Force* (New York: William Morrow, 2017), pp. 349–51.

95. Ayn Rand, *Atlas Shrugged* (New York: Plume, 1999), p. 1012.

96. Ayn Rand, "The Objectivist Ethics," reprinted in *The Virtue of Selfishness* (New York: Signet, 1964), p. 25.

97. David Deutsch, *The Beginning of Infinity: Explanations That Transform the World* (London: Penguin Books, 2011), p. 56.

98. Deutsch, *The Beginning of Infinity*, p. 67.

99. Ayn Rand, *Atlas Shrugged* (New York: Plume, 1999), p. 1038.

100. Sam Harris, *Lying* (California: Four Elephants Press, 2011), p. 12.

101. Ayn Rand, *Atlas Shrugged* (New York: Plume, 1999), p. 1019.

102. I owe this formulation to Onkar Ghate.

103.  Jordan Peterson, *12 Rules for Life: An Antidote to Chaos* (Canada: Random House Canada, 2018), p. 209.

104.  Sam Harris, *Lying* (California: Four Elephants Press, 2011), p. 16.

105.  Aristotle, *Nicomachean Ethics*, trans. Terence Irwin (Indianapolis/ Cambridge: Hackett, 2019), 1146b.

106.  Ayn Rand, *The Fountainhead* (New York: Scribner, 1986), pp. 194–96.

107.  Rand, *The Fountainhead*, p. 606.

108.  *The Life and Letters of Charles Darwin, Volume I,* https://charles-darwin.classic-literature.co.uk/the-life-and-letters-of-charles-darwin-volume-i/ebook-page-36.asp.

109.  Julia Galef, *The Scout Mindset: Why Some People See Things Clearly and Others Don't* (New York: Portfolio, 2021), p. 68.

110.  Cal Newport, *How to Become a Straight-A Student: The Unconventional Strategies Real College Students Use to Score High While Studying Less* (New York: Crown, 2006), pp. 4–5.

111.  Newport, *How to Become a Straight-A Student*, p. 5.

112.  Harry Binswanger, *How We Know: Epistemology on an Objectivist Foundation* (New York: TOF Publications, 2014), p. 228.

113.  These aren't pure cases of false division since both marriage and racism are legitimate concepts—they merely become defined in an overly restrictive way. Genuine cases of false division, where the concept as such is illegitimate, are relatively rare. As a pure false division, Harry Binswanger gives the made-up example of "blins": beautiful blondes with blue eyes, 5'5" tall and 24 years old. This concept would be totally unusable and unnecessary.

114.  Ayn Rand, "The Metaphysical Versus the Man-Made," reprinted in *Philosophy: Who Needs It* (New York: Signet, 1984), p. 24.

115.  Ayn Rand, *Atlas Shrugged* (New York: Plume, 1999), p. 1016.

116.  Keith Lockitch, "Darwin and the Discovery of Evolution," *Objective Standard*, February 2008, https://theobjectivestandard.com/2008/02/darwin-discovery-evolution/.

117. Gregory Salmieri, "Thinking Objectively (OCON 2014)," Ayn Rand Institute, https://www.youtube.com/watch?v=vJcyKHjugXM.

118. Ayn Rand, *Atlas Shrugged* (New York: Plume, 1999), pp. 1016–17.

119. Ayn Rand, *Introduction to Objectivist Epistemology* (New York: Meridian, 1990), p. 35.

120. I owe this point to Onkar Ghate.

121. I owe many of the formulations in this section to Onkar Ghate.

122. Leonard Peikoff, *Objectivism: The Philosophy of Ayn Rand* (Boston: Dutton, 1991), pp. 164–65.

123. I owe this formulation to Alex Epstein.

124. Gregory Salmieri, "How to Be an Objective Consumer of Science," Ayn Rand Institute lecture course (YouTube), May 2020, https://www.youtube.com/watch?v=fuxVVLVtr_A.

125. John Demartini, *The Values Factor* (New York: Berkeley Publishing Corporation, 2013), pp. 11–12. Thank you to Daniel Richards for recommending Demartini's work.

126. Demartini, *The Values Factor*, p. 12.

127. Demartini, *The Values Factor*, pp. 47–53.

128. *Journals of Ayn Rand*, ed. David Harriman (Boston: Dutton, 1997), pp. 28–29.

129. Ayn Rand, *Introduction to Objectivist Epistemology* (New York: Meridian, 1990), p. 33.

130. Ayn Rand, "*Playboy* Interview: Ayn Rand," *Playboy*, March 1964.

131. Gregory Salmieri, "Purpose and Values," Ayn Rand Institute OCON Live! (YouTube), May 2020, https://www.youtube.com/watch?v=TDivgaBGWqQ.

132. Maria Montessori, *The 1946 London Lectures* (Holland: Montessori-Pierson Publishing House, 2019), pp. 151–52.

133. Ayn Rand, "The Objectivist Ethics," reprinted in *The Virtue of Selfishness* (New York: Signet, 1964), p. 26.

134. Ayn Rand, *The Fountainhead* (New York: Scribner, 1986), p. 13.

135. Tara Smith, "Money *Can* Buy Happiness," *Reason Papers* (2003), vol. 26.

136. Smith, "Money *Can* Buy Happiness," vol. 26.

137. Cal Newport, *So Good They Can't Ignore You* (London: Hachette UK, 2016), p. 35.

138. Newport, *So Good They Can't Ignore You*, p. 111.

139. Quoted in Daniel Pink, *Drive* (New York: Riverhead Books, 2009), p. 90.

140. Pink, *Drive*, p. 98.

141. Pink, *Drive*, p. 208.

142. Cal Newport, *So Good They Can't Ignore You* (London: Hachette UK, 2016), p. 105.

143. Pink, *Drive*, p. 79.

144. Newport, *So Good They Can't Ignore You*, p. 28.

145. Newport, *So Good They Can't Ignore You*, p. 37.

146. Ayn Rand, "The Objectivist Ethics," reprinted in *The Virtue of Selfishness* (New York: Signet, 1964), p. 31.

147. Newport, *So Good They Can't Ignore You*, pp. 13, 41.

148. Howard Gardner, *Multiple Intelligences* (New York: Basic Books, 2006).

149. Mihaly Csikszentmihalyi, *Flow: The Psychology of Optimal Experience* (New York: Harper & Row, 1990), p. 3.

150. John Del Signore, "Ira Glass, This American Life" (Interview), Gothamist, October 2007, https://gothamist.com/arts-entertainment/ira-glass-this-american-life.

151. Cal Newport, *So Good They Can't Ignore You* (London: Hachette UK, 2016), p. 88.

152. Arthur Brooks, *From Strength to Strength* (New York: Portfolio, 2022), p. 44.

153. Brooks, *From Strength to Strength*, p. 44.

154. Shonda Rhimes, "Shonda Rhimes '91 Delivers Dartmouth's Commencement Speech," Dartmouth, https://youtu.be/EuHQ6TH60_I.

155. Ayn Rand, *The Fountainhead* (New York: Scribner, 1986), p. 12.

156.    Rand, *The Fountainhead*, p. 613.

157.    *A Companion to Ayn Rand* (Blackwell Companions to Philosophy), edited by Allan Gotthelf and Gregory Salmieri (New Jersey: Wiley-Blackwell, 2016), p. 56.

158.    Edgar Allan Poe, "The Philosophy of Composition," Poetry Foundation, https://www.poetryfoundation.org/articles/69390/the-philosophy-of-composition.

159.    See, for example, Georgios Dontas, "The Getty Kouros: A Look at Its Artistic Defects and Incongruities," in *The Getty Kouros Colloquium: Athens, 25–27 May 1992* (Malibu: J. Paul Getty Museum and Athens: Nicholas P. Goulandris Foundation, Museum of Cycladic Art, 1993), http://www.getty.edu/publications/virtuallibrary/0892362634.html.

160.    See, for instance, Ayn Rand's analysis of how she wrote a paragraph from her novel *Atlas Shrugged* in *The Art of Fiction* (New York: Plume, 2000), pp. 128–32.

161.    Jonah Lehrer, *Imagine: How Creativity Works* (Boston: Houghton Mifflin, 2012), p. xii.

162.    Paul Johnson, *Darwin: Portrait of a Genius* (New York: Penguin, 2013), p. 27.

163.    Johnson, *Darwin: Portrait of a Genius*, p. 33.

164.    D. N. Perkins, *The Mind's Best Work* (Cambridge, Massachusetts: Harvard University Press, 1981), pp. 75–76.

165.    Perkins, *The Mind's Best Work*, p. 76.

166.    Jonah Lehrer, *Imagine: How Creativity Works* (Boston: Houghton Mifflin, 2012), p. 31.

167.    Lehrer, *Imagine: How Creativity Works*, p. 46.

168.    Lehrer, *Imagine: How Creativity Works*, p. 49.

169.    Lehrer, *Imagine: How Creativity Works*, p. 50.

170.    Friedrich Nietzsche, *Human, All Too Human: A Book for Free Spirits*, translated by Marion Faber with Stephen Lehmann (Winnipeg: Bison Books, 1996).

171. D. N. Perkins, *The Mind's Best Work* (Cambridge, Massachusetts: Harvard University Press, 1981), pp. 127–28.

172. Ayn Rand, *The Fountainhead* (New York: Scribner, 1986), p. 38.

173. *A Companion to Ayn Rand* (Blackwell Companions to Philosophy), Allan Gotthelf and Gregory Salmieri, eds. (New Jersey: Wiley-Blackwell, 2016), p. 57.

174. Malcolm Gladwell, *Blink: The Power of Thinking Without Thinking* (Boston: Back Bay Books, 2005), p. 9.

175. David Bayles and Ted Orland, *Art and Fear: Observations on the Perils (and Rewards) of Artmaking* (Image Continuum Press, 2001), p. 13.

176. Brandon Webb and John David Mann, *Mastering Fear: A Navy SEAL's Guide* (New York: Portfolio, 2018), p. 27.

177. Cal Newport, *Deep Work: Rules for Focused Success in a Distracted World* (New York: Grand Central Publishing, 2016), p. 7.

178. Ayn Rand, *We the Living* (New York: New American Library, 2009), p. 101.

179. David Hume, *An Enquiry concerning the Principles of Morals*, Appendix 2: Of Self-love, p. 248.

180. Hume, *An Enquiry concerning the Principles of Morals*, p. 249.

181. Ayn Rand, *Atlas Shrugged* (New York: Plume, 1999), p. 1022.

182. Leonard Peikoff, *Objectivism: The Philosophy of Ayn Rand* (Boston: Dutton, 1991), p. 266.

183. Rand, *Atlas Shrugged*, p. 1046.

184. Adolf Hitler, *Mein Kampf*, trans. Ralph Manheim (New York: Houghton Mifflin, 1971), pp. 297–98.

185. Leonard Peikoff, *Objectivism: The Philosophy of Ayn Rand* (Boston: Dutton, 1991), p. 276.

186. *Letters of Ayn Rand*, ed. Michael S. Berliner (Boston: Dutton, 1995), p. 558.

187. Adam Smith, *The Theory of Moral Sentiments* (London: Penguin Classics; Anniversary edition 2010), II.ii.3.7: 88–89.

188.  Nathaniel Branden, *The Psychology of Self-Esteem* (San Francisco: Jossey-Bass, 2001), p. 109.

189.  Branden, *The Psychology of Self-Esteem*, p. 124.

190.  Branden, *The Psychology of Self-Esteem*, pp. 143–44.

191.  Ayn Rand, *Atlas Shrugged* (New York: Plume, 1999), pp. 1020–21.

192.  Leonard Peikoff, *Objectivism: The Philosophy of Ayn Rand* (Boston: Dutton, 1991), p. 303.

193.  Peikoff, *Objectivism: The Philosophy of Ayn Rand*, p. 281.

194.  Rand, *Atlas Shrugged*, p. 1058.

195.  "Matthew McConaughey Leaves the Audience SPEECHLESS," MotivationHub, YouTube, January 2021, https://youtu.be/68ZcE5GQP9c.

196.  Ayn Rand, *The Romantic Manifesto* (New York: Signet, 1975), p. 38.

197.  Nathaniel Branden, *The Psychology of Self-Esteem* (San Francisco: Jossey-Bass, 2001), p. 71.

198.  Branden, *The Psychology of Self-Esteem*, p. 71.

199.  Ayn Rand, "The Goal of My Writing," reprinted in *The Romantic Manifesto* (New York: Signet, 1975), p. 169.

200.  Ingrid Fetell Lee, *Joyful: The Surprising Power of Ordinary Things to Create Extraordinary Happiness* (Boston: Little, Brown Spark, 2018), pp. 108–109.

201.  Quoted in "19-Year-Old Sylvia Plath on the Transcendent Splendor of Nature," by Maria Popova, *Marginalian*, https://www.brainpickings.org/2014/06/12/sylvia-plath-journals-nature/. Thanks to Kate Sherwood for bringing this quote to my attention.

202.  Ayn Rand, "Art and Sense of Life," reprinted in *The Romantic Manifesto* (New York: Signet, 1975), p. 39.

203.  Rand, "Art and Sense of Life," p. 38.

204.  Ayn Rand, "The Psycho-Epistemology of Art," reprinted in *The Romantic Manifesto* (New York: Signet, 1975), p. 21.

205.  Leonard Peikoff, *Objectivism: The Philosophy of Ayn Rand* (Boston: Dutton, 1991), p. 418.

# ENDNOTES

206. Luc Travers, *Stories in Paint*, p. 16.

207. Lisa VanDamme, "Literature and the Quest for Meaning" (video), Ayn Rand Institute, YouTube, September 2019, https://www.youtube.com/watch?v=JZed0X3-q5o.

208. Ayn Rand, "*Playboy* Interview: Ayn Rand," *Playboy*, March 1964.

209. Nathaniel Branden, *The Psychology of Romantic Love* (New York: Bantam, 1981), p. 74.

210. Branden, *The Psychology of Romantic Love*, pp. 75–76.

211. Ayn Rand, "Philosophy and Sense of Life," reprinted in *The Romantic Manifesto* (New York: Signet, 1975), p. 32.

212. Ayn Rand, "Of Living Death," *The Voice of Reason*, ed. Leonard Peikoff (New York: New American Library, 1990), p. 54.

213. The inspiration for this example I owe to Greg Salmieri.

Printed in Great Britain
by Amazon

35717733R00155